Two Women in the Klondike

CLASSIC REPRINT SERIES
Edited by Terrence Cole

The Classic Reprint Series of the University of Alaska Press
brings back into print classic works of
enduring value and historical significance.

No. 9
Two Women in the Klondike
Mary E. Hitchcock

No. 8
Abandoned: The Story of the Greely Arctic Expedition, 1881–1884
Alden Todd

No. 7
Noel Wien: Alaska Pioneer Bush Pilot
Ira Harkey

No. 6
Across Arctic America: Narrative of the Fifth Thule Expedition
Knud Rasmussen

No. 5
Two Years in the Klondike and Alaskan Gold-Fields, 1896–1898
William B. Haskell

No. 4
The Thousand-Mile War: World War II in Alaska and the Aleutians
Brian Garfield

No. 3
Fifty Years Below Zero: A Lifetime of Adventure in the Far North
Charles D. Brower

No. 2
Exploration of Alaska, 1865–1900
Morgan Sherwood

No. 1
Arctic Village: A 1930s Portrait of Wiseman, Alaska
Robert Marshall

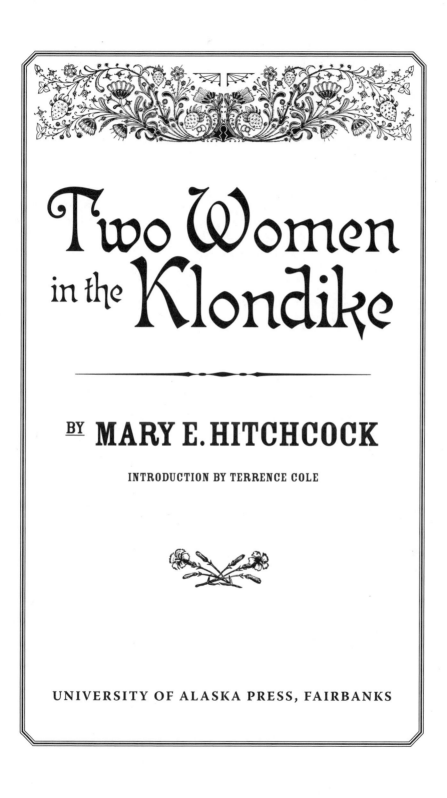

Two Women in the Klondike

BY MARY E. HITCHCOCK

INTRODUCTION BY TERRENCE COLE

UNIVERSITY OF ALASKA PRESS, FAIRBANKS

© 2005 University of Alaska Press

104 Eielson Building, Salcha Street
P.O. Box 756240
Fairbanks, AK 99775-6240
fypress@uaf.edu
www.uaf.edu/uapress

ISBN 10: 1-889963-68-2
ISBN 13: 978-1-889963-68-6

Printed in the United States

This paper meets the requirements of ANSI/NISO Z39.48–1992
(Permanence of Paper).

Library of Congress Cataloging-in-Publication Data

Hitchcock, Mary E. (Mary Evelyn), 1849–1920.
  Two women in the Klondike / Mary E. Hitchcock.
    p. cm. — (Classic reprint series ; no. 9)
  "This volume is an abridgement of the original 1899 edition."
  Includes bibliographical references and index.
  ISBN-10: 1-889963-68-2 (alk. paper)
  ISBN-13: 978-1-889963-68-6 (alk. paper)

  1. Klondike River Valley (Yukon)—Gold discoveries. 2. Alaska—Gold discoveries.
3. Hitchcock, Mary E. (Mary Evelyn), 1849–1920. 4. Castelmenardo, Edith Van Buren,
contessa, d. 1914. 5. Women pioneers—Yukon Territory—Klondike River Valley—
Biography. 6. Women pioneers—Alaska—Biography. 7. Klondike River Valley (Yukon)
—Biography. 8. Alaska—Biography. 9. Frontier and pioneer life—Yukon Territory—
Klondike River Valley. 10. Frontier and pioneer life—Alaska. I. Title. II. Classic reprint
series (Fairbanks, Alaska) ; no. 9.
  F1095.K5H58 2005
  917.19'1041—dc22   2004029694

Jacket and interior design: Dixon Jones, Rasmuson Library Graphics

The text of the title on the title page was composed using Isabella, a typestyle that
was designed in 1892 for MacKellar, Smiths, and Jordan, an American type foundry
located in Philadelphia, Pennsylvania.

CONTENTS

LIST OF ILLUSTRATIONS VII
MAP OF THE 1898 ROUTE VIII
INTRODUCTION BY TERRENCE COLE IX
NOTES ON THE TEXT XXVI
FOREWORD TO THE 1899 EDITION XXVII
ACKNOWLEDGMENTS XXIX

1   HO FOR THE LAND OF GOLD! 1
2   "WITH MALICE TOWARDS NONE" 4
3   LAND IN SIGHT! 7
4   ST. MICHAELS 11
5   A TRIAL OF PATIENCE 14
6   WE MEET OLD FRIENDS 17
7   TRANSFERRED AT LAST 21
8   WE HEAR THE SIGNAL 25
9   UP THE YUKON 31
10   DISCOMFORT OF BARGE LIFE 36
11   NEARING OUR DESTINATION 40
12   THE PROMISED LAND 44
13   WE BECOME SQUATTERS 51
14   THE "SICK BOY" 57
15   OUR FIRST DINNER IN DAWSON 62
16   WE BECOME "FREE MINERS" 69
17   VISITING MINES WITH A KLONDIKE KING . . . 76
18   OUR MAN FRIDAY 87
19   ISAACS, THE IRREPRESSIBLE 91
20   OUR HELPFUL NEIGHBOURS 99
21   A NEW SCHEME 104
22   THE RIDEOUT AT LAST 109
23   THE TRIALS OF BUILDING 113
24   BUSINESS PROPOSITIONS 119
25   A NEW EXPERIENCE 128
26   IN THE NEW HOME AT LAST 138
27   A SERIES OF DISAPPOINTMENTS 152

28 ADIEU TO DAWSON 159
29 THE RACE WITH THE *DOMVILLE* 165
30 THE FIRST PORTAGE 174
31 THE SKAGUAY PASS 177
32 A DAY IN SITKA 185
33 KILLISNOO 188
34 FAREWELL TO ALASKA 191

    INDEX 193

ILLUSTRATIONS

MAP OF THE 1898 ROUTE VIII

EDITH VAN BUREN AND MARY HITCHCOCK XXX

NOVEL MOSQUITO SCREENS 12

CLOUD EFFECTS AT MIDNIGHT 16

THE *WHEELING* 23

A LESSON IN PANNING OUT GOLD 41

EDITH'S FIRST PAN 42

LOG CABINS AT DAWSON 46

MONTE CARLO THEATRE, DAWSON 47

A SLEEPING BAG 52

THE BIG TENT 58

A GOAT TEAM 60

THE BIG TENT ON THE WATERFRONT 64

FRONT STREET, DAWSON 66

EDITH ON HORSEBACK, OFF TO EL DORADO 77

CLEAN-UP 82

DINNER WITH A KLONDIKE KING 88

VAN BUREN AND HITCHCOCK IN THE TENT 93

THE LADIES AND A GUEST 96

ERECTION OF TAMMANY HALL, DAWSON 117

MISS VAN BUREN IN TRAVELLING COSTUME 130

OUR NEW HOUSE FINISHED AT LAST 139

THE *FLORA* 157

THE *DOMVILLE* PASSING US 166

MILES CANYON 172

MRS. HITCHCOCK WITH IVAN 183

OUR ROOMMATE MRS. B— 186

KILLISNOO 189

THE 1898 ROUTE OF MARY HITCHCOCK AND EDITH VAN BUREN
THROUGH ALASKA AND THE KLONDIKE

INTRODUCTION

TERRENCE COLE

RELATIVELY FEW WOMEN went to the Klondike gold fields in 1898, so when a woman was encountered along the trail she was certain to be the object of curiosity and fascination. But none stood apart from the crowd as much as Mary E. Hitchcock and Edith May Van Buren, the eccentric heroines of *Two Women in the Klondike*. This book is one of the most unusual memoirs in nineteenth-century travel literature and a unique, first-hand account of the Klondike Gold Rush.

Hitchcock, a forty-nine-year-old widow, and Van Buren, the thirty-eight-year-old grandniece of President Martin Van Buren, appeared to be the most unlikely pair of prospectors imaginable. The sight of these wealthy, high-society creatures from New York venturing alone into the Yukon in 1898 would have been remarkable enough, even had they not been equipped like a royal entourage.

The load of personal belongings and supplies that Hitchcock and Van Buren shipped thousands of miles to Alaska by rail and steamship, and then nearly a thousand miles up the Yukon River to Dawson City, constituted what another traveler called "the strangest conglomeration of cargo that ever women's wits devised."[1] Readers of Hitchcock's memoir have always marveled at the sheer size and variety of the baggage they brought with them—Mary Hitchcock and Edith Van Buren may have traveled far, but they did not travel light.

Their camping equipment included the largest tent ever seen in Alaska or the Yukon, a giant canvas shelter the size of a small city block, forty feet wide and seventy feet long. Why two single women needed their own four-hundred-pound circus tent (rumored to be capable of accommodating at least seventy-five people for dinner) was no mystery to those who saw the assortment of creatures and cargo it was originally supposed to contain: more

x   than half a ton of luggage and household goods, such as silverware and fine china; air mattresses and easy chairs; a well-stocked library; a soda machine; a graphophone complete with a case of cylindrical records; tinned oysters, lobsters, and asparagus; a one-hundred-pound mahogany music box and a movie projector; a flock of pigeons, a pair of canaries, two Great Danes, and a parrot; an antique Italian mandolin; an ice cream freezer; and a fifty-foot-long portable bowling alley.

Admittedly, the typical gold hunter seldom bothered to bring along a bowling alley. Hitchcock's diary of her peculiar expedition, published in New York in 1899, is hardly a typical saga of frontier fortune hunting either. *Two Women in the Klondike* is a unique portrait of the Klondike Gold Rush and an intimate account of the social, psychological, and physical restrictions that could shape a woman's life at the end of the nineteenth century, especially a woman with a strong sense of good taste, refined manners, and social propriety. These limits were thrown into stark relief as Hitchcock and Van Buren traveled to a land far beyond the bounds of proper society, to a place that their friends believed was no place for a woman.

Mary Hitchcock's biographical entry in the 1914 *Woman's Who's Who of America* described her occupations as "author" and "explorer."[2] Born on March 10, 1849 as Mary Elizabeth Higgins, she was descended from an old and established colonial family in Virginia.

Following the Civil War, the southern belle married Roswell D. Hitchcock, Jr., a young U.S. Naval Officer from New England with his own distinguished heritage and pedigree as a world traveler.

Mrs. Hitchcock's father-in-law was Reverend Roswell D. Hitchcock, Sr., a famed nineteenth-century Presbyterian preacher, biblical scholar, and traveler who was for many years the vice president of the American Geographical Society and a leader of the American Palestine Exploration Society. "It was chiefly through his exertions," one tribute stated at the time of Hitchcock's death in 1887, "that the survey of the eastern and comparatively unknown portion of Palestine was planned and carried out."[3]

Like her father-in-law, Mary E. Hitchcock believed exploring was intrinsically good for the soul and the spirit, and her husband's naval career provided an unprecedented opportunity for them both to see the world (though admittedly her idea of deprivation and hardship was more along the lines of putting up with poor maid service, dining with mismatched plates, or eating unbuttered toast). Until Commander Hitchcock died suddenly in 1892 at age forty-seven from a kidney ailment, Mary Hitchcock often accompanied or followed him on naval and diplomatic missions to Europe, the Mediterranean, the

Bering Sea, and the Far East.[4] She proudly professed to be one of the few women in American history that had ever resided on a U.S. Naval warship, though more typically she would follow behind her husband on a commercial vessel and rendezvous in the next port. Years after her husband's death Mrs. Hitchcock wrote about her adventures on and off Navy ships in a small, chatty memoir with the not-so-memorable title *Tales Out of School About Naval Officers (and others) by A Woman who has lived on a Man-of-War.* While recalling "many strange and amusing experiences" during her two-year stay in the Orient in the early 1880s, she was still angered at the infamous "woman order" of Secretary of the Navy William E. Chandler, which henceforth forbade wives of naval officers from following their husbands' ships. "Some obeyed, some protested loudly," Hitchcock wrote, "saying that they had a perfect right to go where they pleased. They had never sworn to love, honor and obey Secretary Chandler, and had no intention of doing so. He had no right to tell them to go home and live with their parents while their husbands were cruising."[5]

In the summer of 1897 the society pages in New York City announced that Mrs. Hitchcock's only child, Harriet "Nannie" Hitchcock, was engaged to be married to Frederick C. Harriman, a cousin of Averell Harriman, the future diplomat and politician.[6] The Hitchcock-Harriman wedding in November 1897 at St. Bartholomew's Episcopal Church in New York City was one of the most colorful of the year. Mrs. Hitchcock spared no expense in giving her daughter an elaborate ceremony.

"No wedding this season has been more notable for floral decorations," the *Times* reported. Following the ceremony Mrs. Hitchcock hosted a lavish reception at the fashionable Murray Hill Hotel. Standing beside her in the receiving line to greet the guests was her longtime companion, confidant, and traveling partner, Miss Edith May Van Buren.[7]

Mary Hitchcock probably first crossed paths with Edith Van Buren in Japan in the 1880s. Van Buren's father, General Thomas B. Van Buren, was a noted soldier and diplomat who served for eleven years as the U.S. Consul General to the Japanese government. Irrepressible and free-spirited by the standards of the day, Edith had a well-deserved reputation in society circles for a streak of stubborn independence, and was particularly distinguished, an editor once said, "for her adventurous disposition and her travels."[8] She loved training show dogs, particularly Cupid and Fannie, her prize-winning Italian greyhounds.[9] Another passion was raising and breeding horses. At a time when most women in the United States would not dare to drive a team of horses, she was acknowledged in the 1890s as one of America's most skilled horsewomen. An 1895 report on the growing popularity among women of "coaching and driving" claimed that Edith Van Buren was a "whip" of considerable skill with an international reputation, who "even in England…is considered as clever with the reins as any woman there."[10] Van Buren first visited Europe with her family as a young child and grew up to be a traveler of some renown; it was due to her extensive journeys as a single woman in the 1880s and 1890s that she became "well known at the prominent European watering places."[11]

Following the wedding of Nannie Hitchcock in late 1897, Mary Hitchcock and Edith Van Buren found themselves preparing for the boldest trip of their lives, a gold-hunting expedition to Alaska and the Yukon.[12] Mrs. Hitchcock's fascination with the Klondike had first germinated in the summer of 1897, when the initial reports of the gold discoveries along the Yukon made headlines throughout the United States and Canada. She was vacationing at the exclusive resort of Point-au-Pic, Quebec, when the stories about Joe Ladue, one of the Klondike Kings who founded Dawson City, fired her curiosity. Like thousands of others who read those stories that summer, she became determined to go to the Klondike and to get a gold mine of her own.

"My imagination was greatly excited," Hitchcock wrote, "by articles about the founder of Dawson, with which the newspapers were filled. The more I read, and the more I heard of the Klondike, the more necessary it seemed to me to meet this wonderful man, if one would gain information as to where to prospect, where to stake claims, where to locate, and how to gain untold millions."[13]

Swept along by gold fever and the desire "to see one of the few countries unknown to us," Hitchcock and Van Buren made plans to go to the Klondike themselves, despite the strong objections of their friends and families, who thought the idea so outrageous that "we were considered quite mad—fit subjects for an insane asylum."[14] Few people believed they were either capable enough or determined enough to make the trip themselves; that general disbelief was the extra incentive that spurred them onward. With the Great Danes, the canaries, the pigeons, and the parrot, they sailed under the Golden Gate Bridge bound for the Klondike in mid-June 1898. Sadly, they had decided it was necessary for them to make the trip without their maid, a necessary hardship because "the responsibility of taking a young and pretty girl into such regions as we had planned to explore would have been too great."[15]

Two Women in the Klondike tells the story of what Mary Hitchcock heard, said, saw, and did during her four-month-long search for Klondike treasure with Edith Van Buren from June to October 1898. In her mind Alaska and the Yukon were as foreign and exotic as any lands on earth. Mary's journal is rich in details about life in Dawson City that hectic summer, and is written in a high-spirited tone of a marvelous adventure, tinged by a mild but chronic sense of disapproval.

Few things she saw met her own high standards of decency and common courtesy. A typical encounter occurred on the steamship going north when a man asked if he could smoke in her presence; she agreed, but quickly regretted the decision. "Accustomed to the odour of a good cigar," she explained, "I made no objection, but oh! the pipes and vile tobacco! I had not counted upon them."[16] Jeremiah Lynch, a fellow passenger and diarist on the steamship, said Mary had "a most undeniable temper and tongue" and "the captain and various passengers felt the quality of both in infinite variety."[17]

Edith was definitely less particular than her older companion. Early one morning, shortly after 6 AM, while still groggy with sleep, Mary opened her eyes to find herself face to face with a wild creature. "By the dim light of the candle, I saw a mouse running across my bed and into the blankets.... Out of bed I bounded with a shriek that must have aroused every neighbour" and Edith simply "shouted with laughter, saying, 'How can you be afraid of a dear little thing like that?'"[18]

The housekeeping chores and the cooking were Edith's responsibilities, not only because Mary was busy writing her journal, but also because she admitted she was hopeless in the kitchen. On one occasion Mary tried to surprise Edith with a dish of risotto, but the experiment did not end well. Unaware that rice tends to expand in water, she simply loaded the pot on the stove and calmly returned to writing in her journal. When the rice began to boil and bubble she looked up in horror to see it overflowing across the stove. The apprentice cook soon filled every container in the kitchen with a seemingly infinite supply of white blobs of inedible paste. Edith returned home to find the mess everywhere.

"What's this?" Edith said, "as she raised a cover from a saucepan, 'and this?' raising another, 'and this?' looking at a platter containing a white pyramid." Edith professed that she had "once read of someone's having a similar rice-cooking experience, but thought it a fable, never dreaming that anyone could be such a 'ninny.' She begged me to leave the culinary department to her for the remainder of our stay."[19]

Throughout its pages Hitchcock's book reveals the author's fussy style and personality. She adopted what was even then an old-fashioned Victorian custom of never identifying people by their full names, using instead initials, such as A— M— for Alex McDonald, H— S— for Hank Summers, and so on. At the time of publication one reviewer found this "curtailing of proper

XIV names" both irksome and bizarre: "It is hardly probably that *all* of the persons thus designated have objected to the publication of their names in full," he wrote. Why Edith Van Buren's name had been eliminated, when she was one of the "Two Women" in the title, he found unfathomable. "Such apparently unreasonable omissions have not only the effect of prudery on the part of the writer, but are exceedingly irritating to the reader interested in the Klondike and the people who have braved the hardships of the journey there."[20]

Hitchcock's fussy attitude about names was in stark contrast to the utter informality of her surroundings, as the assumption of equality among people assailed her sensibilities on every side. The tension repeatedly highlighted throughout her journal is the contrast between her expectations of proper behavior and the reality of life on the muddy street of a mining camp. While she would never think of addressing a casual acquaintance as "Bill" or "John," the fact was that "every man is known by his Christian name in this part of the world."[21] She felt she had relaxed her standards far enough when she and Edith both agreed that visitors to their tent need not wear "boiled shirts" or "store clothes" because "we are all roughing it and camping out."[22]

"Roughing it" might have been too strong a term for someone "camping" in a nearly three-thousand-square-foot tent furnished with beds, desks, chairs, and complete kitchen facilities that became known in Dawson as "the Big Tent," and was surely the most impractical "two-woman" shelter ever devised. It leaked in the rain, was intolerably hot in the sun, and was none too secure in the wind. In fact, "the Big Tent" proved to be so uncomfortable that the women eventually set up another tent inside it in which to sleep.

Situated in so-called West Dawson, across the Yukon River from Dawson City, "the Big Tent" dominated the skyline. "Our tent," Hitchcock stated modestly, "attracts the greatest amount of attention from each side of the river."[23] One day as she stood among a large crowd on the Dawson City side admiring the tent from afar, Hitchcock watched in horror as the wind began to pick up.

"All eyes were on our tent," Hitchcock wrote, "and the comments were most amusing, as they wondered whether it belonged to the Salvation Army, a merry-go-round, or circus company, but as a gust of wind sprang up, some one shouted, 'Oh, it's a balloon! They're inflating it.' As we anxiously watched it rising and falling with the wind, someone overhearing our remarks on the subject said, 'Does it belong to you two ladies? Why wouldn't one half that size 'a' done yer?'"[24]

Curiosity about "the Big Tent" brought a steady stream of visitors that summer, hats politely in hand, eager to have a look inside. The guests gazed in amazement at the bird menagerie and other assorted animate and inanimate curiosities. "Their pleasure at [the] sight of the pigeons and our other pets was most touching, and their delight in hearing music from our Criterion [music box] was unbounded."[25]

Hitchcock's normal outfit on the trail consisted of what she called her "golf suit," combined with two suits of long underwear and a sealskin cape for cold weather, though she confessed that the sealskin was so warm that on one occasion she had to hire someone to carry it for her. For protection she was equipped with a revolver, cartridges, and gun belt—in one memorable photograph (page 93) she and Edith both posed inside their tent, awkwardly lounging around with their sidearms strapped to their belts—though, fortunately for everyone they encountered, there is no evidence the guns were ever needed. For evening wear, and other more formal occasions, Hitchcock had a sizable variety of outfits to choose from. One fellow gold hunter, a young well-to-do Englishman who first encountered Hitchcock and Van Buren on the steamship from San Francisco, could never forget the sight of the two middle-aged, gun-toting women of considerable girth, decked out in matching suits and cowboy hats. "They were attired in a most peculiar 'get-up,'" Nevill Armstrong recalled, "especially considering they were big women with much *embonpoint*! Both wore blue and white knitted jerseys over tightly laced corsages, leather belts with holsters containing large revolvers, blue serge knickers...stockings and short rubber boots, and on top of all, large, wide-brimmed Stetson hats."[26]

While they might on occasion eat macaroni and tomatoes on a tin plate, the residents of "the Big Tent" were also equipped to enjoy a seven-course meal, such as the spread they put on for the American consul general in Dawson City for their first large dinner party, which included anchovies on soda biscuit, mock turtle soup, roast moose and potato balls, escalloped tomatoes, asparagus salad with French dressing, peach ice cream, and cake, followed by cups of steaming French drip coffee, washed down with glasses of "sparkling Moselle."[27]

Hitchcock maintained that, despite the leveling mechanisms of the frontier, honorable men still respected women like her and Edith who remembered that they were ladies. "It's a fine thing for us to have such ladies around," Hitchcock recorded one man telling her, "it keeps us from getting demoralised.... [H]ow can we have the same respect for women who dress like men, and live like men, and talk like men, and act like men?"[28]

As rare as it was on the Yukon to find women who acted like women, it was just as difficult to find servants who behaved like servants. She resented the fact that on the riverboat "stewards, cabin-boys and cook" felt free enough to be "seated familiarly, at the same table" as all of the passengers.[29] The insolence of the hired help they engaged in Dawson City was almost more than Hitchcock could stomach. When she and Van Buren hired a down-on-his-luck prospector, an irascible Londoner named Isaacs, to be their cook, carpenter, boatman, butler, and "jack of all trades" for five dollars a day plus "grub," he proved to be recalcitrant and unsatisfactory, working at his own pace, and in his own impertinent style. He refused to be deferential. Many pages of *Two Women in the Klondike* are devoted to describing Isaacs' poor work habits. Nevertheless, the women were so fearful of losing his meager services, and being unable to find anyone else to be "our man Friday," that they tried not to complain, even when they thought he was being rude, lazy, or disrespectful.

After serving a round of Curaçao liquor one evening, Hitchcock noticed with horror that "when the glasses were removed we could see our cook wiping the inside of them with his forefinger and then carrying it to his mouth with evident relish. 'Hullo,' he called to one of our guests, 'did you ever taste anything as good as this until these ladies gave it to you?'"

"There is absolute democracy in the Klondike," she concluded; "one person is just as good as another."[30] When they finally decided that Isaacs had to be fired, Edith casually referred to him as a "servant" and he shouted back in her face, "Servant! Servant! Great Julius Caesar! 'Ow dare you call me a servant? 'Aven't I told you a 'undred times that I'm not a servant?"[31]

For all of their annoyance at not being treated in the manner to which they were accustomed, the two ladies found themselves enchanted by the sense of frontier freedom. Strenuous physical activity not only made the food taste better—"truly it is worth the trip to enjoy food as we now do"—but it also provided a sense of physical exhilaration. "How impossible seems the thought of being in the midst of luxuries once more, of having a nice warm room in which to dress, and to choose just what one likes to eat.... Yet how often shall we find the rooms overheated, the atmosphere that of a conservatory, the life limited and restrained, and long for the wilderness and the freedom thereof. A taste of such liberty as this must finally spoil one for civilisation."[32]

Fully aware of the novelty of two society women joining a gold stampede, Hitchcock apparently planned to write a book about her experiences from the very beginning. She kept a detailed daily journal—often writing as much as an hour a day or more—about her adventures. "My pen is...kept busy," she wrote, "in trying to depict in my journal the many novel characters on board, and to write of the warm hearts which show so plainly beneath the rough exterior."[33] Trying to capture the flavor of the local color, she transcribed all speech phonetically. For instance, as she dutifully recorded, their beleaguered "jack of all trades," Mr. Isaacs, privately told Edith he was relieved when he realized that Hitchcock was "book writin."

"I'm sorry I didn't understand you ladies better," Isaacs said, in Mrs. Hitchcock's rendering, "but Mrs. Hitchcock always seemed so 'aughty-like to me that I didn't realise she was book writin' and couldn't be disturbed, but used to get hangry 'cause she never joined in my conversation."[34] Another equally blunt visitor to their tent once asked her: "What are you writin', Mrs. Hitchcock? You're allus writin', no matter how early I comes in the morning nor how late at night, you're as busy as a cat with two tails."[35]

Despite a preoccupation with writing, neither Hitchcock nor Van Buren were too busy to think about getting gold themselves; they may have been rich, but they wanted to get richer. Since 1898 most observers have portrayed Hitchcock and Van Buren as nothing but idle tourists, a habit that started when they first reached the Yukon and the *Klondike Nugget* announced their debut as "the latest additions to Dawson society. The ladies are wealthy and are very well known in the United States. They travel for pleasure, and are simply 'doing' the Klondike country as they have done many other famous points of interest in Europe and America."[36] This picture of them as wealthy women who were "doing" the Klondike out of curiosity has persisted through the years. In his classic 1958 history of the gold rush, *Klondike Fever*, Pierre Berton maintained that out of the multitude of stampeders who went to the Klondike, Hitchcock and Van Buren were the only two taking a vacation. "Of all the thousands who poured into the Klondike that summer," Berton wrote, "it is probable that these two were the only ones who came merely as sightseers."[37] Many of the recent books about the women of the Klondike Gold Rush have repeated the same refrain—that they were merely tourists.[38] Meanwhile a play written for the Dawson Drama Festival in the 1980s based on Hitchcock's book, which highlights the "clash of cultures which resulted when two American society women brought their expectations to the Klondike," was simply entitled *Tourists*.[39]

The tendency to see Hitchcock and Van Buren as two ladies on a holiday spree is largely due to the sheer improbability of their entire venture and the way they went about it—the big top circus tent, the canaries, the pigeons, the bowling alley, and so on. Equipped as they were with the latest, the most costly, and the most modern gadgets, such as the graphophone and the movie projector, they were not particularly concerned with more practical matters. Furthermore, the fact that they were women by themselves has contributed to the tendency to underestimate their efforts, though in truth even a pair of rugged outdoorsmen with such an outfit would have been difficult to take too seriously.

In reality, however, Hitchcock and Van Buren were not so different from their fellow Klondike travelers in 1898, even if they were the only ones carrying fine china and polished silver. Most of the gold hunters had wildly unrealistic expectations about where they were going and what they would find there—they differed only in that few had the funds to outfit themselves in such a grand and impractical manner. Nor were the women the only ones drawn north by the desire to see the wilderness: for most everyone involved, the intoxication of the Klondike was only in part material gain; the thrill of adventure was at least half the lure of the Yukon Gold Rush.

A careful reading of the memoir and other evidence reveals the scope of Hitchcock and Van Buren's ambitious, if unrealistic, plans to get their share of Klondike treasure—plans that went far beyond simple sightseeing. Though they did no actual digging themselves, men wanting them to finance business propositions called constantly. They did grub-stake several miners for a share of future profits, and individually acquired numerous claims throughout the Yukon. They talked of returning to the gold fields the following year and, late in the summer, built a large, comfortable cabin to replace "the Big Tent." In fact, Hitchcock said she did return to the Yukon in later years—perhaps on more than one occasion—to oversee her extensive interests, which reportedly totaled more than one hundred gold-mining claims.[40]

Their most outlandish profit-making enterprise was a scheme to open a combination bowling alley and movie theater. While they never did locate a satisfactory operating partner or secure a location large enough to set up the bowling alley—it required seventy feet for all the machinery—the "animatoscope," an early film projector illuminated with acetylene gas produced by carbide and water, held out real promise of being "better than a gold mine." Hitchcock was confident that the crowds of miners, starved for entertainment, would readily pay to see the two dozen short films they had brought from San Francisco, which ranged from scenes of the Spanish-American War to "Gentleman Jim" Corbett's latest prize fight. In the circles in which she normally traveled, making money was not a subject of polite conversation. As might be expected of someone who had never earned a dollar in her life, she imagined earning a profit to be easier than it looked. Oblivious to the hazards of counting her nuggets before they were mined, she took it for granted that the animatoscope would make a killing. She promised only that she would not feel guilty about pocketing her share.

"I shall be a thousand times more proud of going back with an inexhaust-ible sack of gold earned by my own efforts than if the winter had been passed in idleness in New York, Paris, or London." Edith, who was just as certain that the money would soon be pouring in from miners eager to see moving pictures, pledged she was ready and able to do her share. "I want to work, too. I just want to show my family that I know how to do something and it would be a proud moment for me to carry home a bag of my own earnings—and I want it all in gold dust, too."[41]

Unfortunately for the two novice entrepreneurs, the bags of gold dust never materialized, as a series of technical problems plagued the animatoscope, such as leaking gasbags for the acetylene and a shortage of carbide. Nonetheless, they were proud when the screen finally flickered to life in late September 1898, much to the delight of Dawson City.[42]

By the time the animatoscope was in operation, Hitchcock's thoughts had long since turned homeward. Dreading the prospect that they might have to spend the winter in Dawson City, Hitchcock and Van Buren made their way by riverboat up the Yukon and walked across White Pass to catch the train to Skagway, and then took a steamer to Seattle. It was a rugged journey, espe-cially in a dress. "We picked up our short skirts and waded through shallow streams (bloomers are much safer without the skirts)."[43]

Upon arriving in Seattle (where the memoir ends) Hitchcock said she found herself besieged by reporters and "lionized" by the crowds eager to learn about her experiences in the Klondike. She promised that her forth-coming book, initially to be called "The Novel and Exciting Experiences of Two Society Women in the Klondike," would provide the answers. By the time Hitchcock returned to the East that fall, she was deluged with so many requests for information about the Klondike that she hired two personal secretaries to keep up with her correspondence. Interviewed about her adventures by the *New York Times* in early 1899, she urged capable women, especially trained nurses, to make the journey if they were so inclined. "There is no reason why women should not go. People say it is no place for them, but there are a great many reasons why they should go—they will be most chiv-alrously treated, and there are a great many things they can do. The miners there are nature's noblemen; a women could go quite alone, and she would receive the most courteous treatment." Another piece of advice came from her hard-earned experience. "There is no use in taking a cargo of things there unless you know just what to take."[44]

Gratified by all the publicity, Hitchcock was planning a return trip to the North, this time to the gold fields near Atlin, and a second book to be called

"Expedition No. 2." Her intentions were to travel by dog team and take with her both "a valet and a maid who are under agreement to do anything and everything that shall be asked of them." The valet and the maid would remain on the scene to watch over her interests and stake claims for her. Additionally the maid would be proficient at shorthand. "I shall get miner's stories, and my maid, who is a stenographer, will take down the words verbatim, so that I can have them with all the characteristic expressions" for yet a third book to be called "Tales Told Around the Miners' Campfires."[45]

Though Mrs. Hitchcock never published either of her two proposed sequels, *Two Women in the Klondike* did appear in the spring of 1899 to wide attention but mixed reviews. One journalist said it was "by far the finest book on the Klondike." The *Boston Herald* claimed it was a "racy record" which gave a "fairer and more complete idea of the life of Dawson" than any other book. Though Hitchcock may not have found gold herself, the Boston paper claimed her memoir was itself "a perfect mine of information."[46]

While some readers enjoyed Hitchcock's detailed recollections, others were more inclined to bemoan the fact that she wrote the way she traveled—never leaving any tiny detail out, never leaving a single pigeon or canary behind. Author and explorer Henry M. Stanley, of "Dr. Livingston, I presume" fame, found this book from "the feminine point of view" to be "full of petty details and small adventures" that were "lacking in artistic selection and comprehension."[47] Another critic claimed Hitchcock suffered from a "plentiful lack" of editing. "The style suggests that of a schoolgirl.... The pages are full of petty details which should have been condensed, or, still better, left out entirely." Despite these "glaring imperfections," however, he said that the book would prove of tremendous value "to readers who are eager for accurate information" about the Yukon Valley. "Both the book and the perilous journey that gave rise to it, were big undertakings, and Mrs. Hitchcock evidently attacked the two with an equal fearlessness."[48]

The Klondike would prove to be a turning point in the lives of both Mary Hitchcock and Edith Van Buren. With the publication of her book, Hitchcock became recognized in New York circles as a legitimate explorer and Klondike authority. (The foreword to the book was written by Elisha Dyer, the governor of Rhode Island, and it was dedicated to Mrs. Dyer.) In the years that followed she gave numerous illustrated lectures on her travels, and in 1904 was elected a Fellow of the American Geographical Society.[49]

Hitchcock's Klondike treasure hunt whetted her appetite for further adventures around the world. In 1906 she proposed a highly publicized expedition that could have been scripted by Robert Louis Stevenson. She announced to the press that she intended to lead an exploratory party to the island of Cocos in the eastern Pacific, about six hundred miles southwest of Panama. According to the story she told the *New York Times*, a Klondike miner whom she had befriended had first alerted her to the buried treasures of Cocos, rumored to be worth about $33 million. She claimed the miner had offered "to give me his maps, but I would not have them for anything in the world. Their very possession is a danger. This man is hounded by detectives, but it won't be long before he is free of them and aboard our treasure-seeking ship."[50]

Apparently Hitchcock never found any buried treasure, but another project with which she was involved proved to be more substantial. Around 1904 she founded and became president of a prominent New York City social institution known as the Entertainment Club, which for five years hosted public lectures, recitals, and discussions for women at the Waldorf-Astoria, and featured appearances by travelers, dignitaries, and high-ranking government officials from Europe and the United States.[51] The club prospered until 1908–1909, when a feud erupted between Hitchcock and one of the other members. Allegedly the fight started when "Mrs. Hitchcock criticized the dress which Mrs. Rhinelander Waldo wore at one of its functions." One by one others quit the club in protest until eventually "only a few of the staunchest adherents were left." The club finally disbanded completely in November 1909, when Hitchcock suddenly departed on a visit to India, where, it was said, she had gone to study "occultism."[52] Mary Hitchcock died in New York City eleven years later at age seventy-one, and was buried next to her husband in the Hitchcock family plot in Fall River, Massachusetts.[53]

For Edith Van Buren the most surprising twist of fate that came from her sojourn in the gold fields was that, for better or worse, at the then-advanced age of forty, the Klondike brought her a husband. Among the many letters that Van Buren received shortly after returning from the Klondike was a curious marriage proposal, through a third party, from a "foreign nobleman." Initially both Hitchcock and Van Buren laughed at the idea as preposterous. "Miss Van Buren says that there are a great many ways in which she might invest her money," Hitchcock told the press, "but one thing she never will do will be to invest in a foreign nobleman."[54] Apparently, as time went by, Van Buren reconsidered her position and her other prospects. The Italian nobleman who had asked for her hand in marriage styled himself Count Baron Gennaro Vessicchio de Castelmenardo; clearly she was intrigued by the possibility of becoming the Countess of Castelmenardo—until she heard rumors that the count himself was a fake.

Calling upon her extensive contacts in the U.S. Foreign Service, she asked the U.S. Consul in Naples to investigate whether the count was a "bogus Baron." As Van Buren explained, "naturally one wants to know every thing about a prospective husband. He is remarkably handsome and wears now a small beard, black, and is quite pale and has remarkable brown eyes with very long lashes and is the only well dressed foreigner I ever knew.... Of course I want to know about his character, but it's more especially about the title, and if *he* had the right to bear it."[55]

Ultimately investigators would discover that the count, despite the extent of his sartorial elegance, had no right to call himself a count, though it is unclear whether this was learned before they were married—to the general horror of the Van Buren family—in London in July 1900. Apparently a payment of several thousand dollars was made at some point to make the title legitimate, and henceforth Edith Van Buren would be known as the Countess de Castelmenardo.[56]

The count and the countess were not destined to live happily ever after. In a spectacular case that made headlines on both sides of the Atlantic, the Countess de Castelmenardo had her philandering husband arrested in Naples in 1906 on charges of "brutality, fast living and gambling." The count was ultimately convicted of "cruelty and unfaithfulness" and sentenced to three months in prison for his infidelities.

The countess's actions were recognized at the time as a great step forward for the rights of wronged women. Refusing to be stigmatized for the failings of her disgraced husband, she admitted that Americans would make ideal husbands if only they were not so practical and did not talk too much about business. "Women are romantic," she said, "that is what attracts them to the foreigner, who rarely speaks of his 'work,' if he does work."[57]

When she died eight years later in 1914 at age fifty-four, the Countess de Castelmenardo was remembered as the "American Countess Who Jailed Spouse." As the *Washington Post* stated in a posthumous tribute, "of all the American women unhappily married to foreigners, of more or less authentic title, she was the only one bold enough to take advantage of the laws of continental Europe to have her husband arrested, convicted, and sentenced to a term of imprisonment when she discovered that he had betrayed her."[58] It was such strength as one might expect from the woman who had "dug gold in the Klondike and [had] been presented to the Queen."[59]

Interest in the history of women continues to grow year by year, and for that reason alone the lives of Mary Hitchcock and Edith Van Buren deserve to be remembered, even if their story does not always fit with modern conceptions of how a strong woman should behave. By any reckoning these two women were pathfinders and trail breakers.

Mary Hitchcock claimed she published *Two Women in the Klondike* "in order to show women who feel inclined to make the trip exactly what they may expect."[60] Given the eccentric nature of her Klondike excursion with Edith Van Buren, however, it is unlikely any woman (or man) could ever have used her model as an inspiration, except perhaps for what not to do. But the spirit of the book—the belief that anything is possible—appeals to anyone who has ever tried to beat the odds.

Two Women in the Klondike reflects the journey it describes; a big book of nearly five hundred pages in the original edition, it is extravagant, sprawling, eclectic, and cluttered. In the vast field of gold-rush literature, Hitchcock's book stands apart like "the Big Tent," a symbol of the extremes to which both men and women were driven by the sweet, hopeful song of gold and adventure in the summer of 1898.

NOTES

1   Jeremiah Lynch, *Three Years in the Klondike* (Chicago: R. R. Donnelley and Sons, 1967), p. 18.

2   J. W. Leonard, ed., *Woman's Who's Who of America* (American Commonwealth Company, 1914), p. 392.

3   Quotation from a tribute delivered at a meeting of the Council of the American Geographical Society, June 20, 1887.

4   *Fall River Evening News*, December 6, 1892, p. 4.

5   Mary E. Hitchcock, *Tales Out of School About Naval Officers (and others) by A Woman who has lived on a Man-of-War* (New York: Gotham Press, 1908), p. 95.

6   *New York Times*, June 27, 1897, p. 15; May 14, 1958, p. 33.

7   *New York Times*, November 18, 1897, p. 7.

8   *New York Times*, March 12, 1906, p. 4.

9   For examples of her dog show results see, for example, *Forest and Stream: A Journal of Outdoor Life*, May 6, 1888; October 18, 1888; March 14, 1889; April 11, 1889.

10 *Atlanta Constitution*, August 26, 1895, p. 7. See also *Outing*, Vol. XVI, No. 5, August 1890, p. 411.

11 *New York Times*, May 14, 1914, p. 11.

12 *New York Times*, January 30, 1899, p. 7.

13 See this volume, p. 22. A *New York Times* dispatch noted a slightly different story that appears less credible. The *Times* claimed that Hitchcock and Van Buren initially "started West with the idea of visiting Japan," and only upon reaching San Francisco and hearing the wild tales of the returning Klondikers did their destination shift from the Far East to the Far North. *New York Times*, January 30, 1899, p. 7.

14 See this volume, p. 2.

[15] See this volume, p. 1.

[16] See original text of *Two Women in the Klondike* (New York: G. P. Putnam's Sons, 1899), p. 9.

[17] Lynch, *Three Years in the Klondike*, p. 18.

[18] See this volume, p. 145.

[19] See this volume, pp. 146–147.

[20] Young E. Allison, "Two Women in the Klondike," *Overland Monthly*, September 1899, Vol. XXXIV, No. 201, p. 286.

[21] See this volume, p. 44.

[22] See this volume, p. 54.

[23] See this volume, p. 51.

[24] See this volume, p. 63.

[25] See this volume, p. 53.

[26] Nevill A. D. Armstrong, *Yukon Yesterdays: Thirty Years of Adventure in the Klondike* (London: John Long Ltd., 1936), p. 17.

[27] See this volume, p. 75.

[28] See this volume, p. 113.

[29] See original text of *Two Women in the Klondike*, p. 87.

[30] *New York Times*, February 5, 1899.

[31] See this volume, p. 94.

[32] See this volume, pp. 54, 119.

[33] See this volume, p. 5.

[34] See original text of *Two Women in the Klondike*, p. 296.

[35] See this volume, p. 122.

[36] See this volume, p. 51.

[37] Pierre Berton, *Klondike Fever* (New York: Alfred A. Knopf, 1958), p. 316.

[38] See, for example, Melanie J. Mayer, *Klondike Women: True Tales of the 1897–1898 Gold Rush* (Athens, OH: Ohio University Press, 1989); Frances Backhouse, *Women of the Klondike* (Vancouver: Whitecap Books, 1995); and Jennifer Duncan, *Frontier Spirit: The Brave Women of the Klondike* (Toronto: Doubleday Canada, 2003).

[39] *Klondike Sun*, December 21, 2001.

[40] See this volume, pp. 19, 22, 31, 65, 81, 108, 140; Leonard, ed., *Woman's Who's Who of America*, p. 392; *New York Times*, February 5, 1899. In the spring of 1899 it was announced that Hitchcock and Van Buren had sold their large log home in West Dawson to George Leon, an entrepreneur who used it as the centerpiece for a hotel and summer resort, with cafe and beer garden, that he modestly called the "Villa DeLion." His original plans called for installing the bowling alley apparatus brought north by Hitchcock and Van Buren. See *Klondike Nugget*, February 22, 1899; August 9, 1899.

[41] See this volume, p. 107.

[42] See this volume, p. 155. It is not clear how long the animatoscope remained in operation, though in late November 1898, a showman named George Vogel put

on a moving picture show called *The Wondroscope* (most likely using the films and **xxv** magic lantern slides of Hitchcock and Van Buren) at the Pioneer Hall and the Monte Carlo Theater. See *Klondike Nugget*, November 23, 1898, November 26, 1898.

[43] See this volume, p. 178.

[44] Hitchcock, *Tales Out of School*, p. 155; *New York Times*, February 5, 1899.

[45] *New York Times*, August 22, 1899, p. 3.

[46] Reviews noted in end matter of *Tales Out of School*.

[47] Henry M. Stanley, "Late Books on Alaska," *The Dial: A Semi-Monthly Journal of Literary Criticism*, August 1, 1899, Vol. XXVII, No. 315, p. 72.

[48] Allison, "Two Women in the Klondike," p. 286.

[49] *Bulletin of the American Geographical Society of New York*, 1905, p. 40.

[50] *New York Times*, February 12, 1906, p. 18.

[51] See, for example, *New York Times*, February 17, 1904, p. 9; December 24, 1905, p. x6; February 4, 1906, p. SM7; March 13, 1907, p. 9; January 8, 1908, p. 9; February 13, 1908, p. 9, November 1, 1908, p. x2; *Washington Post*, February 11, 1906, p. 11.

[52] *New York Times*, November 25, 1909, p. 11.

[53] *New York Times*, April 8, 1920, p. 11; Records of Oak Grove Cemetery, Fall River, Massachusetts.

[54] *New York Times*, February 5, 1899.

[55] Edith Van Buren to A.H. Byington, May 13, 1900, Byington Papers, Box 1, Georgetown University Library, Washington, D.C.

[56] *New York Times*, May 5, 1914, p. 11. Edith's brother Harold Van Buren, the consul at Nice, France, was said to have been the person who first introduced Edith to the "Count," but Harold soon became disenchanted with the nobleman (*New York Times*, March 12, 1906, p. 4). On December 10, 1900, Harold wrote to Consul Byington in Naples requesting additional information about "the person who has lately become connected with my family" in order to "safeguard the honor of my family name and that of my near relatives." It was reportedly on Harold's instigation that Edith eventually took her husband to court for infidelity in 1906. (Van Buren to Consul Byington, December 10, 1900; January 19, 1901; undated clipping; Byington Papers, Box 1, Folder 43, Georgetown University Library, Washington, D.C.)

[57] *Washington Post*, November 9, 1907, p. 12.

[58] *Washington Post*, May 10, 1914.

[59] Undated clipping, Byington Papers, Box 1, Folder 43, Georgetown University Library, Washington, D.C.

[60] See this volume, p. 3.

NOTES ON THE TEXT

THIS EDITION OF *Two Women in the Klondike* has been abridged from the original text, published in 1899 by G. P. Putnam's Sons, New York. To create a more accessible narrative, unessential and repetitive material has been deleted; the narrative style and sequence of events in the original account have been retained. While some grammatical and typographical conventions have been modernized, the original British spellings are retained here. The dashes, which so exercised the nineteenth-century reviewers of *Two Women in the Klondike*, have generally been retained, except in the names of Mary Hitchcock, Edith Van Buren, and a few other notable personalities, such as "Big Alex" McDonald, the Oatley Sisters, etc., when it is clear to whom Hitchcock is referring.

FOREWORD TO THE 1899 EDITION

THE STORY OF *Two Women in the Klondike*, written by Mrs. Roswell D. Hitchcock, who with her friend Miss Edith Van Buren, braved all the hardships and dangers of a journey to the Klondike and all the discomforts of a life along the very skirmish line of civilization where the turning of a spade has oftentimes led to the discovery of a fortune, cannot fail to be most interesting and most instructive.

Mrs. Hitchcock is the widow of the late Commander Roswell D. Hitchcock, of the U. S. Navy, who was the son of Professor Roswell D. Hitchcock, for many years President of the Union Theological Seminary, New York. Mrs. Hitchcock herself is descended from Lord FitzGerald. Her grandfather and father were born in Norfolk, Virginia, where many of her relatives now live and where the old family mansion is still a landmark, although it has passed into other hands. Miss Van Buren is a grand-niece of President Van Buren and daughter of General Van Buren, who was United States Consul-General to Japan in the eighties.

The two travellers were born and reared in luxury and refinement and the narrative of their daily life in that terrible Wonderland of the North is of itself not only a tribute to their own perseverance and determination, but to the character of intelligent and fearless Anglo-Saxon women, who, among all sorts and conditions of men, never fail to secure protection and respect.

ELISHA DYER

PROVIDENCE, RHODE ISLAND
APRIL 11, 1899

ACKNOWLEDGMENTS

THE AUTHOR HEREBY expresses her cordial acknowledgment to all those from whom she has received assistance by the contribution either of stories or of photographs, which she has recorded in her journal or has utilised in the preparation of her volume.

Special thanks are due to Miss Edith M. Van Buren for certain facts and stories, and for a number of photographs; also to Dr. Dow, Mr. Arthur D. Spiess, Mr. Von Millengen, Dr. DeCow, and Mr. E. A. Hegg, for their kindness in permitting the reproduction of photographs belonging to them.

Edith Van Buren (left) and Mary Hitchcock
with their Great Danes Ivan and Queen on board the *St. Paul*

Ho for the Land of Gold!

OUR MAGNIFICENT GREAT DANES, Queen and Ivan, met us near the wharf, which was crowded with such a mass of people that it was no easy task for our coachman to guide his horses to the gangplank of the steamer which was about to make her maiden trip to St. Michaels. Although it was still early, her decks were thronged. We slowly worked our way to our cabins, where we found that our maid, who had preceded us, had carefully arranged such articles as she thought necessary for so adventurous a journey. We were sorry to leave her behind us, but the responsibility of taking a young and pretty girl into such regions as we had planned to explore would have been too great.

In San Francisco our outfitting kept us in one mad rush, so that, during the last week, our rule was twenty hours for work and four for sleep; but the work had been so interesting, the various projects so exciting, that the four hours were passed in planning, rather than sleeping, as our brains continued to act, and would not be stilled. At half-past five writing and making up accounts began; then we hurriedly took a cup of coffee while dressing; rushed to reach the shops as soon as [they] opened, had no time for luncheon, and the stores were closing before we were aware that it was time; then dinner, with only half an hour to spare for it, and a hasty comparison of notes before starting to listen to "records" for our graphophone, and music for our "Criterion"; to learn to prepare the beautiful acetylene light with which we intended to illuminate our tent. We were taking extreme pleasure also in outfitting a protégé, whose stories of life in Dawson, and whose many schemes for making a fortune had greatly interested us. Preparations for the trip were often retarded by dear, kind friends who wrote: "Cannot understand your silence"; or, "This is my fourth letter, but not a line have you deigned in reply"; or, "It is hard to believe that you have so changed and have no longer a thought for me." The last night was spent in reassuring those who could not understand.

Thanks be to the Lord! It is all over now and we have before us at least a fortnight of blissful repose—even seasickness will have no terrors. We are just passing out of the beautiful Golden Gate. As we were leaving the dock, Mr. W— appeared with his machine for taking moving pictures, shouted a request for us to stand in the bow of the steamer and wave our handkerchiefs. From his smile of satisfaction we judged that the resemblance would be striking and that we should soon be *en évidence* at some of the vaudeville shows, where "The Departure of the *St. Paul* for the Klondike" might be announced in loud tones. Such is fame!

This longing of ours to see one of the few countries unknown to us had created such astonishment among our friends and acquaintances that we were considered quite mad—fit subjects for an insane asylum. The remarks we heard on all sides were also far from flattering or consoling. At each stage of our journey from New York to San Francisco, reporters by the dozen came to interview us. Such questions as these were asked us: "Do you mean to say that you really intend to give up all the luxuries and comforts of home life to camp out and endure such privations and hardships as we read of? Have you ever climbed mountains? Tramped through swamps? Stumbled over rocky precipices? Lived among rough miners? Do give it up—you have no idea of all the perils that are in store for you."

In Colorado Springs we were charmingly entertained, but not one of our friends there believed that we really would carry out our plans. In Denver a party of us went to visit a famous mine in Georgetown; we were shown every attention and courtesy, and deep interest was expressed in the success of our plans. "She oughtn't to have any future," growled an old miner standing near; "any lady wot leaves a fine home an' fine friends and luxuries to take up with hardships wot's hard enough for strong men to bear ought to be locked up in an insane asylum."

Upon inquiry, we found that the reputation of the Alaska Commercial Company was so high, their ships so well manned, and their contracts so carefully carried out, that we went to the office to ascertain how soon one of their steamers would be leaving for the desired land. We were informed that the *St. Paul* had just been finished; was fitted with all modern conveniences; that a reception on board was to be given that very evening, and were urged not only to attend but to bring our friends. We did so, were received by one of the courteous owners most charmingly, treated with distinguished consideration, and told to select whichever cabins we pleased, as, although all were engaged, the passengers, being composed mostly of men, would "willingly change in favour of ladies." We were next taken to the dining room for a champagne supper; after tasting the chef's bouillon and one or two other dishes, we immediately decided that the wants of the inner man would be well cared for and booked our passage at once, so charmed were we with the equipments and many advantages of the *St. Paul,* to say nothing of the extreme courtesy of her officers.

And now begins a most truthful account of incidents just as they happened, copied from the journal of daily events, in order to show women who feel inclined to make the trip exactly what they may expect.

"With Malice Towards None"

STEAMER *ST. PAUL*, **THURSDAY, JUNE 16TH** ❦ Wakened early. Opened the blind, and was sitting up in bed rapidly jotting down a dream-inspired article, when the curtains parted, the head of a man appeared, and a big, hearty voice called out: "Hulloa! How are you this morning? Why don't you get up? I'm up! Have a piece of orange? I've been seasick for four days. This is my first day out of my cabin. Have been awfully generous. Gave the captain the ocean, and the purser all the land we've left behind. Didn't think I should ever want either of them again; but, say—why *don't* you get up?" "Because it is so much more comfortable resting here than walking on a wet deck, and so much easier to write." "Writing—do you have to write? What yer writing about? Write a letter to me; I'm your next-door neighbour. Suppose you don't mind my looking in your room and trying to jolly you up?" "As for the 'looking in,' one grows accustomed to that on this ship where the cabins open on the promenade deck and kind neighbours feel it a duty to cheer up those who are supposed to be ill, and Miss Van Buren and I intend to 'rough it,' and to live and do just as the people of the country do." Later—same voice: "One o' your dogs is loose. What yer going to do with them when you get to the first landing place? I'll help you look out for 'em and get 'em ashore, while you carry your revolver, as the other dogs will all pounce on 'em and it won't be a fair fight—twenty against two. What! You don't know how to use a revolver? That don't matter. Just fire in the air, and the dogs'll run. Why, women shoot better than men, anyhow. I didn't know my wife could shoot until I offered her a pair of gloves for each time she hit the bull's-eye. She did it twice before I was sure it was not an accident, and then I cried quits. So long; I'll come and jolly you again by and by."

[Another] face appears: "I've got some very bad news for you, Madam." "Not the dogs?" I cried in alarm. "No, Madam." "Nor the parrot?" "No, Madam, but one of the canaries is dead. I did all I could for him, and left him two hours ago bright and lively, but returned to find the other mourning his mate, who was lying cold in the bottom of the cage. I'm very sorry, but as the two dozen pigeons are in perfect health, you must see that I have given great attention to your birds and animals."

Face number one again: "Say! I've thought of a splendid scheme for you. There's plenty of old canvas on board. Why don't you hire one of the sailors to sew a tent for your dogs out of it? On the quiet, of course. You can do anything on the quiet. I'll get one for you. Here, Bo's'n, this lady wants a tent for her dogs. Look in this window an' you fix it with her, an' she'll fix it with you afterwards—that's all right. Say what was your friend kicking about this morning? She looked thundering black at me while she was talking in your window to you. Oh! She didn't like our talking outside her door! Wanted to sleep later! Well, why the deuce didn't she say so? You can bet your life we wouldn't 'a' done it if she'd 'a' said she didn't like it. Well so long! I'll come back and jolly you some more if you don't get out soon. I'm feeling fine! Your mandolin disturb me last evening? No! Bless your soul! If I'd known you had a mandolin I'd 'a' been in. Next time you play it you can count on me as a sure enough visitor."

FRIDAY, JUNE 17TH ☞ I am not enjoying much of the rest to which I so longingly looked forward. Letters home must be written, and my pen is also kept busy in trying to depict in my journal the many novel characters on board, and to write of the warm hearts which show so plainly beneath the rough exterior. I hurried through dinner and went to my cabin for a quiet hour's practice of zither and mandolin. With closed door and spirit far away in the realms of music, I was brought back by hearing: "Ain't that the sweetest music you ever listened to?" "Egad! I could stop here forever if she'd never stop playing." "What's she playin'?" "Why, a zither," and the informant, bolder than the others, worked his way inside of the tiny cabin and seated himself on the washstand. Another dropped into the corner of the sofa, while still another seated himself on the doorsill. Shouts of "A whale! A whale!" sent the entire party forward, and music [was] forgotten as we watched the sport of several monsters of the deep.

SATURDAY, JUNE 18TH ☞ "Thought you'd like a flower," a voice shouted early this morning, as the curtains were pushed aside and a rose fell on my bed, stopping my hurrying pencil. "Bet you don't know where I got it from, but I was sure you'd appreciate it. Still writing? I say! You work hard, don't you? Why don't you come out and enjoy yourself like the rest of the people?" and the man

6 who had offered to look out for the dogs at the first landing place disappeared, as Edith entered to give me the morning news. "Do you know who your friend is, the one who gave you the rose?" she laughed. "His name is J—, and he keeps a saloon in San Francisco." "Saloon or no saloon," replied I, "he is much more polite and considerate than your friend, who, representative of an enormously wealthy syndicate though he be, bows to a lady without seeming to remember that he has a hat to touch." "Oh, he's absent-minded," said Edith. "I've already spoken to him about it, though. He and the Judge are wild to know why we are taking such an enormous tent to Dawson. They have spent the entire week in trying to discover for what purpose it is intended, and say that it is the first time that they have ever found a woman who could keep a secret; so they are waiting to see if they can't prevail upon you to divulge the great mystery."

Upon leaving the dinner table early in order to indulge in music before all the world and his wife should start upon the evening promenade, a refined-looking young man, with delicately cut features, approached, saying: "It's very dull on board, and I enjoy your music so much that I thought by coming early you might allow me to listen, and may I bring my mandolin and try some duets with you?" The request was willingly granted, but only for a short time were we permitted to indulge uninterruptedly in practice. The crowd soon discovered us. . . . Had a delightful chat with two modest Italian priests. They had expected to be sent to Dawson, and had made all their plans to that effect, but orders had been changed and they were going to an unknown region. No comment did they make—no unkind criticism at this unexpected news: they were in the Master's service, their only thought to do good and to lead souls unto Him. May they reap a rich reward.

Our evening entertainment on the *St. Paul* ended with *My Country, 'tis of Thee*, after which a collection was taken for the stewards who had so well helped us to pass an hour, the generous captain heading the contribution. As I was being escorted to the cabin by half a dozen musical acquaintances, my attention was attracted by something to me quite novel: it looked like a searchlight coming from the bottom of the ship. On questioning, I was told that instead of irritating the nerves of passengers by the old-fashioned method of hoisting and throwing overboard cinders or ashes, they were washed out in a stream of water. That explained the unusual quiet, so different from the noise endured on my last long voyage.

Land in Sight!

SUNDAY, JUNE 19TH ☞ Towards evening there was a great commotion on board. A head appeared at the window and a voice said: "Pardon me, but land's in sight, and we shall reach Unalaska before midnight." What a delightful announcement! Scarcely had the head disappeared ere I was dressing rapidly and soon joined the excited passengers. Oh! The grandeur of the scene before us! A long chain of mountains on either side. Snow everywhere, and above the snow the most beautiful blue clouds, not with silver lining, but golden. As we approached the entrance, three islands lying on the left seemed to be surrounded by fishing boats, and we gazed eagerly; but, upon drawing near, they proved to be only rocks. Sea birds flew before the *St. Paul* as though carefully guiding the good ship on her first voyage; smaller birds flitted to and fro across the bow, while sea fowl skimmed the water in search of prey. The icy wind was so penetrating that my companions soon sought the warmth of Social Hall, but the inspiring scene chained me to the deck, and my soul was filled with gratitude towards Him who in His infinite mercy had brought us safely across the ocean.

MONDAY, JUNE 20TH ☞ Evening—such an exciting day on shore! A large party of us pushed off in the steam launch, and after all were comfortably placed I took a seat in the doorway to be sheltered and also to enjoy the beautiful view. A young woman, finding it too cold outside, asked if there were room for one more in the cabin. I willingly moved aside to allow her to enter, instead of which she coolly took my place and allowed me to remain standing. We passed a rock completely covered with gulls, which reminded me, I scarcely know why, of a certain rock in China which was pointed out to me as the one on which superfluous girl babies were placed to be disposed of by the birds of the air. On reaching the wharf, great was our dismay at finding it towering high above

8 our heads, necessitating a perpendicular climb on slats which shook under the feet of lighter weights than ours. As we were thinking sadly of turning back, Edith had a happy inspiration. A rowboat was near, and its occupant hailed. He quickly came to our rescue. We had but to transfer ourselves to his boat, and presto! We were landed safely on the beach. Several women who had followed our lead dashed on with never so much as a "thank you" to our assistant. We stopped to offer him remuneration but he assured us so cordially of his pleasure in having been able to oblige us, that we thanked him profusely and decided that we were going to like Alaskans.

At the very end of the town we came to a collection of tents. At the entrance was a sign which read, "Laundry by the Lake." We inquired if we might enter and inspect the "Laundry," and the request was readily granted. After peeping first into one tent and then another Edith at last said to the good-looking young woman in charge: "But where is the laundry?" "Here," said she, pointing to the tub in which her arm was immersed. "Are you getting rich?" "Oh, no! Madam; I did not come for that. The laundry is only to keep me from feeling lonely while the men are away, as the days would otherwise be too long." "May I take a picture of your laundry?" said I. "With pleasure, Madam; but may I have the time to put on my red shawl and my cap?" "By all means, and call some of your friends to join in the group." A shout brought a number of men, who entered into the spirit of the thing and posed to make an interesting picture. One threw a bag over his shoulder, another caught up a grip-sack, a third pretended to prepare a mess of porridge in a pail; while a fourth looked hesitatingly as though to inquire whether he were really wanted. "Come along," cried Edith, "we are waiting for you; the picture would never do without so handsome a fellow," and the others laughed at his embarrassment and pleasure. The laundress, who had been searching unsuccessfully for her cap, was obliged to pose without it.

Our next visit was to the cemetery, which we reached after climbing a short hill. Many mounds were unmarked; others had a wooden cross, but no name. There was one with a marble slab and the inscription "Sheltered at last" and three with pretentious iron railings which looked incongruous. As we wandered back towards the little town, we stopped to gather many beautiful wildflowers and violets, that seemed so out of place under the snow-capped peaks. I stopped at the "Jesse Lee Home," to make inquiries in regard to this mission, feeling that the information would be grateful to those who could hear but seldom. On sending in my card I was ushered into a sitting-room, and while waiting I was pleasantly entertained by an interesting young couple who had been boarding at the "Home" for a fortnight. They were waiting for the Yukon to be free from ice that they might continue their journey, and were enjoying their stay immensely. "There is always something going on," said they. "The officers of the *Bear* have entertained us extensively, and many little festivities have been given in our honour." One of the teachers then entered, and, telling me that she was in the midst of great preparations for an exhibition to be given in the evening, asked if I would accompany her to the "village store and post office," thus allowing her to kill two birds with one stone, and talk to me while at the same time accomplishing her errands. She spoke of her love for the work of helping and educating Indian girls, but said that the immorality in the village was so great that it was often most discouraging, for instead of having the assistance of the mothers, they seemed rather to encourage their daughters to intimacy with the white men. She also stated that the Russian priest, disapproving of their sectarian teachings, tried to undermine their influence, and to wrest from them their charges. Here we reached the post office, and our ways parted. I was cordially invited to the evening entertainment, also to pay another visit on the morrow. I left, sad and pensive, to think that here among those dedicated to the service of the Lord, instead of love and brotherly aid, there should be dissension, strife, and bitterness! Why, if both were equally earnest, could they not work in unison?

TUESDAY, JUNE 21ST ☞ A steady drizzle, but I dressed and went up to feed the dogs, who were softly crying at sight of the land which they could not reach. Our plans were made to spend the day in a trip to Dutch Harbour, close by, a visit to the Russian church, also to the mission. The rain alone would not have prevented, but the thought of trying to climb up the wharf on slippery, shaking slats, of being pushed by those from below, and pulled by those from above, of the trouble we would give the men accompanying us—this all combined to cause us to remain on board, consoling ourselves that we might be able to carry out our programme on the return trip. The few merchants of the place might have made a good investment by arranging an attractive landing place, as there were a number of small articles which we would gladly have purchased.

FRIDAY, JUNE 24TH ☞ Shouts of "land" awakened passengers this morning, and King Island was announced, but, unfortunately, it was too far off for pictures to be taken. After luncheon there was great excitement, and the upper, or shade deck, was crowded by many who gazed upon icebergs for the first time. Down they floated towards us, singly, and in fantastic shapes. We steamed through them carefully—then the pulse-beats of the engine were slowed, as we saw in the distance what seemed to be an impenetrable barricade, and we began to realise the meaning of the old saying, "We could hear ourselves think."

10 A man was sent aloft to indicate a passageway. To our inexperienced eyes, that long wall of ice before us seemed to shut out all hope of entrance, but the sailor guided us to a narrow doorway through which we passed into a clear sea. Not for long, however, did we steam at full speed. Far in the distance a small cake of ice appeared, then another, and still another, until we were soon in what could only be termed an icefield, with the stillness of death around and not even the voice of a bird calling to its mate to be heard. It is difficult to describe the solemn stillness which pervades this vast region, dotted with ice floes speeding noiselessly to destruction; the silence unbroken by a single sound save the throbbing of the steamer as it advanced slowly through this wilderness of space. Language becomes too poverty stricken to express the awe and admiration which fill the soul at such a time.

We were aroused from reverie by hearing, "Yukon's broken up, sure enough. Wouldn't 'a' believed she could a' held so much ice. We're all right to go in now if the river boat's waiting for us as the Company promised, and we'll be the first ones in, too. Won't 'the boys' give us a rousing welcome!"

St. Michaels

SATURDAY, JUNE 25TH ☞ The dropping of the anchor, the shouts, the lowering of boats, brought many a head to the windows. Three bells struck. Only half after five, and no further sleep, for there is St. Michaels, flat and uninteresting in appearance from this distance; nothing to be seen but a few houses and tents, several ships and barges. We hear the shout, "River has been open two weeks," so, expecting to be transferred at once, packing begins, and plenty of it there is, too, after a fortnight at sea. At eight o'clock we were told that there was not a river steamer in, and that we might be obliged to remain on board a week or more. After luncheon everyone hung about the gangway in "store clothes," ready and waiting for an opportunity to explore St. Michaels. Good Father R— approached, and, listening to the complaints, which were loud and long, insisted that we should be allowed to cross before the work of changing freight began. He was assisted in his efforts by a man who seemed to be in charge of the St. Michaels department of the Alaska Commercial Company, and who proved to be as helpful as their employees generally are. He quickly called for the gangplank, had the ropes cast aside, and a happy lot of passengers were soon on the tug. We found the point of attraction to be the store of the Alaska Commercial Company, a large roomy building with post office in one corner, similar to the arrangement at the settlement of Iliuliuk, Unalaska. The hooped veils were being inquired for by men as well as women, who expected with such protection to be able to escape the mosquito pest which makes life miserable in these regions. A very funny picture was thus presented as we looked at one another through such novel screens. The supply soon gave out, so an enterprising passenger purchased netting and wire from which she soon fashioned the required article, for which she charged and received one dollar each.

On to the Custom House I went, but the door was locked, and the Indian on the porch informed me that the Inspector was taking a walk. He pointed

NOVEL MOSQUITO SCREENS

him out in the distance. I followed, soon reached the end of the plank walk, then struck into the grassy, muddy soil, jumped several ditches or crossed on a plank, until a particularly marshy spot was reached, over which the Inspector, his wife, and friend had easily passed, being properly shod for such soil, but as they were within hailing distance, I called out and told my errand, which was, that as our Government does not take our word, even under oath, it would be necessary for me to have my sealskin wrap stamped before going into British territory, in order to prove on my return that I was not swearing falsely as to having been its lawful possessor before crossing the boundary line; otherwise I must be deprived of it, no matter how cold the weather, or submit to unjust payment. Truly, a brilliant idea, which Uncle Sam would never approve of could he but realise the humiliation thereof.

When the St. Michaels inspector was informed that I had been told in San Francisco that it would be easier to have the stamping done by him, he replied, "Oh, yes! They think we have nothing to do up here, but I have no appliances whatever for that sort of thing; however, if you will send in an application describing the wrap, and have the purser or someone sign that you purchased it in the United States, then I will make out a paper with the official seal, and you may sew it inside the lining." This ended my first interview in St. Michaels. I took snapshots of many of the little one-story houses that faced the water, made groups of small Indian children, who seemed always ready to be photographed and obeyed readily the motion of the hand. The interesting pamphlet arranged by the Alaska Commercial Company tells us that:

the natives about St. Michaels and all over the big Yukon delta, are Eskimo belonging to that strange race which stretches from the domain of the Aleuts on the west to "Greenland's icy mountains" on the east. They have nothing in common with the Chukchi of the easternmost Siberian land, any more than they have with the Aleuts of the islands, which fact has gone against the theory of the original settlement of America by way of Bering Strait. These people form a most interesting study during the brief wait at St. Michaels, while baggage and freight are being transferred from the ocean liners to one of the swift and commodious river steamers. They are among the mildest, and unquestionably the filthiest of humankind. Personal cleanliness in the winter is entirely unattempted. The Eskimo diet consists principally of rotted fish and rancid seal oil, which give to their habitations an odour from which the nostril of the white man recoils. Though lazy and improvident past all belief, they are tractable, have the powers of mimicry exceptionably developed, readily unravel the puzzles of white children, and even master chess in a way to put to shame their missionary teachers.

It then goes on with a description of the geese, ducks, snipe, and other waterfowl in countless thousands, willow grouse, deer, caribou, and larger game, while the fishing "is merely a matter of dropping in a line with properly baited hooks, when the creel of the angler will soon be full."

Time and space will not permit me to give further extracts in regard to the history of St. Michaels, nor the romantic story of how a massacre was averted by a warning given through an Indian maiden to her white lover in the fort; while, as for the "outfit" instructions, already too many books have been published on the subject. I paid a visit to the Russian priest, but he proved so uncommunicative that, aside from learning that he had been there since 1882, there was no other information of value to be obtained. He devoted but five moments to showing me the interior of the church.

It was pleasant to return to the cool, comfortable ship after such unwonted exercise. Those who had visited the native quarters, advised us by all means to avoid them. Old Alaskan travellers on board told of a dance that could be seen, by crawling through a hole and then dropping into a cavern. The dancers enter from a subterranean passage, and perform until exhausted. The greatest objection to being one of the audience (we were informed) is, that one reaches daylight with clothing so covered with vermin that it is unfit for further service. I innocently asked if we might not hire the dancers to entertain us in open air, but was laughingly told that underground performances would not be appropriate to such changed surroundings. Six bells! And it was still light, and difficult to imagine that it lacked but one hour of midnight.

A Trial of Patience

SUNDAY, **J**UNE **26**TH ☞ Now the question is asked on all sides, "How soon may we leave St. Michaels?" In San Francisco, where many Alaskan companies were trying to cut each other's throats, we were told at different offices: "Our river boats are at St. Michaels waiting the arrival of our ocean steamers. No matter what you may be told by other representatives, they have no river boats there, of that we can assure you, and you may be obliged to wait at St. Michaels all summer if you fail to exercise great care in the selection of the line by which you go. We make immediate connection, and, by booking here, you will be the first up the Yukon to Dawson." Well, we followed the best of advice, selected the line of the oldest and most reliable company, and here we are, and here we are likely to remain, the Lord knows how long; for the water in the Yukon is so low, we are told, that all of the Company's river steamers are high and dry on bars. The pessimists say, that "the tide will not rise sufficiently to release them from imprisonment, and that even should we succeed in reaching Dawson there will be no possible chance of returning before next year." Such stories, however, are always received by me with a very big grain of salt; so I am not ready to listen to the wiseacres who say, "Take my advice and turn back ere it be too late."

MONDAY, **J**UNE **27**TH ☞ So many wild tales of detention here were floating about the ship last evening, that, when we heard that according to the latest yarn we should have at least a fortnight to remain, it seemed to me quite necessary to get facts from headquarters; so, sending for one of the owners, who was himself a passenger from San Francisco to St. Michaels, I requested him kindly to put all doubts and conjectures at an end, and reveal to us our fate. He said that only once in ten years could it happen as at present, that there would be nothing ready to take us up the Yukon. The boats of the Alaska Commercial

Company had always been the first to enter the river, but this year, owing to the very low state of the water, they are grounded, and their new steamers are not quite finished. "However," added he, "one is so nearly ready that we hope to be able to transfer the passengers in a day or two. It will accommodate about forty, while the others will have good quarters prepared for them on the freight barge." To my question as to how the cabins would be lighted, he smiled and said, "Oh, you won't need artificial light where you are going." He then kindly offered to have my sealskin marked, to save me the trouble of visiting St. Michaels again. At 10 PM, while sitting on deck reading by the light of the setting sun, the "cherub" came to inform me that the *Roanoke* was coming into the harbour, towing two river steamers, which, we were informed, were freighted, and ready to make the trip to Dawson without delay. How we groaned! We, who had had the advantage of being the first to reach St. Michaels, could not bear the thought of being passed by the *Roanoke*, or any other ship. What sympathy we felt for some of our fellow passengers who were taking in large cargoes whose value would be greatly depreciated in case of not arriving on time, and here we had not only the *Roanoke* to contend with but another steamer of the Columbia Navigation Company. Two rivals!

TUESDAY, JUNE 28TH ☞ Still in the harbour of St. Michaels with "all hands" impatient and growling at the detention; however, the old saying that "misery loves company," seems most true in this case and few there are who are not delighted to know that although the *Roanoke* and the steamer of the Columbia Navigation Company towed their own river boats, for some as yet unexplained reason they are not able to go farther. Those who have cargo on board are almost frantic at the thought of prospective losses through this delay, while the less interested members of the party fear that the best claims, houses, and sites will be gobbled up before our arrival. Meanwhile, all are praying that the *Portland*, with our new river boat, may be seen soon entering the harbour, and are straining their eyes in search of her. What a lottery is life! And how our fortunes hang upon the slightest contingency. This afternoon, while almost all our passengers were on shore, I remained to give the dogs a run, and was well repaid for it by a visit from a New York man who is on his way home, having "made his pile." Only eight days ago he was in Dawson, so was able to clinch the "Yukon lies," and give me late information. According to his story, the river has never before been so low. Steamers are lying aground all along its banks. They have little chance of coming down, nor have we of going up, unless a heavy rain sets in, for the snow and ice have already melted and disappeared. Nothing can go through now drawing more than scant four feet of water. My informant

CLOUD EFFECTS AT MIDNIGHT

left Dawson on a tiny steamer scarcely fitted to carry twenty-five of the hundred men who crowded it, but so determined were they to reach the "outside," that, although they were literally wedged in like sardines, no complaint did they utter. He was surprised and amused at the questions that people put to him simply because of his having wintered in Dawson, and said indignantly, "Why, one woman even asked me how much money I had made this year, and did not seem to realise the impertinence of the question, so I told her seven hundred and fifty thousand (might as well have said that as anything else), and she replied, 'Oh, how nice! Annie, come here! Here's a gentleman who's just made seven hundred and fifty thousand dollars in Dawson this winter! Just look at him!' And they stared at me as though I were a wild animal!" He laughed heartily at the tale that we should be obliged to pay one thousand dollars a month ground rent for a place to pitch our tent, and said, "Although Dawson is now so crowded that men jostle each other in walking, prices have not begun to reach that figure except in the business street on the waterfront." Upon telling him that I had the option on a house and lot with a spring on the ground, for two thousand dollars, he advised me not to conclude the bargain until after having seen the habitation.

We Meet Old Friends

WEDNESDAY, JUNE 29TH ☞ Did not go on shore today as the water is so rough and the facilities for landing so poor that the temptation was not sufficiently great. Those who made the trip were obliged to climb ladders and perform gymnastic feats, before reaching *terra firma*, while some waited hours for the return tug, as rowboats were out of the question. The New York man called again, and among other stories, told us of a Klondiker, who had taken a frozen turkey to Dawson, for which he was immediately offered one hundred and fifty dollars, but refused, preferring to raffle it. The result was that he pocketed three hundred dollars by this proceeding.

The monotony on board was varied this afternoon by the kindness of Dr. D— and Mr. H—, who gave me my first lesson in developing photographs.

FRIDAY, JULY 1ST ☞ After many days without going ashore, I went this morning under the escort of the doctor, who assisted me over the ditches, in the tramp to "Hotel Fort Get There." Many times we stopped for a group or a novel view. The exterior of the modern hotel was really far superior to anything we had imagined. There were rocking chairs on the balcony and a piano in the drawing room. Crowds of miners everywhere. Mrs. U— (who, in common with all other passengers of the *Roanoke*, had been landed at St. Michaels, there to remain until time for the departure to Dawson) was at home, received us at once, and complied readily with my request to allow me to peep at her room. I supposed it would be very tiny, but that it would be at least all her own. Tiny it was, but to my astonishment there was a bed in each of the four corners, and above these beds four more. There were two women dressing in the small space in the centre. Handsome silk gowns hanging on rusty nails looked most incongruous. Just a board floor with not even a rug. Two Chinamen rapped at the door to ask if they might "do the room, Missie?" I begged permission to

18 photograph just one corner, which was granted upon condition that I would not send the photograph to H—, "for she will be sure to say," added Mrs. U—, "same old Minnie—room always in disorder." The light was so poor that the result is sure to be unsatisfactory. I asked for a glass of water, which was brought in a tin cup! The colour of the water was that of weak coffee, but the taste was delicious. With Mrs. U— accompanying us, we inspected the storehouse, but the mosquitoes were so thick and ravenous, that, although men and women were heavily veiled, there was not much relief to be found, as the insects, which have not learned to sing as do their cousins at home, were able to crawl under the screens undetected.

Every carpenter in St. Michaels had been secured to work night and day, so we still have hopes of reaching Dawson before the others, even though we are making a late start. On returning to the *St. Paul,* we photographed four natives in their kayaks, which they handle in the most marvellous manner. Our passengers, who try them for the first time, are unable to balance themselves, but the Company's pamphlet tells us that the Indians "venture in these skin-boats into troubled seas; with a flirt of the paddle turn themselves completely over, bobbing up after completing the underwater round as lightly as so many corks, and in these frail cockle-shells hunt the leviathans of the deep."

An interesting visit this afternoon was from a man who carried mail over the Pass to Dawson. Government facilities being far from satisfactory, the miners at Dawson rich and poor longing for news from home had promised one dollar a letter to anyone brave enough to undertake the perilous trip. "I needed the money," said our visitor, "and so took the job, but was detained and delayed by many hard and unpleasant experiences, until, just before getting back, a friend came to meet me and said that as I had been so long on the trail the miners had held a meeting and decided that they would not pay me. I just walked right in, put the mail on the table, put my shooter on top of it, and said, 'Gentlemen, you are several hundred, and I'm one and unarmed, but not a man touches a letter without paying his dollar for it; otherwise, back they go to the post office from whence they came.' Well, I got four thousand dollars on that one job. I came here without a penny, from a farm that didn't pay. The first year I sent three hundred and fifty dollars home to my wife and children; the next year seven hundred dollars; each year more, and now I'm sending three thousand five hundred dollars at a time. Have been out here seven years, and intended to go home this month, but my three partners all went home at this season of the year, and the summer heat killed 'em. So I'm a-goin' to wait till autumn. I've got plenty o' claims an' I'll sell every one so soon as I can get my price," added he, with a wink, as he went over the side to take the tug for shore. "What did you think of your visitor?" said a passenger to me. "Most entertaining," I replied. "Other people think so, too," said he, "or at least I suppose so, as he has earned the name of 'Windy Bill.'"

At 10:30 PM Dr. D— approached rapidly, saying, "Come to the stern of the boat; I want to show you an unusual sight." The "cherub" and I followed, wondering and silent, until the doctor said, "Look!" A great ball of fire was rising in the east—in the west, a similar ball of fire was sinking. The grandeur and magnificence were so impressive that we gazed in silence upon the wondrous works of the Lord.

SUNDAY, JULY 3RD ☞ A cold, rough, rainy, windy day, the steam turned on, and everyone trying to keep warm. At half after eleven Captain S— came to take us to lunch with him on the *Wheeling*. We were obliged to watch our chance as the seas dashed against the side of the boat and jump into the steam launch as she rose. After an exciting spin across, we found ourselves once more upon the deck of an American man-of-war. We were so delightfully entertained, that we might have found it difficult to make our adieux had we not happened to see the arrival of another steamer from Dawson, the sight of which put us in a feverish state of excitement to obtain the latest news from our future home.

Wild stories were circulated by the new arrivals, and we could choose for ourselves those we thought most worthy of credence. Some said they were leaving enormously rich claims behind them, as it did not pay to work them with Canadian laws becoming more stringent and the royalty so exorbitant. They had come to the conclusion that a syndicate was trying to force the true owners out, and take possession of the abandoned property. On one side we heard that those in Dawson were so wealthy that they did not care what they paid for desired articles; on the other, they were so poor that they were unable to raise the money to leave the country; as for our informants, they declared that they were taking out two million among them, while there was five hundred and fifty thousand dollars in the safe of their steamer, which may or may not be true.

The doctor, who has become enthused with the unlimited possibilities in this wonderful country, has decided finally to remain for the winter, and is now fitting himself out with furs and other necessary articles, as are many of the passengers, who came only "to see," but remain hoping to conquer. Edith and I have already grub-staked trusty men, to go to the rich Koyukuk River—two we have sent in with supplies for two years each, while to another we have given a sufficient amount for assessment work on six claims. All in life is a lottery.

20   One prize from this river, which we consider the richest in Alaska, would more than repay us.

Midnight. Such excitement! The *Bella* came in from Dawson this evening, towing a barge containing over two hundred passengers, and, although it was still raining, they had but a canvas cover over their sleeping accommodations. As the barge was made fast to the *St. Paul*, we watched the crowd of returned miners to see if we might judge by their faces whether they had been successful in their search for gold. The greater number were clothed in jerseys, and trousers made from blankets. The gangway ladder was let down. The purser stood at the head of the landing, and the miners came up in the most orderly fashion, after having made room for the half-dozen women to precede them. Some had grips so heavy that it was necessary to set them down on each step for a moment's rest. Others were so burdened by a bag on the back that it needed no X-rays to tell us of the gold within; then came men with weighty boxes, followed by men whose necks were decorated with what looked like bologna sausages, as they dangled at their sides, but were only skins stuffed with gold dust. "They're just carrying their gold that a-way for effect," whispered one of the women from the barge, "and they'd oughter have it stolen to teach 'em not to put on so many airs."

Two men climbed the ladder, staggering under a box over which they had stood guard from Dawson. We were told, also, that it contained seventy-five thousand dollars. Then came two men with an enormous valise on a stick, an end of the stick on their shoulders—the weight bending them almost double. After that, followed the reverse side of the picture—a poor fellow carried on board with frozen feet and legs; another, too weak from scurvy to walk, borne in the arms of two men; still another who had been blinded by snow was carefully led up the ladder. As we watched those who had been unsuccessful, we were filled with great pity. Those who had started out with high hopes only to return helpless! Pity also we felt for those who had gained enormous riches, knowing but too well of the many traps prepared for them, and from which some of their number might not escape.

Transferred at Last

TUESDAY, JULY 5TH ☞ At 11 AM, not having received any orders, we decided to go on shore for the mail. Scarcely had we boarded the tug, when the gong was sounded and we heard the shout, "Passengers from the *St. Paul* return and take over their luggage to barge." As we rejoiced loudly that the summons had come at last, a returned Dawsonite exclaimed, "You wouldn't be so happy if you could realise where you are going."

We had some difficulty in getting our pets off. The dogs were crowded into the pilothouse, leaving room only for the man at the wheel; the parrot was scolding at being disturbed; the pigeons were frightened and fighting each other; only the canary was contented and continued to sing merrily. We had heard such exaggerated stories about the river boats that we were pleasantly surprised at the reality, but preferred accommodations on the barge, as the cabins had but two berths, while those on the steamer *Leah* had three—one just off the floor, one very near the ceiling, and one between the two. Neither Edith nor I felt equal to the gymnastic performance required to "turn in" and "out" and were decidedly averse to sleeping where we could not sit up without bumping our heads and bending our backs double. The cabins on the barge, although very primitive and constructed in the cheapest possible fashion, were new and clean, with comfortable mattresses; the beds, table linen, and blankets were also all new, and the basins, carafes, and toilet articles of enamelled agate. We could nowhere see prospective discomforts such as we had read of, so started out determined to enjoy all that was pleasant, and to close our eyes to anything which must be endured because it could not be cured. A table of pine ran through the centre of the barge, but as the galley was not quite complete, all barge passengers were to have their meals on the steamer *Leah*, which was to take us in tow. Her dining room was far too small for so large a number,

22 consequently it was first come, first served, and the stools at the table made one feel as though at a lunch counter.

There was a rush for rooms, but, as Mr. S— had distinctly told us that in case there should be a sufficient number of cabins Edith and I should each have one, we made no effort to "scramble" with the others, but went on shore to give the dogs their first run since leaving San Francisco. We had been many times warned that the native dogs would attack them in a body, so we kept as near to headquarters and the miners as possible, knowing that the latter would be ready to help us keep our beauties from a fight; but we had neither the attack from the native dogs, nor the enjoyment of seeing Ivan and Queen dashing in mad joy and rolling on the turf. They walked sedately by our sides as though they had never been weeks from shore, while the enemy skulked in the rear, waiting for a chance to bite and run, and were so cowardly that they disappeared if we but raised our hands in a threatening manner. A very unexpected thing did happen though. The few cows of the place, that had never been known to seem aware of the existence of other dogs, immediately gave chase to ours, and in such a determined manner that the men had to stand in front of us and pelt them with stones, shouting to us to seek cover. After the danger was over, the cows followed down a side street, in a manner which we should not have believed possible had we not been eyewitnesses, hiding behind the small houses to dodge the men and stones, but peeping around the corners as though to watch a chance to break through the ranks.

The Collector of the Port took the greatest interest in Ivan. An old man stopped to ask many questions about his pedigree, saying that he had owned a descendant of one of Bismarck's dogs. All whom we met were very talkative; one poor fellow said he was coming "out" after a five years' stay in Dawson, thoroughly broken up with malaria. On our return to the barge, we were informed that there were at least two in each cabin, so that Edith and I made no complaint at being at last obliged to room together. "There is some advantage in being unpopular," said one of the passengers. "Everyone on board has absolutely refused to share X—'s room; consequently he is triumphantly telling that he is the only one lucky enough to have a cabin to himself, all unconscious of the reason for his solitude."

About a year ago, while sojourning at Point-au-Pic, my imagination was greatly excited by articles about the founder of Dawson, with which the newspapers were filled. The more I read, and the more I heard of the Klondike, the more necessary it seemed to me to meet this wonderful man, if one would gain information as to where to prospect, where to stake claims, where to locate, and how to gain untold millions. Dreams developed into plans, arrangements

THE *WHEELING*

were made for the trip to the promised land, and Joe Ladue's* hand held the key which was to unlock the golden chests. Suddenly appeared a notice in the *New York Herald*: "Joe Ladue will sail from San Francisco June—for the Klondike." "That is to be my steamer," cried I; but to my great disappointment, on reaching California, it was only to learn that Ladue had already sailed, and was "going in" over the Pass. So I read with avidity all articles in regard to the promised land, in order to gather the information which I had hoped to obtain from him.

And now (after this prelude), to go back to our first evening on the barge, as I sat talking to one of the passengers, a tall, fine-looking man came on board, and stopped a moment to greet my companion, who, after he had passed, said to me, "That's Joe Ladue; did you ever hear of him?" "Hear of him? More than of any other man of this part of the world." "Do you want to meet him? I'll go and get him," but, after a few moments, he returned, saying, "I'm very sorry, but he's so surrounded I couldn't get near him. I'll introduce him, however, before night." After dinner his promise was fulfilled, and a most interesting chat we had. The information which he gave us was most valuable, and when we asked what chance there was of getting a house in Dawson, he immediately said, "I'll give you one rent-free." "For how long?" said I. "For a year," he replied. "Is there a stove in it?" inquired practical Edith. "You can buy all the stoves you want in Dawson," said Ladue. "It must be a curious sensation to go alone to a place, and watch its development, as you have done," I remarked. "Oh, yes; but if I had it

* Founded Dawson in 1896.

24 to do over again, I'd do differently," said Ladue. "I'd have a cinch on everything, and that's what I didn't do in the first place. But do let me give you ladies a bit of advice. Don't go to Dawson; people are dying there like sheep, and they will probably have an epidemic this summer," and off he went to watch the trial trip of his new steam launch.

It seems strange to have no light and no heat on board, and not to feel the need of either in this Arctic Circle, but we had no difficulty in undressing by the dying rays of the sun.

WEDNESDAY, JULY 6TH   A long, enjoyable tramp on shore, with an Englishman. We finally went to the Alaska Company's stores, which were crowded. The men kindly offered to make way for me, on account of my sex, but, their time being as valuable as mine, I followed the example of other women, and sat on the counter until my turn came. How we laughed at each new experience! My purchases consisted of a pair of muck-a-lucks, four dollars, which they say are worth three times that in Dawson; a small tin of ginger wafers, fifty cents; and a bottle of lime juice, seventy-five cents. Not such extravagant prices as we had been led to expect.

A nasty, rainy afternoon. Nothing to do but to sit on deck, talk with returned miners, and listen to the fascinating stories of Klondike life. Some of them so alarmed Edith about the many dangers in store for the dogs, that she suddenly decided to send Queen back to San Francisco on the steamer *St. Paul* in charge of the porter who had cared for her when outward bound. Such tales never affect me, as I have learned from long experience that they are generally greatly exaggerated, so Ivan remained. After dinner, another most agreeable visit from Ladue, who brought his agent with him, instructing him that should our stores not reach Dawson in time we were to be allowed to help ourselves to his.

We Hear the Signal

THURSDAY, JULY 7TH ↾ After this morning's shopping experience, will retract all written yesterday about prices. Ordinary single blanket for Ivan, the cheapest made, seven dollars; a very common skirt braid, two small pieces, twenty-five cents; writing pads, twenty-five cents each; ink, twenty-five cents for a five-cent (retail) bottle; and the slimsiest kind of calico, twenty-five cents a yard, all to be carried home by the purchaser.

After dinner a breeze sprang up, and great excitement was caused by the breaking of the barge rudder. Many of the passengers declared that it was defective when we started and, on investigation, it was discovered that the tools required for making repairs had been left on the dock. Another story was circulated that the barge was leaking; one of the men declared that he had been down below, that the pumps were being used and the cargo ruined. I finally appealed to the purser, telling him that our outfit was of some value, after which he assured me that he had made a thorough investigation and that the story of a leak was absolutely false. We were next informed that the rudder of the steamer was showing signs of weakness, and as we had sixty miles through Bering Sea to make before reaching "the bar," the passengers were very much frightened, and declared their intention of remaining dressed and ready for emergencies should any arise. The barge was then placed in front of the steamer and pushed instead of towed. The floor of the barge vibrated with a serpentine motion as though each wave would prove fatal, and, recalling the accidents that had taken place so recently, many of the passengers crossed to the steamer and remained on deck until 3 AM; the men, seemingly, were more alarmed than the women, as we were told that some of them slept in life preservers. Plans were made as to our actions in case of disaster. One of the Englishmen said that if I would promise to keep cool and only rest my hands on his shoulder he could easily save me by swimming to shore. Heated discussions ensued among the passengers at things having been so rushed—the same passengers who had protested vigorously against the long delay. At 3 AM we came to anchor and, on retiring to our cabins, the light of the coming day was so strong that we were obliged to hang our wraps before the window.

Friday, July 8th ☞ Still waiting outside the bar! No one could tell why, so I inquired of the captain, who replied, "Barge rudder broken, shy on the steamer rudder, and the tools to repair them were left on the dock." There is a carpenter here, but he is wanted everywhere at once, consequently the skylight is not yet finished, and the opening is covered with canvas, excluding light, but admitting rain, to the great discomfort of the passengers, some of whom are now shifting their quarters to the *Leah*. This leaves a few vacant rooms, and Edith at once informed the purser and the steward of Mr. S—'s promise. The former said, "Have you got it in writing?" The latter, "His words don't go here," and we were obliged to accept the inevitable, as we saw that others were taking advantage of what had been given to us conditionally. Moral, be sure and have everything in writing before you start! Indians came with salmon and plover for sale. They wanted whiskey in exchange, but that, being too rare and precious, could not be given—not from conscientious scruples—so they took tea instead.

Saturday, July 9th ☞ After luncheon, we stopped to put off a couple of French missionaries. They entered the compartments fore and aft of the tiny canoe, leaving the Indian guide and boatman to take the seat in the hole in the centre. Not a complaint did they utter as they squeezed into the tight-fitting box and were paddled towards the solitary and uninviting shore. Such bravery showed a noble spirit of self-sacrifice. As they heard the shouts of "Good luck to you," they waved a last adieu and said, "We shall pray for you."

Had a most interesting chat with the wife of the archdeacon, who, although a great sufferer from seasickness and a martyr to neuralgia, is bravely returning for another seven years in the Arctic regions. She and her good husband first entered the country from the Canadian side in small boats over the lakes. This, which seems to the majority so primitive a style of travelling, is, to them, by contrast, most luxurious. Their hearts are filled with love for the work they have attempted, and no discouragements are allowed to interfere with the anticipated glorious results.

At 11 PM we tied up to the bank for wood. Indians by the dozens lined the shore, but the light was not sufficiently strong for snapshots. A white man came on board enveloped in a mosquito shield (as was everyone else except the

Indians). He was greatly surprised that we had but ninety passengers, instead of the expected two hundred. In answer to our question he said, "We call this Andreafsky, though Andreafsky is twenty miles beyond. We stopped here to build a boat which is to take us to Dawson, and the name of our camp is Black Foot." That explained the red flag with a black foot in the centre, which was flying under the American. One of the passengers asked for my decanter that he might fill it with pure water from the spring. It was deliciously cool. A— brought me back a big bunch of ferns, bluebells, pink flowers resembling clover, and cotton buds. Poor Ivan, whom he had taken for a run, returned almost frantic from the sting of mosquitoes and sand flies, which had taken possession of his entire body.

SUNDAY, JULY 10TH ☞ Have searched the Alaska Commercial Company's pamphlet to glean some information about our stopping place last night. It must have been Kollik, of which it tells us that "it is near the discharging point of the Aphoon mouth," and adds: "Here there is a rude Russian church, the store of an ancient Russian trader who dominates the place, and the driftwood dwellings of a small settlement. The surroundings are characteristic of the entire delta—flat, rich soil which might support a nation, if in a kindlier clime, but which, frozen to within a short distance of the surface, produces nothing but thick grasses, and low scrub-willows, or other Arctic trees. Waterfowl flit in every direction, or chatter continually on the flats. Here, too, the traveller has the first experience of taking on wood for fuel. The Eskimo cut up and split the drift logs, and pile them on the bank. Then, when the steamer hauls up at the landing, the natives, who compose a greater portion of the crew (not so on our ship) bring on the wood as rapidly as their naturally sluggish natures can be spurred to work."

Upon leaving the cabin this morning, late, I found that we were again "taking on wood," not that we needed it, but simply to prevent one of our rivals from obtaining it, and thereby overtaking us. The men were on shore with their rifles. The "cherub" brought back a very pretty tame fox in a box. The women purchased the skins of muskrats and swans. Mr. A— was the last one to return, with a beautiful bunch of wild roses. He was held up several times and robbed of one or two sprays, but handed the remainder to me, saying in his modest way, "Mind you don't cut your hands, as they're full of thorns." The doctor, who is an enthusiastic amateur photographer, was delighted at having been able to get a good light on the tomb of a princess, saying that the box containing her remains was kept on top of the ground, while on a board were nailed the paddle of her canoe, her bracelets, hunting-knife, and many trinkets of value.

28 **Monday, July 11th** ⊱ No respect for Sunday is shown by a large number of passengers. Last evening, after dinner, a dance was organised, J— leading and calling out "the figgers." The orchestra consisted of Mr. P— with his violin, Colonel B—, with his fiddle, and one of the waiters with a mandolin. The dancing being too tame to suit J—, he shouted, "Here, give us some ginger! We must have some ginger! This dancing ain't got no spice in it." We sat on deck and watched the glorious scenery until eleven. Scarcely had we retired to our cabins, when the assemblage adjourned to the top of the barge, which was very near our heads, and commenced a march to the accompaniment of songs and shouts. The poor Archdeacon and his wife, who had been sitting on deck with us during this desecration of the Sabbath, were most unhappy, but there was no one to whom to complain, so the dear lady, with "a splitting headache," was obliged to wait until the crowd disbanded.

While dressing late this morning, the whistle blew and we saw a town in the distance, with a beautiful Russian church standing out prominently. We hastily finished our toilet and hurried on shore; but no sooner had Ivan touched land than the native dogs came dashing from all directions, and as they failed to run away at my shout of "Moosh!" which only evoked peals of laughter from the Indians, the poor beast, who was quite ready to whip every dog there, had to be sent on board without his exercise, as I did not wish the winner of twenty-two prizes to be debarred from further honours by disfigurement. Salmon was hung out to dry before every house, and all along the banks. A small boy of not more than three years of age was smoking a pipe. As I turned the Kodak in his direction he took the pipe from his mouth to refill it from the contents of the bag which he held in his hand. I motioned to the father that the pipe should be replaced in the child's mouth; he understood the gesture, and an interesting group was taken, as the father had a tiny papoose in his arms. Mr. A— kindly escorted me to the Russian church, but service was over, and we had not the time to photograph the interior. We climbed to the graveyard, but the mosquitoes were so ravenous and attacked us in such swarms, that we beat a hasty retreat, only stopping to gather a few flowers. At eleven we returned to the ship and as my English friend said we had been visiting "the most swagger place on the Yukon," I immediately read the following in regard to it from the pamphlet heretofore quoted:

> Ikogimut [Ikogimiut], or the Russian Mission, as it is generally called. This mission has been established many years and is the principal station of the Greek Church in the northern portion of Alaska. The church itself is a picturesque structure, and its services most interesting. This is a favourite place for picking up curios and small furs. The water in the river at this point has been sounded to a

depth of four hundred and eighty feet, indicating that it flows through an ancient crater. Here, too, the birchbark canoe of the upriver Indian begins to be seen in competition with the skin kayak of the Eskimo, for Paimut, about five hours' run up the stream from the Russian Mission, marks the dividing line between the Innuits and Ingaliks. The Eskimo and the Indians of the interior were, in former years, frequently at war, but it has been many years since any great battles were fought. Still, they occasionally shoot on sight, when hunting parties chance to meet on the ranges.

TUESDAY, JULY 12TH ☞ Pandemonium let loose! Last night after a sunset so glorious that it surpassed all others, we retired as usual at eleven. At 2 AM, we anchored, or rather tied up to the bank at Koserefsky [Holy Cross]. As we had read in the same pamphlet, this "Holy Cross Mission is maintained by the Sisters of Saint Anne and the Jesuit Fathers. Here the voyager will be greatly interested in the gardening, which shows what may be done in the way of raising the hardier vegetables whenever an increasing population shall put Alaska to the test of its capacity for supporting life. Turnips, radishes, lettuce, potatoes, cabbages, and celery are grown with more or less success, and continuous experiments are made with different seeds. The work among the Indian children shows their wonderful capacity for receiving a certain measure of instruction, although as yet the moral results have not been all that the devoted missionaries have hoped for." We had been anticipating with great pleasure a visit to the church and the wonderful gardens, but, unfortunately, the hour of arrival was not propitious, and we again sought repose in sleep. Alas! That was impossible, for, having no officer on the barge at night, the Indians were allowed to board her, and roam at will, not only on the narrow ledge outside our windows, but to congregate in groups before our doors, or tramp through the hall, chattering like magpies. Then came the whistle from an approaching steamer, and we were soon aware that the long-expected *Alice*, from Dawson, was being secured to the barge.

In a few moments many of her two hundred passengers had landed on our decks, and were loudly calling for those whom they hoped to find on board. One or two of the most popular men were surrounded, and their conversation would have been of great interest at any other time. The same advice was reiterated on all sides. "Turn back. Don't go to Dawson. People are dying there like rats in a trap." Only one man was affected sufficiently to follow this counsel, and his companions said that he was dreadfully homesick, and only too glad of an excuse.

After luncheon we stopped at another small village, the name of which it was impossible to learn, and there remained until five, leaving stores on shore. Mr. A— escorted Ivan and me for a short walk, but the sun and mosquitoes soon drove us back; we watched, with great concern and anxiety the purser bargaining for more dogs, and groaned as first one and then another was purchased and sent on board, where the howling and crying make such an agonising concert that the passengers would gladly have clubbed together and paid the higher price demanded farther up the river, rather than suffer night and day. Many of our passengers decided that the hot sun was conducive to laundry work. Even the dignified and pompous Q— found a tub, and no laundress could have put more energy into the work, but his indignation was great when he found that the doctor had secured a fine picture of him at his novel employment. My English neighbour said that someone had offered to teach him how to wash his linen, that he had taken great interest in the lessons, but never succeeded in learning until the work was quite finished.

Up the Yukon

WEDNESDAY, JULY 13TH ☞ During breakfast we stopped at another small settlement for wood, and again at lunchtime, when we had an opportunity to take a very short walk and to get a few photographs. The squaws all covered their heads at sight of a camera. We thought them bashful, but a young Indian girl explained: "They want you to pay them for being allowed to take their pictures." At four, another stop, long enough for some of the passengers to have a swim in the Yukon, and for the camera fiends to obtain some good views; a delightful chat and tramp on shore with a new passenger, Mr. —, who gave me most interesting information about Dawson.

While reading after dinner, who should approach but Colonel B—, saying, "Do yer mind if I take one o' your nice easy cheers? It looks so comfortable an' there ain't no one a-usin' it. My wife she's got a nice rockin-cheer in her cabin, made special for her; yer see she's so fat an' so heavy she can't sit in no ordinary cheer. She weighs nigh onto three hundred pounds. You'd oughter seen her when we was married, tho', the slimmest thing yer ever sot eyes on."

THURSDAY, JULY 14TH ☞ At two o'clock this morning, we tied up at Nulato, where we remained cleaning boilers, so we were told, until eleven.

We started for a tramp with Ivan, but the native dogs, which dared not face him, set upon him in a pack when his back was turned, causing him to be ignominiously sent on board. A large rowboat from the Koyukuk, containing two men and a woman wearing a sunbonnet, interested us greatly, and still more, when the latter told us that just around the bend, in a boat with a tent, was a Mr. N—, partner of one of the men whom we have "grub-staked" and whose stories of his life on the Koyukuk were so thrilling that we were strongly tempted towards that river rather than to make the trip to Dawson. His nuggets were so large and so valuable, his plans so wonderful, that had it not been for fear of the Indians who we were told were very savage, we should have joined our man and his family on the small yacht which was being prepared in San Francisco. We had a short interview with the partner, met a great number of men who had "gone in" with our man the previous year, and heard his story and learned of his daily life and what he had accomplished up to the last moment of his departure for home to sell his mines.

After dinner, we were comfortably ensconced in our easy chairs in the bow of the barge, admiring the scenery, which was still wonderfully beautiful, the air balmy and soft as that of springtime at Lenox, when someone wished aloud for an ice. Edith said, "Your wish can easily be granted, if you can get our freezer from down below." Up jumped J— and two other men, and in a few moments the freezer was on deck, taken to the steward, who supplied the sugar, cream (tinned, of course), and extract, and half an hour later we indulged in the first ice cream, according to all accounts, that had ever been served on the Yukon.

Many boats have passed us today, containing from two to eight miners returning home. Everyone shouts the same question, "How far ahead is the other steamer?" (Meaning the one belonging to the Columbia Navigation Company, which started two days before us.) Latest information is, that we are separated only by four hours, consequently we are wild to overtake her, and most impatient at any detention. Just before retiring, J— came to me and said, "I'll give you ten dollars for your freezer." "It cost fifteen before paying fifteen cents a pound freight," I replied. After some reflection he offered Edith twenty dollars for her half, but she told him that he could not have it at any price.

Friday, July 15th ❧ We were glad to have our attention diverted by the boat's stopping at Novikakat. Edith stopped at an Indian tent, where she had just concluded the purchase of a lot of marten skins at four dollars each, when one of our passengers entered, and, being a half-breed, engaged in a fluent con-versation with the proprietor in the native tongue, which Edith, consequently, was unable to understand, so was filled with astonishment when informed that the skins were not for sale. Shortly afterwards a relative of the Indian maiden came on board, with the skins of which Edith had been deprived. My time on shore was spent in gathering wild pink roses, with which to decorate the dinner table, and quantities of a flower the colour of heather, but with very long stems. I have omitted to say that at the preceding stopping place we found groundsel growing wild, and many were the offerings to the only canary on board, who appreciated it immensely. We sat in our easy chairs in the bow of the boat enjoying the marvellous scenery, and the freedom from gnats and mosquitoes which here are replaced by enormous horseflies. Tales were being related of the different passengers who were anxious to be grub-staked, and Mr. R— said, "Women are certainly incomprehensible. Let a man go to them as a gentleman, and offer them fine claims! Do you think they will listen to him? No! They suspect a swindle every time; but he has only to pose as a rough miner to be at once believed, and to fill their souls with confidence."

Towards evening, the *Margaret*, belonging to the Alaska Commercial Company, was seen coming toward us, and excitement was rife as she tied up alongside. The usual rush was made for letters to send home. Instead of asking us for war news, her passengers told us that papers of the 29th had already reached Dawson from "over the Pass," bringing tidings that although we had captured Havana, Hobson and his brave men had been shot, and two of our ships lost.

They also warned us to turn back, as had all those in the small boats passed during the day; but such advice only creates laughter, as the constant repetition seems ridiculous to those who have more than half finished so long a journey. We lost but one of our passengers. The Indian maiden who had interrupted Edith's purchase of furs, being on her way to Dawson to meet her sister, found that she was on the *Margaret* "going out," so her gripsack was quickly packed, and she departed. The *Margaret* was crowded to that degree that men were sleeping on tables, under tables, and even on the cords of wood on deck, and they informed us that, as there are still thousands waiting to "go out," there was little chance for newcomers to secure transportation down the Yukon. Before reaching the *Margaret* we had a pilot who had landed us on sandbars twice during the day, so we speedily exchanged him for the one who had brought this craft safely down the river.

SATURDAY, JULY 16TH ☞ If the scenery yesterday was grand, what can be said of that through which we have been passing today? Mountains, and relays of mountains, narrow gorges, rapids, all that is most wild and picturesque! We had been too rapt in admiration even to read, but, as there must be ever a slight blot on all that is beautiful, so this scene was partially marred by the gradual approach of a heavy fog, as we thought it, until the air became laden with smoke, and, as night came on, we saw that the mountains on all sides were on fire. Truly a gorgeous sight, which would have been still more brilliant had it not been for the ball of fire that hung in the west, making all else insignificant by comparison. All day we had steamed without stopping. At last in the distance we beheld great stacks of wood piled high on the shore, so all made preparations for a short tramp, until the captain shouted, "How much for the wood?" "Fifteen dollars a cord," was the reply. "Keep it," and on we went. Just beyond, another lot was plainly visible, but for that seventeen dollars a cord was asked;

34 at the third place, twenty, which caused the passengers to discuss the likelihood of being called on to fell trees, in order that the Alaska Commercial Company should not be obliged to pay such exorbitant prices.

At last, Fort Adams was in sight, and as we had read of the "Episcopal Church and Mission," where the children of the school were "particularly proficient," and that there was also "a trading post and something in the way of gardening," we were looking forward to an interesting half-hour, only to be disappointed, as no one was allowed to land.

We remained on deck until eleven, hoping to catch a glimpse of Rampart City, but found that we were not to make that settlement until 2 AM. We might just as well have remained up, for when we did get there sleep was impossible. One of the passengers had brought out some whiskey, and was treating the crowd in the hall before our door. Such a babel of voices! And we were told the following day that the supply of whiskey in Rampart having given out, the citizens were offering our passengers nine dollars a bottle. We breathed a sigh of relief as the whistle blew, the men rushed for shore, and we slowly steamed away; then came the howling and yelping of the dogs, which lasted until drowned by the clattering of dishes and preparations for breakfast.

SUNDAY, JULY 17TH ☞ Women in the dining room sewing; men on deck with rifles, waiting for something at which to shoot! At ten we stopped at a bank where there was a coal sign. The usual question was asked, and as this fuel cost only ten dollars a ton we took on board a goodly quantity of stuff which looked like black dust. We were told that this condition was due to the coal's having been frozen, so that it could not be extracted in large bits. Poor Ivan was let loose from the terrible heat of the engine room and the howling of the other dogs, which is so racking to the nerves that we now fear his good habits may be spoiled and his training prove ineffective by association with these "Siwash"* mongrels. To think that sixty dollars was the price paid for such quarters and companionship just from St. Michaels to Dawson, and we supply the dog's food! How we longed for Sunday peace and quiet after such a night, but it was not to be.

Scarcely were we again on our way when our ears were pierced by the rasping noise of a badly played violin, which had to be endured until the bell rang for luncheon. Later in the day, the sky grew dark, then leaden coloured. A

---

* "Siwash" generally meant "Indian." The term is derived from the French word *sauvage*, which became "siwash" in Chinook jargon. See Russell Tabbert, *Dictionary of Alaskan English* (Juneau: Denali Press, 1991), p. 54.

storm was brewing. Nervous women, terrified at the thought of a thunder-storm amidst the mountains, flocked into the dining room like a herd of sheep only to be together. The scene soon became one of most imposing grandeur, in which I revelled, seated alone in the bow of the boat, well protected by cap and mackintosh, as the rain came down in torrents.

Shortly after, the doctor came to ask if I would not like to meet and talk with the famous Hank Summers,* saying, "You don't want me to bring him out here in the rain, so let us all sit inside." Following the doctor, I soon came face to face with the new passenger, one of the noted miners of this part of the world, who, having passed eight years in Alaska, had left Dawson only eight days previously, consequently, his conversation was of intense interest; but he gave us the same advice as we have heretofore received from all others: "Better turn back, even at this late day, for typhoid fever and malaria are raging. Even those on the hill are not free from what may soon become an epidemic, and there are not steamers enough to transport those waiting to leave. Unless this exorbitant Canadian royalty be soon repealed, there will be no more mines worked, as even the richest claim owners are unwilling to pay ten percent to such extortionists." Mr. Summers then showed us the beautiful big nugget he had first panned out, a ring made from gold taken from one of his claims, and told of the man who had first grub-staked him, to whom he was able to send twelve thousand dollars in ninety days. But grub-staking is rarely so profitable, for many tales do we hear of these men who, after striking it rich, forget those who have assisted them in time of need, sell their claims, carrying the result where it cannot be reached by the rightful owner, who, according to miners' laws and agreements, is entitled to half.

Towards ten o'clock a turn in the river showed Fort Hamlin directly before us, and a small steamer tied to a tree. We prepared for the anticipated tramp, but to our keen disappointment there was no wood to be had, so on we went, after having "slowed up" long enough to talk with the captain of the *Victoria.* The rumour was that she had come to assist in towing our barge over the Yukon Flats, but we went on without her.

---

* Summers made a fortune on El Dorado Creek in the Klondike.

Discomfort of Barge Life

MONDAY, JULY 18TH ☞ Last night on reaching my cabin, mattress and pillow were wet with the rain that had leaked in, but having learned the lesson that "kickers" are treated with contempt and discourtesy, the only thing to be done was to bear it uncomplainingly, and roll up in blankets with a life preserver for a pillow. Wakened at 5 AM by the *Victoria* bumping against the barge, men running along the ledge before the windows, and directions being shouted to make fast alongside; then followed the awful howling of the dogs; then preparations for breakfast, and no chance to sleep for another eighteen hours at least. From overhead we heard shouts of "Moose" and "Bear." Men called excitedly to others to get their rifles, as the animals were swimming across the river, but nothing came within reach.

At our next stopping place we were met by two men from Halifax, who had spent eight days in Dawson, had had enough, and were on their return trip. They managed to live by chopping wood for river steamers wherever they happened to camp for the night and received from our purser fifteen dollars a cord.

During the entire trip, men have been complaining from time to time that their cargo was being ruined. Notwithstanding this, matters were left without investigation, until one of the captain's favourites went down to procure some articles from her trunk. She returned most unhappy over its condition and must have gone at once to him, for scarcely had we finished dinner, when he accompanied her to the hatchway, had it opened, sent some of his men down and had all trunks brought on deck. Up they came, covered with mould, then wet mattresses, and small tents mildewed; the passengers on all sides looked on, groaning, "What a shame!" "D—d outrage!" "Our goods packed where they can be ruined and the Company's goods nicely stored in high, dry space on the steamer!" However, we are lucky to have our boxes up, even though our stores are still in the dampness, and we are told that our beautiful new tent is not fit to be seen.

TUESDAY, JULY 19TH ☞ A very quiet day! Scarcely anything to record except stopping at 10 AM to take on six cords of wood, where, unfortunately, the banks were so steep and the woods so filled with mosquitoes, that few of us were able to land. There is always a pleasant breeze while travelling on the Yukon, no matter how intense the rays of the sun. At 4 PM another hour at a woodpile, but the driftwood was so thick along the banks, that one walked with difficulty, as it cracked and broke under the feet at each step. The protest against early dinner has had its effect, and the bell was not rung until after five.

The nights are deliciously cool. Hardly do we finish dinner, before an icy breath passes through the air and robes and wraps are in demand. Not a star has been visible in the heavens since we left St. Michaels, and tonight as we sat in our little corner of the barge peacefully discussing that and other astronomical subjects, we were startled by an unusual invasion of mosquitoes, which attacked so ferociously that even our shields afforded little protection, and we were driven to our cabins, there to wage war until 5 AM, when the attack suddenly ceased. We fell into a delicious sleep, which lasted about fifteen minutes, then chairs were dragged from under the tables, and the stewards, who were sweeping the dining room, engaged in loud conversation. Groans were heard on all sides, and when the bell rang calling passengers to breakfast they would gladly have had quiet and sleep in preference to all the delicacies of the season.

WEDNESDAY, JULY 20TH ☞ We are all indignant this morning. The *Sovereign* passed us at six o'clock and here we are three hours later, tied up again to the bank, and have been for the last hour and nobody knows the reason why, although questions have been freely asked. We are chafing under the detention.

9:30 AM. The *Victoria*, having repaired damages, has now overtaken us and is alongside ready to assist in towing. Predictions are rife that she will bring us bad luck. We are now in the Yukon Flats, of which our guidebook says:

> These extend from Fort Hamlin clear to Circle City, a distance of about four hundred miles. The river widens and the water flows in many channels, between numberless islands; undoubtedly there was once a great lake in the basin, larger than any lake of today. At the Ramparts there probably was a fall greater than Niagara, before the water cut its way through the mountains, and drained the lake into the sea. After the waters subsided the flats became the home of the mastodon, the fossil remains and ivory tusks of this great animal being found here in profusion, especially on Mammoth Island, which seems to have been a

burying place for them. Indian stories come drifting along occasionally to the effect that some of these monsters are still alive in the comparatively unexplored territory around the head waters of Copper River, but the yarns are probably apocryphal.

THURSDAY, JULY 21ST To our great disgust, we were soon tied up to another woodpile where we remained until midnight, groaning and suffering under attacks of myriads and myriads of ravenous mosquitoes and vicious gnats. Some of the passengers assisted in preparations for arranging two new rudders, without which the captain dared go no farther into the Flats. A short walk on shore through the driftwood and dead branches resulted in a torn skirt and defaced shoes, only compensated for by a few new photographs.

FRIDAY, JULY 22ND At noon, to the anger and disgust of all the passengers, the *John C. Barr*, of the North American Transportation Company, passed us, those on board waving handkerchiefs and hats, hurrahing, hurling shouts of derision, calling that they would wait for us in Dawson, etc. Then the "kicking" from our passengers began, and these expressions were heard: "What did they tell us in San Francisco? That we should be the first ones to arrive! That no other company would be able to keep such a promise. Oh, no! And here we are, sent on a steamer towing a heavy barge, crawling at a snail's pace, so as to carry in the Company's freight. Last night we was within thirty-five miles of Circle City and here we are, nearly eighteen hours after, tied up at a woodpile, with still ten miles to make and everything on the river passin' us. Oh! We're in luck, we are! The *Sovereign*, the *Monarch*, and the *Barr* all ahead of us, their passengers to get the good claims, the best cabins, the best of everything, while we who paid extra for just such luck are left here to kick our heels on the bank!" Such an unhappy lot!

We had half an hour's tramp on shore, where we were surprised at being able to gather mulberries, currants, and raspberries, which grew wild. We had an interview with Rip Van Winkle's double, who has lived here some years raising turnips, radishes, lettuce, and carrying them over the trail to Circle City. He was doing well until the river rose and carried away his entire garden. What a delicious luncheon we had—fresh radishes and sweet potatoes, which never before had we properly appreciated. At 4:30 PM we reached Circle City, and were delighted to see the *John Barr* tied to the banks, but alas! She pushed off even as we arrived and her passengers shouted, "We will deliver our own messages in Dawson, thank you, and will not trouble you, who have tarried so long by the way, to give them." The plank was soon out, and here some half-dozen passengers left us to tempt fortune in a strange land. The French girl who had informed us that she was to be married on arrival, as her fiancé had sent for her, had basely deceived us if a newcomer was to be believed, who said that she had been sent for to be their cook at one hundred dollars a month.

We were greatly astonished at the size of Circle City. We went first to the post office, simply to see it, expecting nothing and receiving nothing. We concluded afterwards to post our letters home from there, although [we were] told that they would go more quickly via Dawson and the Pass; still, we wanted the Circle City stamp on the envelope, for who can tell how much longer the town may exist. The doctor overtook us, and presented the famous pioneer, Mr. McQuesten,* who has been thirty-five years in Alaska, and has a handsome Indian wife. He informed us that, although Dawson has a population of from ten to forty thousand, Circle City contains more houses, and is much healthier, as the former is in a frightful sanitary condition. We peeped into the dance hall, and were told of an entertainment that had taken place the previous night which, in the words of our informant, "even the nicest people from the other steamer attended, and they didn't put on no airs, but followed the rule of the mining camp, and danced with every fellow what asked 'em. They don't ask nothing to go in, but you have to order a drink fer each girl you dance with, and every drink costs a dollar." We also peeped into a couple of restaurants, saw fine-looking bread at twenty-five cents a loaf, pies fifty cents each, clam chowder fifty cents, and the tables covered with dainty white linen.

After dinner we were grieved at being obliged to say farewell to Mr. S—, one of the most popular of our passengers. May good luck attend him! His hand was shaken again and again by those who were sad indeed to leave him behind, and his loss will be mourned by more than one. We had two new and entertaining arrivals who contradicted many of the stories we had heard of Dawson. In fact, all stories in this part of the world seem to be told but to be contradicted. According to the newcomers, Dawson is exceedingly healthy, prices are very low—bacon only twenty cents a pound, whereas we are paying fifteen cents a pound freight, while this, added to original price and duty to be paid, would prove it wiser to start empty-handed and purchase provisions at the journey's end.

Our pigeons have attracted great attention, and we have received many fine offers for them, but prefer "squabs on toast." The man who wants the ice cream freezer has gradually increased his bid, which now stands at eighty dollars, as he has heard he can get ten dollars a glass for ice cream!

---

* Leroy Napoleon "Jack" McQuesten, the pioneer trader at Circle City.

Nearing Our Destination

SATURDAY, JULY 23RD ☞ For the first time we were able to sleep soundly from midnight until 6 AM, when awakened as usual by the stewards.

Someone has been, and still is, dancing a hornpipe over head with such force that the boards above bend with each emphatic kick. Thank the Lord, Dawson is only three hundred miles distant, and this tedious fight against the seven-miles-an-hour current of the Yukon will soon be ended. If we had only dared cross the Pass "going in," taking this means of leaving the country, we should have had this tremendous current aiding us the entire way. The day has been passed in silent admiration of the grandeur of the mountainous scenery—chain upon chain of rocks crowned with trees, which seem to be growing from the solid stone, and down the sides to the water's edge, with never a sign of earth to support the roots. Smoke on all sides fills the air, as campfires are built and not extinguished, and the flames slowly climb the mountainside, destroying the much-needed wood, and spoiling the picture otherwise so beautiful.

SUNDAY, JULY 24TH ☞ So chilly today that shirtwaists have been discarded for thicker garments and wraps, and few can remain out of doors. The mess-hall is filled with card players. The missionaries and those devoutly inclined shut themselves in their cabins, but that does not prevent them from hearing all that takes place in the universal sitting room. Before luncheon a great shout went up, followed by shrieks, hurrahs, catcalls, "We'll meet you in Dawson." Looking through the cabin window, I saw the *John Barr* replenishing with wood, and the cheers of our passengers meant that we were slowly but surely leaving her behind. "Don't you be so cocky," they called; "wait until you need wood again, and then our turn will come."

4:30 PM. The shrieks are recommencing, which announce to those below that the *John Barr* is again passing us. Shouts of triumph from her passengers and of despair from ours are wafted on the air. Now the *Leah* blows her whistle, and we are off again, probably for an exciting race, should the channel prove sufficiently wide.

MONDAY, JULY 25TH ☙ The exciting event today was "crossing the line." We were at dinner when someone called out, "We're just going into a foreign land." J— left the table, and opened his cabin door, so that we who were seated opposite could obtain a fine view of the termination of the possessions of the United States and of the entrance to the Dominion of Canada.

Several bouquets which had been gathered in the vicinity of the different landing places were brought to me during the day. We were greatly surprised to find flowers growing in such abundance. We are becoming so weary of this never-ending voyage that we have been asking concerning the difficulties of the Pass, so, after dinner, Mr. P— came with maps and plans in order to explain to us all the dangers in store for those willing to attempt such an undertaking. Notwithstanding, both Edith and I are longing to see the other part of the country, and are carefully weighing the pros and cons, hoping to find that we can try the trail without imprudence or risk.

===== A LESSON IN PANNING OUT GOLD =====

EDITH'S FIRST PAN

TUESDAY, JULY 26TH ☞ Facing us, and to the right as we approach, is Forty Mile. Nestling on the edge of the water, at the foot of high hills backed by the mountains, lie Forts Cudahy and Constantine. At the right are two small houses, a few warehouses, a flagpole with a red flag flying, and nine one-story houses. Beyond is the mission where the bishop lived and worked for many years. Quite a number of passengers left us at Forty Mile. Others started for a tramp and we waved adieu to them as the *Leah* steamed across the river for wood.

After luncheon, Mr. L—, of Circle City, asked if I would like to pan out some gold, as the ground in the vicinity looked rich. No second invitation was needed—my pan was in my hand and went with me on shore in less time than it has taken to write this. Mr. L— brought a shovel and helped dig, then showed me how to wash the gravel, which I did with great impatience, shouting with excitement as the colours began to show, until, in a few moments, passengers and stewards had joined us with their pans. The result of my first work was between fifty cents and one dollar to the pan, and L— told me to stake off the ground at once, and record the claim. Of course there were the usual remarks about someone having salted it, but that did not deter others from digging with a will in this lucky hole, offering to give me a percentage of whatever they found for permission to do so. The whistle blew, calling us on board, and back we went to Forty Mile to pick up our stranded passengers. They brought us the following war news which they had gathered on shore: that Spain's navy had been completely wiped out; that the *Oregon* had chased and sunk Spain's last ship, but that in capturing Santiago we had lost eighteen hundred men; that "Teddy's" Rough Riders had received worse treatment than those in any other regiment; also that Admiral Cervera had been caught and held as hostage for Hobson, who had not been shot as according to former report. Mr. L— presented us with a couple of oranges, the first seen since leaving St. Michaels. "Oh, my!" said a woman to Edith, "do you know that them there oranges is worth fifty cents apiece? It's like eatin' so much money. How kin you do it?"

The Promised Land

WEDNESDAY, JULY 27TH ☞ We made such fast time during the night, that we are now nearing Dawson at a rapid rate and find the scenery on all sides far grander than we had anticipated. Here is Dawson at last! No pictures we have seen, no descriptions we have read or heard, compare with the reality. Those who were here last year tell us that it has grown at least one hundred percent. The three long wharves are so packed with people that we expect to see them precipitated into the water by the addition of a feather's weight. Miles and miles of tents of all sizes and descriptions fill the town, and are pitched everywhere on the hillside. Skeletons of many warehouses which are being constructed and a few log cabins are also to be seen. Stores of all kinds line the main street and riverfront, some being less than ten feet wide, as rent for ground is ten dollars a foot per month in the business part of the town. From the landing up to the Klondike River, boats of every style line the waterfront, reminding one of the houseboats about Canton, although those belonging to this settlement are of a much more primitive character. As we neared the wharf of the Alaska Commercial Company we searched in vain for a familiar face among the thousand before us. Such perfect discipline seemed marvellous. We tied up at the dock, but not one man stepped on board, no one attempted to land, and yet there were only two Canadian officials on duty. There was much handshaking across the boat's side, shouts of "Hulloa, Bill!" "Why, there's Jim," etc., for every man is known by his Christian name in this part of the world.

We felt indeed that we were strangers in a strange land, when who should evade the police and jump on board, after having rowed around the *Leah* in a canoe, but Mr. M—! A case of the bread which we had cast upon the waters returning to us in a moment of need. We had become interested in him when we were in California. He was land-poor and just about to go to Dawson over the Pass. He looked delicate, and after all the tales that we had read of the hardships of that terrible trip, we felt that he might never live to reach there, so Edith and I talked it over and finally decided to send him in by steamer and allow him to "pay up" when his mines should prove valuable. How glad we were to receive his cordial, hearty greeting! After lunching with us, he accompanied us on shore to look at accommodations.

We first went along the main street to a new hotel* which was to be opened that evening with a big dinner, followed by a dance. The house, built of wood, and three stories high, quite towered above the tents and cabins of its neigh-bours. The only entrance that was finished was through the new and elaborately furnished barroom, within whose walls many a sad history will probably be recorded during the coming year, as we are told that "the liquor business here is bigger pay than the richest mine," and that "even the smallest barroom realises between five hundred and a thousand dollars a night." Separated by a hallway from this saloon is the dining room, beauti-fully clean, table covered with damask, and even napkins (something unusual in this part of the world) at each place. The menu, beginning with "oyster cocktails," caused us to open our eyes wide with astonishment, after all that the papers have told us of the starvation about Dawson. We next visited the kitchen adjoining, where there was a stove that would have gladdened the heart of any cook at home. The chef was said to be from Marchand's, of San Francisco. The proprietress explained to us that she had sent for chairs, which had arrived without legs, they having been left on the dock at St. Michaels, one of the inconveniences that one has to bear through the negli-gence of transportation companies, so she had carpenters at fifteen dollars a day manufacturing new legs.

On the second floor, a long, narrow hall separated rooms that were about double the size of an ordinary cabin on shipboard. Each room contained a primitive wooden bedstead, but there was no space for wardrobe, closet, or dressing table. Evidently the pride of the hostess's heart was centred in Brussels carpets and lace curtains, to which she called our attention as having been introduced into Dawson for the first time. The price of one of these tiny rooms was six dollars and a half a day, food five dollars extra, or two dollars a meal. On the third floor the carpenters were busy preparing for the evening dance, after which the large hall was to be partitioned off into small rooms, at five dollars a day each, providing that the sojourn of the guest should be at least of one month's duration, otherwise terms to be increased accordingly. We were

* Belinda Mulrooney's Fairview Hotel on Front Street.

cordially invited to return for the dinner at 10 PM, and also for the dance. Noticing that there were no panes of glass in the windows, which were simply covered with cheesecloth, we asked what happened in case of rain, and were told that it very rarely rained, but that when it did there would probably not be sufficient to do any damage. Glass also had been ordered, but, as usual, it was impossible to tell when or by what steamer it would arrive.

From the hotel we continued our walk as far as the banks of the famous Klondike River. But of it and its attractions later—in case we have the courage and good fortune to tramp in that direction to pan out gold on a claim of our own. Then to the other end of town, to a small cabin 12 x 18 on the hillside, it being the one upon which we had an option for two thousand dollars. As it was crowded in by tents on all sides, with the sun beating down upon it, and as we were exhausted by the long tramp after a six-week voyage, we were finally persuaded to row across the Yukon to West Dawson, which was described to us as being on high ground, healthy and cool, and just the place for our tent. Our guide invited the doctor to accompany us in his canoe. Going over is very easy, as the current carries the boat at the rate of at least five miles an hour, if not more, but the return trip requires strong oars and stout arms.

We landed at the foot of a picturesque bank, which was already in its favour, as compared with the marshy swamp on the opposite side. Plenty of room there was for an ordinary tent, but it was difficult to find space sufficient for our 40 x 70. Finally, we came to a bit of ground belonging to Mr. —, who told us that, as

LOG CABINS AT DAWSON

he was leaving the following day, he would gladly give up to us his rights of possession, before starting on a prospecting trip. The miners from all the tents in that vicinity were sitting outside, enjoying their evening meal, from which they rose to give us cordial welcome, and to tell us that in case we were prevented from turning up on time they would allow no one else to "jump" the site. They also begged us not to hire men to pitch the tent, as they should like the pleasure of doing it for us. Although they were clad in rough miners' costumes, their gentle and kindly manners showed that at home they occupied positions of no slight prominence. At 9 PM the sun was still lighting us on our way, and we decided that with three steamers in port, it would be a fine occasion for "doing the town" as it is called here.

We were first escorted to the dance hall of the place, and slipped through a private entrance into a box that was curtained, so that we were free from observation while able to see all that took place. Nothing could have been more highly proper than the dancing, which consisted of waltzes, polkas, and military schottisches, interspersed with occasional square dances, which seemed more like caledonians than lancers or quadrilles. The "girls," as they were called, seemed to be between twenty-five and thirty years of age. A lot of Dawson "society" men were dancing with them. According to the rule of the house, drinks at one dollar each must be ordered after every dance. In case the "girl" does not care to drink, her partner gives her a check which she is allowed to "cash in" later, receiving twenty-five cents from the proprietor of the dance

MONTE CARLO THEATRE, FRONT STREET, DAWSON

hall. She is also paid twenty-five dollars a week for dancing, or at least so we were informed. In the rear of the hall was a stage and there were ensconced five men who composed the orchestra, and very good music they produced. We heard one or two songs from the Oatley Sisters, and then adjourned to the Monte Carlo Theatre, where we witnessed a thoroughly respectable variety show, which came to an end a little before midnight, after which we were escorted safely back to our barge through crowded streets, where law and order are wonderfully well maintained.

THURSDAY, JULY 28TH ☞ The first visit that Edith and I paid this morning was to the post office, to inquire for the large batch of mail which we supposed had been sent in to us over the Pass. To our great astonishment there was but one letter. We sent for the postmaster, who listened most courteously as we told him of the books, magazines, and papers which we had ordered to be forwarded long before our departure. He politely explained that a very small mail had been sent in over the Pass, but that the greater quantity would come by the *Alliance* according to contract made by our government. First disappointment.

The Alaska Commercial Company is very generous in allowing passengers to remain on the boats until they have found comfortable accommodations. On returning to luncheon we were greatly interested in the different plans. The old fiddler said: "There ain't nothin' here for me. The whiskey business is over-done—saloon on every corner, and a dozen thrown in between; restaurants everywhere; houses with only one room, the cheapest of 'em a hundred dollars a month; me an' my wife's goin' back on this same steamer." One of the most energetic passengers was a German, who, with her daughter and two sons, had already visited every available site in town, had purchased a controlling interest in the swimming bath, and was planning to partition from it one side, which she intended to run as a laundry; the other for her daughter to serve ice cream, cakes, and "soft drinks." The colonel's wife was most unhappy, as the German had engaged the two "servant girls which I've raised and brought up here," said she, "and now they won't go back with me."

Before leaving San Francisco, we had supplied ourselves with certificates of deposit on the Bank of California, worth fifty dollars each, which we were told were not only "as good as gold," but "command a premium of from ten to fifteen percent in Dawson." Imagine, then, our surprise at being obliged to pay two dollars and a half a hundred for the privilege of exchange. Another surprise was when, after luncheon Edith and I started on a shopping expedition, she was greeted by a man who had travelled through Egypt in her party in '95. After dinner we were asked to accompany a few friends on an exploring expedition, but, feeling exhausted, preferred sitting in our easy chairs on top of the barge, from which point we commanded the entire town. Our first visitor was Mrs. —, a former passenger, whose husband is a Dawson physician. He accompanied her, and we were greatly amused by the experiences which they related. "Our cabin, although large for Dawson," said she, "is too small to contain trunks, furniture, and a stove, so we do without the latter and take our meals at restaurants, but oh, how I hate to see four dollars passed out three times a day just for our food! As for the doctor, he is so accustomed to receiving seventeen dollars for a visit that he doesn't mind."

Good Father R— joined our party and told me that one of the Sisters at the hospital here had been in the hospital at St. Josephs, Victoria, during my stay there, and that she was anxious to see me. How delightful it will be to meet her again in this faraway corner of the world! Mr. L— then presented the correspondent of the *New York Herald* and a Mr. J—, who we were informed was the rightful owner of the land which we have been inspecting in West Dawson. He told me that he and his partner had staked out one hundred and sixty (or perhaps many more—have forgotten the number) acres. They had paid the commissioner a deposit of fifty dollars on the land, which he had accepted. They had spent many thousands in clearing it and in starting a fine garden. Just as radishes, and many other delicacies (for that part of the world) were springing into life, the squatters came, and, as the government had failed to protect his rights, this garden had been abandoned, and he would be delighted to have us as neighbours. Some miners were here introduced, among them one of the "Klondike Kings." I begged for a story, whereupon he said that one of the most amusing things that had happened to him was the receipt of the following letter, which he kindly allowed me to copy:

Dear —: Doubtless you will be surprised to receive a letter from your native land in far-off America, but seeing your picture in the paper with details of your sojourn in the Gold Regions, and pleased with your courage and Perseverance thought I would like to make the acquaintance of one that has spent 8 *long* years in the Yukon after so many reverses becoming the Mineing King. How true if you don't succeed at first try, try again and you surely have been rewarded for your trials and hardships endured which I suppose was many and *hard* at the time. Yet wherever we are, there are more or less hardships to bear. Though my younger days were spent with *much* Happiness haveing everything that Heart could *wish*. Then I married one of the *best* men of the world and my life was a pleasant Dream of *love*, until he died leaving me alone in this cold, cold world. Not haveing children, I have spent most of my time with relatives here and in the West. I am very fond of travelling, and have been fortunate in that respect. The paper speaks of your Wandersome disposition. True, that is very well when we are young. My experience is that there is no place like a Pleasant Home, with a *loveing* and *devoted* husband and it seems to me that a bachelor of your age, would conclude that life was not worth *liveing*, without a *dear* little Wife to look after your Happiness in sickness and Health with plenty of this world's *goods*, to make *everything* comfortable. *I* have always been *use* to plenty and have an income that keeps me *very* comfortable, but the *Loneliness* of this life. I have been of a *bright* and *Lively* disposition and enjoyed Life untill the passed 3 years but now every thing seems faded and life not worth liveing. I cannot enjoy *anything* without *some* one to share that Happiness. I am rather tall, brown hair, and blue eyes, fond of music and the *fine* Arts; have studdied both. Now that you have *almost* finished reading my letter, I hope you will *reflect* and think *kindly* of me, and answer this poorly composed and written letter through *Friendship* and that *some* day, *some* where we may meet and not be *sorry* that this letter was written. I can give the *best* of Referrence and *of course* expect the same. Thinking you would be pleased to see your picture in the paper, I enclose the same then you can tell me in return if it is *really* you. I *wish* you would send me a Photo then I will return the compliment. Since July, I have constantly been with my Invalid Mother who has been very ill most of the time and not expected to Live long, as she is 75 years old and one of the Sweetest in this world and I feel that when her Spirrit leaves that *poor old Body* that it will get to that Land of Rest where all is Piece and Happiness. If you are *pleased* with this letter and wish to *answer* I will promise a Better one in return. Respectfully your *true* and unknown Friend

Mrs. —

FRIDAY, JULY 29TH ☞ As the *Leah* and the barge were about to pull out of the harbour this morning, carrying many of our former passengers, J— (who had concluded to try Dawson rather than Rampart) said, "Mrs. Hitchcock, if you're going to live across the river you'll want a boat and there's a man 'going out' on the *Leah* who will sell one for ten dollars." "But I know nothing of boats; let me wait and consult M—." "You can't," said J—, "he's off now." The owner then sung out, "You may have it for five," and with a woman's love for a bargain, after a hasty glance at the boat, I handed out the money and was very proud to be told afterwards that in this part of the country the lumber alone is worth between twenty and thirty-five dollars, and still more proud that the *Joseph* was able to hold all our household goods and provisions, weighing over a thousand pounds.

We spent the morning at the Custom House, paying about one hundred dollars in duties. Our tent had already been taken across and was being prepared for our reception, but as it weighed over four hundred pounds, we engaged men to put it up carefully, unwilling to impose upon the good nature of our neighbours.

We Become Squatters

AND NOW WE ARE SQUATTERS on the land staked out by Mr. J— and his partner. Our tent attracts the greatest amount of attention from each side of the river. Tents, as a general thing, run from eight to perhaps twenty feet but one this size! The *Klondike Nugget* wrote of it: "West Dawson is taking metropolitan strides. From this side of the river can be seen a large number of cabins going up, and within a few days has been erected the largest tent in the district. The West Dawsonites are to have the first church services in the town there next Sunday, which will be conducted by the Rev. Dr. D —." The same sheet added in its personal columns: "Miss Van Buren and Mrs. Admiral (!) Hitchcock are the latest additions to Dawson society. The ladies are wealthy and are very well known in the United States. They travel for pleasure, and are simply 'doing' the Klondike country as they have done many other famous points of interest in Europe and America. They came in by way of St. Michaels, and expect to go out again before the freeze-up, and possibly by way of the Chilkoot Pass."

To return to the subject of the tent. It took four men to transport it from Dawson. Our neighbours worked under the direction of an experienced man at fifteen dollars a day, with his assistants at one dollar an hour. We had given an order for planking the entire ground, but when we saw as we entered, the wildflowers and plants, or rather weeds, two feet high, the place looked so picturesque that we concluded to allow it to remain in its natural state. The pigeons, permitted to fly about, looked so pretty in the high grass and perched upon the screen; the canary and the parrot made the interior attractive and homelike the general effect that of a conservatory. Mr. L— sent us a large bearskin, while our neighbours contributed half a dozen smaller ones. Mr. J— sent radishes from his garden, and after they had all worked hard and were ready to enjoy a well-earned rest, we started the graphophone which many of "the boys" (they are all "boys" here) had never before heard. How delighted they were and how quickly the evening passed! As they left at 11 PM, we hooked the flap of our tent and made preparations for retiring. It seemed impossible that I, who had insisted, when at home, upon having doors locked, bolted, and barred, and who had never gone to bed without looking under it, as well as in the wardrobe and every conceivable nook and cranny, and who had also started for the Klondike with revolver, cartridges, and belt, should now be entirely free from fear, realising that the tents of honest miners were all about us, and that, were a burglar to present himself, one call from us would bring the man to justice so quickly that he scarce would have time to repeat a prayer.

We had been advised to purchase air mattresses, as being lighter and more convenient than any other. Ours came from one of the best-known firms in San Francisco. We had them made to order, ordering at the same time canvas hammocks with a boxing all around so that they should be firmly held. Imagine, then, our indignation to find that this boxing was too flimsy to stand, while the air pumps or bellows had been forgotten, although we had repeatedly charged the clerk not on any account to fail to pack at least two with the mattresses. Let me say just here that it is almost necessary to watch one's goods put into the box and the cover nailed down, no matter where one may outfit nor how responsible the firm, for it rarely happens that articles arrive with everything needed. Then begins a search in the stores and junkshops for the one essential thing, and should one be so unusually fortunate as to find it, the cost would surely amount to five or ten times more than one would pay for it at home.

Edith and I spent an hour in trying to "blow up" our mattresses, but laughter at the funny situation retarded work. Finally we rolled up in two ten-pound blankets each and tumbled into the hammocks on one side only to roll out on

A SLEEPING BAG

the other side, as our novel bed swung, landing us on the soft ground. After a little practice, however, we managed it and slept a few hours until awakened by the icy wind. We then bundled up in heavy wraps, and, as our air pillows were too cool, we substituted those of down from our deck chairs, which were decidedly more comfortable. After another short sleep we again wakened, shivering with cold. Edith called to know if it were not time to start the fire, as it was so light it must be late, so we prepared for breakfast and then looked at our watches—2:30 AM!

SATURDAY, JULY 30TH ⇒ The "boys" promised to find us a cook, but as he failed to materialise, Edith made some delicious soda biscuit and we managed with great difficulty to open a tin of butter and of sardines. We had some nails, so drove one with a log of wood into one of the posts supporting the tent, and what do you suppose was the first thing we hung up? Why, a mirror, of course. Some of the "boys" had opened boxes for us the previous evening, and we had as much fun and excitement in looking through them as though they had been Christmas boxes from home. As we had neither shelf, nor peg, nor table, we could only look into them in order to know where to find things when needed. By ten, the sun came out and shone with such power that it was too hot to continue the inspection, so we placed our chairs where we could get the breeze in the door of the tent, from which we had an unobstructed view of the river, the mountains, and Dawson nestling at the foot of this magnificent background. We began to read the three latest papers from San Francisco and Seattle, but were soon interrupted by visits from our neighbours, the miners whose tents surrounded ours. People came during the morning from all parts, to have a look at our wonderful tent, the fame of which seems to have gone far beyond Dawson. As they showed a disposition to see the interior, we gave them permission to enter, which they did in the most respectful manner, hats in hand. Their pleasure at sight of the pigeons and our other pets was most touching, and their delight in hearing music from our Criterion was unbounded.

We may be surrounded by rough miners, but never have we met men more courteous or more ready to lend a helping hand, not only to women but to men. Before starting from California we had read that here each man was for himself and had no time to assist his neighbour, nor was he willing to offer him the smallest portion of "grub." All untruths for no such generosity exists in any other part of the world. Lunchtime and no cook! We are beginning to feel the pangs of hunger, but do not dare attempt filling the coal oil stove. We look outside and see our next door neighbour cooking a delicious-smelling mess on his stove out in the open air. He glances towards us and asks if we would like

54 some stewed oysters. We are divided between a longing for them, and the fear of robbing him and his partner, but his offer is so cordial that we accept, upon condition that he will take our box of sardines, which he does reluctantly. How we relish the oysters, and with what an appetite we devour them! Truly it is worth the trip to enjoy food as we now do. Edith borrows a place on her neighbour's stove and makes herself a cup of cocoa. Another neighbour goes to town and brings us two loaves of bread at twenty-five cents each, accepting the money most reluctantly, as they all want to be not only hospitable but generous. Another neighbour presents us with lemons; still another with oranges, which are given in such a way that we cannot offer to pay for them without fear of offending these kind souls. One of the "boys" tells us that in a tent near by lives an English physician who had the pleasure of meeting Edith in Yokohama when her father was consul-general to Japan; that he wishes to call on her, but has no "boiled shirt" ready, nor "store clothes." To this we exclaim, "But our visitors must not stand upon ceremony. We find that we must keep to jerseys and short skirts while here, and the men must make no changes in their costume on our account. We are all roughing it and camping out, some for one purpose and some for another, and we desire to be treated as are others in West Dawson." In a very short time the doctor made his appearance, handsome in his jersey, and needing no "store clothes" to show him to better advantage. How we did enjoy talking over the Orient and those we had known in China and Japan! Thus occupied, the afternoon sped by rapidly.

Towards 5 PM the tent grows delightfully cool. M— appeared with delicious salmon steaks for dinner and we could hardly wait for him to fill the coal oil stove, so famished were we. It did not take long to light the fire and to heat some of Van Camp's delicious tomato soup. This is one of the articles of food we brought in which more than equals our expectations. Edith also cooked the salmon and heated a tin of corn, all of which we enjoyed more than any feast. Edith was then allowed a well-deserved rest, while M— and I washed and wiped our aluminum dishes and hung them up on the high weeds. Poor M— had been scouring the town all day for a cook but the search was in vain. "The boys" came and sat in the tent door after dinner, while we had some of our best Criterion music, and it was delightful to see how they enjoyed *Lohengrin* and *Tannhäuser*, as well as Italian opera and Sousa's compositions. All parties break up here at eleven. So at that hour our tent flap was closed, and we followed the directions given to us by our neighbours and had a fine night's rest. We put rugs under the hammocks this time, so that the dampness from the ground should not rise; then we made a bag of one pair of blankets, stepped into it, and rolled into the other instead of getting into a carefully made bed, and, although the night was quite as cool as the previous one, we slept as warmly and comfortably as if at home. One amusing thing occurred. The fur robe was under Edith's hammock, while under mine was placed the pair of blankets purchased for Ivan, but which we were told he ought not to be allowed to use so early in the season. Hardly had we fallen asleep before the dog recognised his blankets and tried to crawl under my hammock in order to take possession of them. As he pushed under on one side, the hammock tipped over on the other and sent me rolling out on the grass, which caused me quite as much merriment as it did Edith, whose laughter was soon hushed, lest our neighbours should be disturbed.

SUNDAY, JULY 31ST ☞ Another glorious day! Temperature delightful. While Edith lighted the fire and heated some of our tinned stores, I fed and watered the pigeons, parrot, canary, and dog. By the time we had finished breakfast and our few chores, it was too late for church. Some of our neighbours came to invite us to row across in Peterboro canoes, which are considered the safest boats to use against the tremendous current, but we have a deadly fear of anything bearing the name of canoe, so had private services at home. Lunch hour, and still no cook, although the "boys" are scouring the town in search of one. We cooked a bit of salmon which was brought us from Dawson, heated some tinned vegetables, and, with our appetites, it was a feast.

As we were sitting resting and reading at our tent door, who should appear but our shipmates, Mr. R— and Dr. D—, bringing with them a very handsome fellow named A—, who has been in this part of the world so long that he thinks it would be difficult to live at home again. Hardly had they seated themselves, or rather thrown themselves on the rugs (for we have but three chairs), when Mr. M— and Mr. R— joined the party. They had all rowed across and were hot and thirsty. We remembered a powder which had been prepared for us by our San Francisco chemist, so we mixed it with the cool springwater, making a delicious cider. As our guests had come to spend the afternoon in the country, we treated them without ceremony, and opened a box containing the latest periodicals of all kinds, which they had not yet been able to obtain, so that they could enjoy the illustrations as well as conversation. M— spied my mandolin, and told me how charmingly R— played, and he was right. He drew from it more exquisite music than I had ever heard, even in Italy. Such a restful, peaceful Sabbath! We also heard the songs of the Salvation Army, as the airs floated across the Yukon to us.

We were sorry to tell our guests *au revoir*, but could not feel lonely, as one neighbour after another stopped to see if we needed anything. Mr. O—, who

56   is three tents away from us, came to ask if he could row one of us over in the morning. Edith gladly accepted, as she is to do the shopping. O— said there were two great causes of excitement in Dawson, from which town he had just returned. One was the preparations for the departure of the *Bella*; the other, the arrival of two of our pigeons, which were quietly seated on the roof of a low building, with an admiring crowd about them, as many had not seen pigeons for years, and were revelling in the sound of their cooing. "I hope they won't shoot them for seagulls," said Edith. "Never you fear," replied O—. "Every man, woman, and child knows that they belong to you two ladies, and they would be only too ready to bring them back to you, did they not think they would come of their own accord." Just then M— appeared with a fellow whom he introduced as his friend Mr. Isaacs, saying: "He is in hard luck just now. He took out last year eight thousand dollars from one of his claims; went home to find his father had died, gave his mother seven thousand to pay off a mortgage on the old home, then put the remainder in an outfit and returned to Dawson. After a short rest, he started out on the trail, and after locating one or two claims, returned to find that his tent and entire outfit were burned to the ground. But his pluck never deserted him; he determined to take the first job which presented itself, so he is willing to be your cook, boatman, and jack-of-all-trades for five dollars a day and his 'grub.'" The news of our acquisition was soon spread abroad, and we are now spoken of as millionairesses and are told that we shall probably have claims offered us by the thousand.

14

The "Sick Boy"

MONDAY, **A**UGUST 1ST ⯐ Mr. O— had promised to row Edith to Dawson at nine o'clock. At ten he had not yet turned up, so we sent Isaacs to inquire whether he had changed his plans. He quickly came to tell us that he had been sitting up with a sick boy all night, and had just finished breakfast, but would be ready in a few moments. I immediately went to the "sick boy" to see what he needed. He was sleeping in a small tent, on a bed made of pine boughs, covered with a fur robe; his head was in an uncomfortable position, with no pillow; he was feverish, and able to retain nothing on his stomach. To get him a nice cool air pillow, to bathe his head and give him the juice of an orange, was the work of a few moments, and then I left, fearing to weary him, but giving him a whistle with which to call me in case of need. The poor fellow said he had never been ill before, and would rather be dead than on his back, but he had had a long, tough tramp over the mountains, "which knocked me out," said he.

Edith returned from town, having purchased the commonest kind of a wooden table for eight dollars, but glad to get it at any price, although it was badly warped. Upon expressing a wish that we had half a dozen of them, Mr. J—, who was calling upon us, said, "I have one that I'll gladly lend you, and it won't be depriving me a bit, as it's too large to go in my cabin." Edith had also purchased moose steak at a dollar a pound, but, although she had searched all the shops of Dawson, she was unable to find at any price a tub, large or small, for bathing purposes. She brought an invitation for Wednesday evening. Mr. M— had asked us to dine, in case we would not mind eating as the miners do from a table with no tablecloth, and from saucepans instead of dishes.

While at luncheon, five passersby put their heads into the tent; they were evidently from a distance, and were abashed as they caught sight of us, but we had been inspired by the hospitality of our neighbours, and called out "Come

THE BIG TENT

right in if you want to see the tent." They entered almost on tiptoe, and twirling their hats between fingers and thumbs, but at sight of the birds their feelings overcame them. One sat down near the canary and almost wept as he listened to its beautiful notes. Another said: "I used to have a parrot at home, an' it knew my footsteps so well that whenever I came into the house it always hollered, 'Papa! Papa!' Many a one tried to deceive it by walkin' like me, but it warn't no use, it never hollered for anybody else. Tell you what, parrots 'ez got a heap er sense. Another thing yer couldn't fool my parrot on was this: yer'd take some money out o' yer pocket and shake it, en' she'd holler, 'Gimme a nickel, gimme a nickel'; but yer might shake other things that sounded like money all night, an' though she could only hear it an' couldn't see it, she'd look as wise as an owl, an' never say a word." The appreciation and the deep feeling shown by these guests to whom chance had revealed some relics of home life were most touching.

Towards evening I went again to the tent of the "sick boy" who seemed very much better and thanked me most heartily for the air pillow which had been such a comfort to him. There was a heavy towel on his forehead, which I replaced with a soft handkerchief, dipping it occasionally in the icy spring water until he assured me that his head was greatly relieved. As there was only a box on which to sit, Isaacs brought over one of our steamer chairs, and the invalid listened attentively as I read to him some of the war news, for which he begged in preference to stories from novel or magazine. He interrupted occasionally to tell me of his life of wandering, of his adventures, and how, recently, he had been lying and watching, from his cot in the tent, the burials that took place across the river, "sometimes five to ten a day," said he. "But you must remember that the population is said to be nearly forty thousand," said I, "and that the Dawsonites are living in a marshy swamp, while we are on high, dry ground." Just then a blonde head appeared, and a pleasant voice exclaimed, "How are you feeling, Mr. Jones?" "Oh, much better, thank you," and turning to me he said, "Mrs. Hitchcock, let me make you acquainted with Mrs. A—" and I was soon deeply interested in listening to Mrs. A—'s experiences in crossing the trail from Dyea, which she declared to be so wonderfully beautiful that it more than repaid one for all the perils of the undertaking.

Although this is mainland, we call it "our island," because it seems to us, as though we are leading a Robinson Crusoe life. We went on an exploring expedition this afternoon and our imaginary boundary lines are an eighth of a mile on either side, consisting on the left of a poultry yard and small slaughtering establishment, from which the odour was so unpleasant that we hastily retraced our steps; on the right, a rivulet or creek coming down from the mountainside which supplies us with drinking water. As walking over this boggy ground is ruinous to shoes, we have decided to imitate the neighbours and wear either muck-a-lucks or rubber boots. We were greeted pleasantly from each cabin, where the miners are taking their summer's rest after a hard winter's work.

Edith and I have both grown tired of hammocks and want something more stationary, so Isaacs, with the assistance of our neighbours, cut down some trees, made them into four bedstead legs, which they drove solidly into the ground, nailed across these side poles, and then pieces for the head and foot. The frame being finished, a double thickness of burlap was tightly stretched across it, and this was Edith's bed, upon which her hammock and mattress were placed; a similar one was then constructed for me and finished by 11 PM, and it was still too light for a candle. Isaacs had had an unusually hard day's work, but had been unwilling to leave until he had made us thoroughly comfortable. The "boys" had divided their time between rendering him assistance and entertaining us. Mr. A— gave us his experiences in crossing the Chilkoot Pass to which we listened intently, wondering whether we should be able to screw up our courage to the point of attempting so difficult a feat. He said that, like many another, he had quarreled with his partner and made the usual division—cut the tent in half, the boat in twain, and even divided the stove. All night long the rain continued.

Tuesday, August 2nd ☞ Not enough sun to dry anything, but it is a blessing that the rain has ceased, and we are praying to be protected from rheumatic pains, for dampness reigns supreme this morning. It was quite ten before we were able to have breakfast, but that is an hour earlier than any of our neighbours, who are seldom about before noon. Isaacs prepared us a delicious breakfast, and we are thankful for such a perfect oil stove, which is always ready at a moment's notice for cooking of any kind; we had nice fresh salmon taken from our Klondike refrigerator, which, by the way, I have not yet described. By digging from one and a half to two feet underground, one strikes ice, so we have a large subterranean ditch in the kitchen corner of the tent, in which we place boxes containing meat, fish, or whatever one would preserve on ice at home.

Mr. O— and Mr. J— paid a friendly call to ask if we wished to be rowed over to town, but we were so very busy unpacking and decorating our tent, that we had to depend upon them to bring us back a roast for dinner. Isaacs busied himself making a couple of benches for our table; chopping trees, and breaking boxes, from which he made us shelves and a couple of stools. It was three o'clock before we knew it. Isaacs prepared soup from a "beef-stock powder," while Edith made most delicious scalloped tomatoes. We partook of these dishes and hot biscuit with keen relish, while our cook, being such a hard worker, got the remains of the moose meat of the day previous, with some "evaporated" potatoes.

At four o'clock Dr. H— brought two most attractive young Englishwomen, who had come from Dawson to have tea with him. They had "come in" over the Chilkoot Pass. One had crossed the summit, suspended in a basket, one thousand feet above sea level. Naturally we were deeply interested in their

A GOAT TEAM (PHOTO BY E. A. HEGG)

descriptions. Mrs. F— had lived in Victoria, British Columbia and knew many of my friends there, so the visit seemed all too short.

5 PM. Mr. S— has just been here, attracted by our pigeons, having raised fancy pigeons at home for his own amusement. He gave us much excellent advice in regard to building their cotes, and kindly offered to assist in their construction. He sat on the ground, Japanese fashion, outside of our tent door and related some of his experiences. He said that most of the "boys" had struck it rich, but that his turn had not yet arrived, as he did not intend to work his claims until those on either side had found plenty of pay gold, after which it would be easy for him to trace the vein. "There's nothing makes a man cuss so much," said he, "as continuous but unsuccessful hard work. Why, I cuss by the hour sometimes, an' it's like a thunderstorm—it clears the air."

6 PM. "What you doing? Writing up all your troubles?" said Mr. O—, as he stood at the entrance to our camp. "How could we have any," I answered, "with such kind neighbours, and where all is so peaceful?"

At 9 PM a pleasant voice said, "I reckon I'm the only neighbour that hasn't called on you. I'm Mrs. B—, and the busiest woman you ever met; moved over here from Dawson to be quiet, and indulge in literary work, but it's no use; everyone is so kind that there is never a moment in the day without visitors, and so I haven't had time to come before," and in stepped Mrs. B—, dressed in an Indian buckskin suit with two rows of fringe around the bottom, a most picturesque figure; and for the past two hours she has entertained us with such stories of hairbreadth escapes, in Arizona, New Mexico, and coming over the Pass, that they far surpassed in excitement the most thrilling tales ever written.

We expressed great astonishment at her courage and daring, but she said that her love for work among the Indians was so great as to cause her to forget all fear and thought of self. Before leaving she asked if we would like to go on a stampede. We both jumped at the suggestion and were so wildly excited at the plan she unfolded that we had little sleep that night.

Our First Dinner in Dawson

WEDNESDAY, AUGUST 3RD ☞ Another rainy day! Consequently, no stampede, as one would sink beyond the knee at each step. Isaacs was late, so Edith made some of her delicious biscuit and broiled some bacon, while I attended to the dining room and fed and watered the many pets. Just as we finished, our man Friday entered, in time to do full justice to the remnants of our repast, although, as we had furnished him on the previous day with a month's "grub," the agreement was that he was to do all his cooking and his eating in his own tent. So fearful were we, however, of losing our cook, butler, boatman, and jack-of-all-trades, that we dared not enter a protest. We had lines stretched across the rear of the tent, and prepared to empty the trunks, which were covered with mould from having been stored in damp quarters while coming up the Yukon. We found many of our gowns ruined beyond redemption, or in such a condition that it would be impossible to wear them again at home; but the Alaska Commercial Company has the reputation of being just and honourable, so the loss will perhaps be made good to us on our return to San Francisco.

At noon M— arrived, bringing with him some veal for luncheon, which he remained to share with us; we had also some delicious potato balls, made from desiccated potatoes, and macaroni and cheese, in which we were indulging with ravenous appetites when Mrs. B— appeared, bringing with her Dr. D—, a Presbyterian clergyman. The result of this visit was that we promised our tent for religious services next Sunday morning, at eleven o'clock, granting permission for notices to be posted both here and in Dawson proper. In the midst of an interesting conversation we heard a voice outside calling, "Dinner is now ready in the Pullman car," and in this manner Mrs. B— informed the clergyman that his time was up. "Is it the third and last call?" we shouted, and upon hearing a reply in the affirmative Dr. D— bade us *au revoir*. After luncheon we were informed by Isaacs that the pigeon cote was ready to be lifted to the top of the four poles which he had embedded in the ground before the tent. "Now we'll see," said he, "how many of your neighbours who's been a-hoffering to do heverythink for you will 'elp me up with this 'eavy box. I expect they will all be deaf, dumb, and blind when I calls upon them," but he soon discovered his mistake, and the cote was soon high in air near the river bank, giving the Dawsonites and the West Dawsonites another novelty to admire. Two good hours it took to drive the pigeons out of the tent, after which the flap had to be closed, as we discovered for the first time how like cats they are in their love for home. This work finished, it was quite time to dress for our first dinner in Dawson.

We had seen so much of showy silk gowns and draggled feathers on the other side of the river, that we preferred the quiet elegance of a well-made "tailor suit" with "boiled collar" and silk tie. Just before starting, O— came to inform me that the "sick boy" would like to have a little of our Van Camp's soup, so over to his tent I went with it; found him in good spirits and with a ravenous appetite. He expressed himself as delighted that we were "going to dine with such nice people, and to see something of the better class of life." Just starting again, when Mrs. B— came to tell us that she also had an invalid on her hands, who thought he could relish the same soup, a tin of which we gladly gave her. She said, "In this country, one must always take something in return for such a gift; what shall it be?" But we were speedily out of sight and hearing, as we stepped into the boat with Isaacs in the role of boatman, and a powerful one he proved to be, easily rowing it against the tremendous current.

Scarcely had we landed when such a tremendous shower came down that we rushed for protection to the vestibule of the store of the North American Transportation Company, where we found many others seeking shelter. All eyes were on our tent, which we were facing, and the comments were most amusing, as they wondered whether it belonged to the Salvation Army, a merry-go-round, or circus company, but as a gust of wind sprang up, someone shouted, "Oh, it's a balloon! They're inflating it." As we anxiously watched it rising and falling with the wind, someone overhearing our remarks on the subject said, "Does it belong to you two ladies? Why wouldn't one half that size 'a' done yer? Is it Salvation Army?" "No, but there are to be services there next Sunday morning." "Free to all?" "Most certainly." "Well, then, we're a-goin', an' many a boy who never goes to church'll come, too, an' plenty o' others who want to see the inside o' that there tent."

Just then our host, Mr. M—, and his chum R— discovered our retreat; the rain stopped, and we were escorted to their one-roomed cabin. "I thought you'd like dining in here, and seeing just how we live, better than going to a restaurant, and so here we are," said M—, as we took a high step into the room, gorgeous with a magnificent fur robe in one corner, a library in the other, in the third an oil stove and a few kitchen utensils, while facing that was the dining corner used for multifarious purposes. We were at once seated on empty grocery boxes for chairs at a pine table without a cover, according to the custom of the country. On tin plates before us were caviar and sardines on toast, which our host had previously prepared. There were two other guests, one of whom handed me an envelope containing a letter of introduction from a son of Judge B—, who wrote: "It is a matter of much regret to me, that I am leaving here before your arrival, for I had looked forward to the pleasure of meeting you, and thought, moreover, that I might be of some assistance to you. However, I am sure I cannot do better than by introducing my friends of New York. Anything they can do for you and Miss Van Buren I am sure they will be most glad to. With best wishes for a pleasant sojourn, I am sincerely yours." We were soon well acquainted, as F— and C— were college mates of Edith's brother, and she had already heard much of them through him.

While we were chatting and enjoying the first course, our host was putting a spoonful of soup stock into each of six tin cups filled with hot water; he then passed them to us, saying, "Your medicine is now ready to be taken," and very good medicine it was, too. Our host then reached over to a frying pan on the small stove, stirring with one hand a mess of oysters and cheese, while in the other he held his soup cup, from which he took an occasional sip. The pan was then lifted from the stove, and its contents distributed on our tin platters, and

===== THE BIG TENT DOMINATES THE WEST DAWSON WATERFRONT =====

proving to be a most palatable concoction. M— ate with us, heating macaroni and tomatoes at the same time; and how we enjoyed it all! After carefully cleaning our plates, we received upon them a bit of mince pie (a great luxury), which had been nicely divided into six portions, with a tiny scrap left over, so that no one should be rude enough to take the last piece, said M—. How we laughed over this novel entertainment, and wished for photographs of such an unusual spectacle as that of college-bred youths in rough miners' costumes enjoying this repast with more pleasure than the finest entertainment they could be given at home. We wondered what the different members of our families would have said could they have had but a momentary glimpse of the scene. Certainly, no one dining with all the luxury known to civilisation could have enjoyed delicacies of the best market with more appreciation, or had a more delightful feast of reason and flow of soul, than had we in our primitive surroundings, talking so rapidly that one scarce could wait for the other to finish a sentence. The dinner ended, our host suggested that we must "do the town," so off we started.

We finally reached Main Street, which was as crowded and as light at ten o'clock as any fashionable promenade would have been at that hour in the daytime. At each corner we were stopped by greetings from former fellow passengers, and, finally, by one of the men we had grub-staked, who said: "I've been trying all day to reach West Dawson to see you on important business, but could get no boat. There is a big stampede to — Creek. I've been out there and located claims for you two ladies, and have done enough work to be certain that the ground is rich, so I've come in to pack a lot o' grub back, and want all your orders in case you should leave before I git through prospectin'. Anyway, when you come back next year you may look for big returns from these mines, even if I don't get to stake another." The party waited patiently while we listened to these glowing accounts and then rejoined our escorts, quite excited over the brilliant prospect. Our host then proposed that as our beverage at dinner had been water, we should stop at the Hoffman House, which he was anxious to show us, for a liqueur.

Filled with curiosity we entered, joined by Mr. M—'s "big brother," as he calls him. We entered what would seem at home a small room, but which, here, is of unusually good size; at the end was a stage where five musicians played *Cavalleria Rusticana*, as well as I have ever heard it.

Edith and I being the "Chee Charkers" (otherwise known as strangers or people to be preyed upon by sharks with wildcat schemes) attracted general attention. We remained long enough to hear two songs from a man with an exceedingly fine voice, and then were invited to the Combination Company Theatre. Our party had grown to eight, so we felt sufficiently well protected

Front Street, Dawson (Photo by E. A. Hegg)

to follow the custom of the country and enter the parquet through the bar-room—a proceeding so common here (in fact one has to wade through deep mud to reach the side entrance) that it caused no remark. We were then shown up a pair of stairs and told to take our choice of the unoccupied private boxes; only four of our escorts could be comfortably accommodated, so we had two boxes, and the men continually changed places with one another. We could see and not be seen, protected as we were by the curtains. We looked down upon a sea of sombreros, not a woman in all the audience, as the boxes are reserved for them and their escorts. We were the only ones who sat with drawn curtains, consequently curiosity was rife. We were more amused by watching the occupants of the boxes than with the performance on the stage, which was of the usual variety order, not very refined, with plenty of coarse jokes, but nothing absolutely vulgar. The young lady from the first box left her escort and descended to the stage, and entertained us with a song of a poor little country maid on a visit to town, where the young men made to her many suggestions, to each one of which she sang, "Will it do me any harm?" in the most innocent way. This so pleased the "boys" in the audience, that they threw an abundance of chips and nuggets on the stage, all of which she carefully picked up, and stowed away in her stocking. A jealous actress in the next box said in a stage whisper, "She'd never get so much money for her voice; it's all because the 'boys' like to watch her trick o' stowin' it away."

We listened to the mandolin playing of one of the prettiest girls I have seen for an age. The men said: "You should encourage such a person as that; beautiful as she is she is about the only virtuous girl in Dawson; let us send for her, that you may speak a few kindly words, which she will greatly appreciate. Besides, you won't have seen this show nor be able to write it up unless you have an interview with Adèle." Adèle was sent for, and talked and behaved most modestly; but when the drinks arrived she made a dash for the chips before they could be handed to us, besides stealing some extra ones from the waiter, who begged her to return them so that he would not be obliged to make them good; but this thrifty young person had them tightly tied up in her handkerchief and no amount of persuasion or argument could induce her to return one. The men excused her by saying, "She knows that you only want to show them as souvenirs in New York, and one is sufficient for that, while to her they represent so much cash."

The show over, the benches were quickly taken out and the hall cleared for a dance. We remained to look down upon a waltz and a quadrille, which were eminently proper in every respect. The men told us that this would last until five or six in the morning and that, notwithstanding the drinks which would follow each dance, it would be no more noisy at the termination than in the beginning of the evening. We had instructed Isaacs to wait for us at the Alaska Commercial Company's wharf, but saw him among the dancers. [We were] delighted to accept the offer of M— and R— to row us across in a Peterboro canoe, although I had solemnly sworn never on any account to put foot in a canoe. Seated, however, in the very bottom of it on the coats of the men who rowed us, all alarm faded away, even when we were in the midst of the powerful current.

We found our tent almost collapsed from wind and rain, but it is always easy to find a dry place, owing to its enormous size; still, it is aggravating in the extreme to look at the Catholic church tent opposite, tight as a drum and beautifully put up, and compare it with the one put up by a so-called first-class workman at fifteen dollars a day. The tentmaker had written most elaborate and detailed instructions, so that even in the Yukon he might be proud of his work, and begged us to have it so well arranged as to do him credit. But here it stands waving, swaying, swelling, dropping with the different light winds which take it in charge, looking a most slovenly affair, and criticised by people on both sides of the river. We have been in it a whole week now, and the man who put it up, though sent for many times, has not had pride enough, or a sufficiently keen sense of honour to come to our rescue; so we emptied again the jelly bags of water and "turned in." There were so many slack places in the

68 canvas around and above us that the air came in on all sides and we nearly froze to death, although we were covered with as many wraps as we could bear the weight of. The extremes are very great. An icy coldness during the night and intense heat about the noon hour, so powerful are the rays of the sun, and yet we are told that one never takes cold here.

Thursday, August 4th ☞ Nine o'clock and no Isaacs; ten, ditto; at half-past ten he made his appearance and when he found us already at breakfast said, "Why, I thought you ladies wanted to sleep late, and so I didn't dare to come before." Scarcely had we finished when Mrs. B— and Mr. T— came to spend the morning, and laughed most heartily over our experiences of the previous evening. Mrs. B— said, "That is just such a trip as I ought to take for my newspaper work, but, being alone, never have had the courage to do so; you must let me go with you should you ever do the town again." We faithfully promised, although not expecting to repeat the expedition; at least, not more than once before our departure, and not even then, unless there should be something new and particularly worthy of record. When we told triumphantly about the checks we had received our guests looked at each other and Mr. T— said, "I see you ladies do not recognise the meaning of many things, and treat all experiences in this part of the world as a huge joke; be careful that this be not misinterpreted, as those you meet may not understand you as we do." While deeply appreciating this kindly advice, we felt, however, quite certain that no action of ours could be misinterpreted.

As Isaacs left the tent on an errand, Mr. T— observed, "You did not get your man Friday very early this morning, and might have had him an hour later still, had it not been for the fact that when I heard him shout from his tent (which adjoins mine), at eight o'clock to know the time, again at nine, and again at ten, each time rolling over for another snooze, I called out to one of my neighbours, 'I hear the ladies in the Big Tent are looking for another cook.' There was a great scrambling, and, instantly after, the head of your major-domo appeared, saying, 'What's that about the Big Tent?' 'Oh, nothing,' I carelessly replied; but the effect was that desired." After luncheon M— appeared. "Well, I heard about you last night," said he. "What?" "Oh, that you were invited to occupy every box in the Combination Company." Shortly after came another guest, saying, "What a sensation you two ladies made last night; can't help it if you were behind curtains all the time. Every nice man in the house wanted to be introduced, as they hadn't seen so much style since leaving home ten years ago."

We Become "Free Miners"

FRIDAY, AUGUST 5TH ❧ As the tent flap was turned back this morning to admit the sunlight, for which we have never before been sufficiently grateful, the "sick boy" appeared to renew his thanks for our kindness and to return the dishes and steamer chair. His gratitude was so much greater than the little we had been able to do for him warranted, that we protested against further thanks, made him rest, and tried to persuade him not to row over to town until his health was fully reestablished; but our advice was as useless as it generally is when man has determined upon a plan. Immediately after the departure of John Jones, otherwise the "sick boy," Mr. S— arrived. This most picturesque-looking Virginian, whom Mrs. B— calls with a smile, "too lazy for words," said that he expected to go on a stampede in the evening—a real one—not, as he had done on several occasions, make a pretended start, with such hustle and bustle that all the boys in town followed in his footsteps, to be left in the lurch, but a quiet, secret affair. As he said *au revoir* however, he remarked that he might back out at the last moment, unless he got fine news from his partner. An Indian next appeared in the doorway, and is the only person whom we have not greeted pleasantly since our arrival; but our fear of the tribe is so great that we sent Ivan to lie across the doorway, but this had no effect upon the noble red man, who continued to gaze until he had fully satisfied his curiosity.

Then came from across the river Dr. D—, to tell us that he was soon to leave for the Koyukuk; of his brilliant prospects; the congenial society in the party; and to beg us to call on his wife on our return, and give her details which no letter can supply. Another visit from Mrs. B—, who expressed much astonishment that we should have been inhospitable to so good a member of the tribe as the Indian who had recently honoured us. She told us of the country about the Tanana, for which she is soon to depart, where there are said to be cannibals, and that there is a reward of forty thousand dollars for anyone who penetrates the region, as some of our worst criminals are in hiding there. She has been offered the assistance and escort of the marshal or police representatives, but considers that would be but an impediment, as she can do much better work alone. The only thing she dreads is being deserted in an unknown country by her guides, but she added, "I can feel instinctively when they are afraid to go farther, and when there is no doubt of their intention, if I can get the drop on them first, I should not hesitate to kill them and feed them to my dogs."

At two o'clock Mrs. B— took us over to Dawson to purchase a miner's certificate. Mr. F— who was holding court, left long enough to come downstairs and be presented to us as the widow of Admiral (!) Hitchcock and the grandniece of President Van Buren. From there we went to the office of Mr. W—, the Crown Timber Agent, as Mrs. B— thought it very important that we should know and be properly introduced to the officials before starting on our claim hunting.

We did a little shopping at the Alaska Commercial Company's warehouse, which is headquarters for everyone in town, where we chatted with a dozen or more acquaintances. On going out we saw the utter collapse of our tent. Dr. C— at once offered to row Edith across the Yukon, Isaacs assisting, while I went on with Mrs. B— to keep an appointment with one of the Sisters at the hospital, stopping to inquire for the mail, which arrived yesterday (Thursday), but which will not be ready for distribution before Monday! The reception room of the hospital is the most comfortable, homelike spot yet visited, with its stove, carpet, curtains, desk, and real chairs. Father greeted us most cordially, and sent for Sister —, who had been at St. Josephs, in Victoria, B.C., and who gave me pleasant news from the dear Sisters there.

At the wharf we found Isaacs, but no boat; someone had borrowed it, and there was none for us to hire. After applying to a young man in a fine-looking Peterboro and being courteously but decidedly refused on the ground that the boat belonged to an official, Mrs. B— asked as one having Masonic rights, and before we had time to breathe the boat was ours. On reaching the other side, what a sight met our gaze! I felt as one who had been evicted for non-payment of rent. Our tent was flat on the ground, our furniture and household goods, books, magazines, music, even my beloved diary, were scattered all over the ground, while the two carpenters, aided by our kindly neighbours, were pulling at the tent, ropes, and tackle with all their force.

Mrs. B— proposed that while waiting we should walk over to Sheep Camp to have a look at some fur robes which were offered for sale, one at one hundred dollars, the other at eighty-five dollars, as the man who had them was "going out," and had never used them. We passed dozens of tents from which we received kindly salutations, reached the small chicken farm, and beyond that a place where cattle had been killed; making a detour we approached a good-sized pen filled with sheep. Still on, passing an occasional cabin, until we entered a clearing in which were comfortable quarters.

In the open air, at a rough table, partaking of their evening meal, sat three men in shirtsleeves. They rose as we approached and cordially welcomed Mrs. B—, who introduced me as the owner of the Big Tent, a globetrotter who had been many times around the world, and was now in search of new experiences. "I hardly suppose so grand a lady would condescend to take supper with rough butchers," said the spokesman; "but it would be a great pleasure." "Condescend! Why, I'm simply starving; my tent's down, so I can get nothing to eat for an hour at least, and if you had not invited me, I should have asked myself, or have stolen something that smells so good." This little speech so pleased the miners, that they gave me the best seat on the bench. One helped me to salmon, another to bread, and the third to fried potatoes filled with onions, and though the latter have always been avoided by me they were now eaten with hearty relish, and never was a meal more thoroughly enjoyed. The men apologised again and again for having no butter, and offered to cook us a bit of moose steak; they could hardly understand that we preferred finding them and their meal just as we did. We asked for a leg of mutton and some brains, which latter cost one dollar apiece, but they were not able to fill our order until next week. They insisted, however, on our taking as a small souvenir a package of sheep's tongues and a couple of brains each. Then we asked to see the fur robes, but the lowest price for me was two hundred and fifty dollars for the two, a beautiful lynx robe and a wolf robe. "Why should you ask Mrs. B— one hundred and eighty-five dollars and me two hundred and fifty dollars?" queried I. "We told Mrs. B— that we paid one hundred dollars for one and eighty-five dollars for the other, and she did not add to that freight at twelve cents a pound, and the profit that one naturally expects from such an investment," said the honest butcher. "I can sell the lynx tomorrow for two hundred dollars, and in the winter it will bring three hundred dollars, but I don't care to keep and bother with them, as I'm 'going out.'" After much argument, as he was unwilling to deduct one iota from his price, he agreed to bring them over for Edith's inspection, which would give me an opportunity for consulting the fur experts who were raising our tent. On our return our friends carefully examined the robes, thought one particularly fine, but advised us to see first what we could do in town, so my friends the butchers offered to leave them with us until we had tried them and examined others. Now I know why they are so highly recommended for use here, as never have I had anything so perfect in which to sleep; no shivering, no icy, penetrating

72 wind, no fear of rheumatic pains. To roll up in a lynxskin makes the couch soft and downy, and keeps one so warm and "comfy," that it seems like being once more among home luxuries.

Saturday, August 6th ☞ "May we come in?" said the voice of John Jones, "I want to make you acquainted with Mr. McDonald,"* and one of the great men of the Klondike entered, was made welcome, and remained for an hour or more, telling stories so interesting that we deeply regretted when it was time for him to take his departure. John Jones said, "I was tellin' Mr. McDonald as how you ladies was so very kind to me whiles I was ill, and as how you wanted to see a 'clean-up,' and pan some gold yourself; so he is going Monday to one of his mines and has come to invite you to go with him." "Just what we've longed to do, but we never expected to have so fine an opportunity. Please explain the road, however, so that we may judge whether we are capable of such an undertaking."

"My plan is to start Monday between noon and four o'clock," said McDonald, "go over the trail two miles to the ferry, cross the Klondike River, and land at the mouth of Bonanza; there Miss Van Buren may take a horse, and if you can walk three miles an hour that will be a sufficiently rapid gait; after twelve miles we reach the Grand Forks Hotel, Bonanza. You will find it very rough; the men are only screened off from the ladies, but you can rest assured that every man would defend you with his life in case of need." "Oh, I intend to take my tent along for the ladies," said John. "It's just big enough for the two of them and they'll be much more comfortable than shut in with us men." "The next morning," continued McDonald, "we'll take a short walk before breakfast down to some mines very near there and see a clean-up,† and you can pan out your first gold; later in the day we'll go to B—'s clean-up, from there to my claim at El Dorado, only three miles; then to another claim of mine at El Dorado, which yields pretty good-sized nuggets. You know ten claims make a mile, so you can easily tell how much you will have to walk there; there are some bench claims near that have not been located, so that you and Miss Van Van Buren can stake

---

* "Klondike King" Alexander McDonald (d. 1909) was one of the major characters of the Klondike gold rush era. A Nova Scotian (some sources say a New Brunswicker), he came to the Klondike in 1896. As one historian wrote of McDonald: "In Dawson he had a finger in almost every pie, buying lots, erecting buildings, having interests in every sort of commercial enterprise." McDonald also gave generously to Dawson and paid for the construction of a new Catholic church building after the first structure burned down. See Dale Morgan, ed., of Jeremiah Lynch's *Three Years in the Klondike* (Chicago: Lakeside Press, 1967), p. 337.

† The "clean-up" occured when miners "cleaned" the gold out of dumps of pay dirt with running water.

them (now that you have your miner's license), and return to the Forks that night, unless you care to go on and stake on Dominion and Sulphur." We were filled with delight and excitement at the prospect.

Ivan and I went for a short walk on "our island" after a nine o'clock dinner. The first thing which attracted my attention was a notice tacked on the dovecote that had been placed there by the Rev. Dr. D—:

> Presbyterian Church
> Sunday service in the large tent at 11 AM
> Everyone cordially invited

Our walk was a short one. Two miners hailed me with, "Excuse me, marm, but must we dress up to come to church tomorrow? If so, we shall not be able to attend service, 'cause our dress suits are in our other trunk." We all laughed at the joke, as few have trunks, and they seemed relieved to hear, "We are all to attend in our jerseys—no boiled shirts or collars." Mrs. T— then came to the door of her tent saying, "I hear you are going with McDonald and Jones to locate claims and see some clean-ups; they took Mrs. H— and me last time; it is the most wonderful experience imaginable, and we enjoyed it so much that I'm wild to go again. People at home could never understand the wonders of it."

Just then we were joined by Mr. O—, who presented a Mr. H—, and another Klondike millionaire stood before us, with a dazzling diamond on his shirtfront, and another of enormous size on his finger. After a few moments' chat, Mrs. B— called out that she was coming to pay us another visit, and so I returned. "It's a pity to bore you so often," said she, "but I feel so lonely and homesick today that I can't stay by myself, and thought perhaps you'd give me a little music. Seeing you and talking of home has quite unnerved me. I don't mind when I'm among the Apaches—then I enjoy their wild life, and forget homesickness."

"May we come in?" said Mr. O—, entering with Mr. H—, the Dane. "You are just in time to help us select the airs to be played for church service tomorrow. It is too dark to read this fine writing, so we must try them all." The committee listened, selecting *The Lost Chord, Nearer My God to Thee*, and *Portuguese Hymn*, but Mr. H— was ruled out as he pleaded for Strauss's *Blue Danube*. He told us that he left Denmark many years ago and never has had a homesick day; but he expects to "go out" this year. After they left, Mrs. B— remained until midnight, and as the moon's rays came through the open door of the tent and we listened to her thrilling experiences, time was forgotten, also the cold chills of night, as we wondered at the daring courage of one lone woman.

74 SUNDAY, AUGUST 7TH ☞ When Isaacs arrived this morning, he brought us the news that many of the "boys" wanted to come to service but did not dare lest they should meet some of our "city friends" in store clothes, so we instructed him to make the rounds and say that all had been requested to wear jerseys, women as well as men. Shortly after we heard, to our horror, the loud ringing of a cowbell, and a voice crying "Church, church—no collection and no dress-up. Mind and don't be late; service in half an hour. No collection." It was too late to stop our zealous assistant, who returned with the bell behind his back and slipped in the back door. We threw our shawls and robes on the grass, and placed the three steamer chairs, some empty boxes, and a few benches made by our jack-of-all-trades. The British and American flags were draped back of the pulpit, which consisted of a pine table and a bench made from a box. This was decorated with some yards of mosquito netting loaned by a neighbour. We placed a Bible on the stand and Mrs. B— supplied a big tin basin of flowers. Facing the pulpit we had an old screen and, as that was not large enough to hide the kitchen and sleeping apartments from view, Isaacs strung a rope across on which we draped thirty yards of cheesecloth which we had brought for other purposes. To this drapery we pinned pictures of Dewey, Sampson, Sigsbee, and General Lee; also photographs of dear ones at home.

First came the Rev. Dr. D—, with two men and a large package of hymn books. Then the miners, many with noble faces, began to arrive, throwing themselves about on the grass in all-unconscious picturesqueness. Mrs. T— and Mrs. B— were the only other women present at the opening, which was as solemn as it could have been in the grandest church in the land. My seat was a box placed close to the screen so that I could slip behind and start the music at a sign from the clergyman. We began with the orchestral cylinder *Prayer from Moses*. The entire service was most inspiring, and the sermon good and earnest. As the clergyman, who evidently put all his heart and soul into his work, spoke of being "Nearer my God to Thee" the orchestra's solemn strains were heard and after that the hymn was taken up by the chorus of miners and those who had come late. As they sang, the miners, who had not the courage to enter, stood outside the door with bowed heads. Only one unfortunate mistake occurred; as Dr. D— was reading a chapter about Joseph and his coat of many colours, a pigeon perched on the music box of the Criterion and started once more *Nearer My God to Thee*. There was no stopping the hymn until the end, but there was not a smile, and it was listened to with as dignified attention as though it had occurred in the right place. At the close, Dr. D— spoke of the ladies who had so kindly loaned their tent, and said that he would be more than glad to officiate regularly in case they would extend the same hospitality in future. Those who would attend were asked to raise their hands, and all hands were immediately high in air. After the service, one of the miners said to me, "Beg your pardon, madam, but by what mission are you sent out?"

We gave our first dinner, and this is what we read of it in the *Klondike Nugget*, almost before the entertainment came to an end.

> Mrs. Admiral (!) Hitchcock and Miss Van Buren, the two distinguished ladies who are "taking in" the Klondike just as they have taken in Paris and London, gave a select dinner in honour of the United States Consul-General [James C.] McCook, now stationed at Dawson. The ladies are in camp over at Dawson, and the dinner was given in what was probably the largest tent canvas in the Klondike. Mrs. B—, the popular scientific lady stationed for the winter at West Dawson, aided the two hostesses in entertaining the guests of the evening. The ladies carry their own chef and the repast was much enjoyed. After dinner the party adjourned to the new cabin of Mrs. B— and it was there that the late reports from the scene of war were received. The party immediately devoted themselves to adoration of "Old Glory," and the cheers were enough to alarm that peaceful neighbourhood.

Under ordinary circumstances it would be bad form for a hostess to give her menu or to refer to the food presented to guests, but I really must state how well we lived in that corner of the world where so many are supposed to be starving:

1st. Anchovy on soda biscuit.
2nd. Mock turtle soup.
3rd. Roast moose and potato balls.
4th. Escalloped tomatoes, prepared so deliciously by Edith that each one asked for a second helping.
5th. Asparagus salad, for which I made the French dressing.
6th. Peach ice cream.
7th. A very delicious cake made by Isaacs.
8th. Edith's French drip coffee and all washed down by sparkling Moselle.

After dinner we adjourned to Mrs. B—'s cabin, where we sat on her home-made divan, on benches, and on flour-bags, and told stories until midnight.

Visiting Mines With a Klondike King

MONDAY, **A**UGUST **8**TH ☞ John Jones came after breakfast to tell us what to pack. After he had taken his departure, Isaacs said, "I hope you're going to take me with you, marm, to do the cooking and for to carry the pack, as I don't think you'll care for what you'll get to eat along the trail, and I can carry from sixty to a hundred pounds. Besides, I'd like to stake some claims, too, for when Alex McDonald tells you where to stake, you're sure to make your pile. That's a mighty fine man for you to know. He's got fifty millions, and knows more about mining than any man in this country. I've known him all my life just as well as I've known that parson that Mrs. B— brought to call on you; and yet I can't go up and speak to them because you ladies seem to think that I ought to stay in the kitchen instead o' coming in and talking to the visitors that I know. Holy Moses! You don't realise how embarrassing it is for me only to be able to speak to them on 'the outside.'"

We lunched hurriedly, after which the neighbours came to inquire what they could do for our pets during our absence. Mrs. T— kindly offered to care for them, and to take charge of the tent. Jones had a boat in waiting at the foot of the bank. Isaacs carried the pack, consisting of fur robes, blankets, flannel wrappers, and toilet articles. We were soon across the Yukon, where we were met by Big Alex. Edith went to purchase a cowboy hat for the trip, and Isaacs a harness for his back, so we appointed the usual place of rendezvous, the Alaska Commercial Company's stores, from which point we were to be ready for the start in half an hour. Many of our friends were there to help Edith on to the horse and to see the start. "No horse for me," said I; "walking is far more enjoyable." So Edith rode alone in her glory, while McDonald, Jones, and I tramped by the side of the horse when the road was sufficiently wide, or single file, with Isaacs in harness bringing up the rear. At first, it was a gradual ascent on a good road; we were soon high on the hills back of Dawson, and were astonished to see so many log houses, while many more were being built.

After a long tramp, we reached a bridge of logs. Edith's horse forded the stream, while I clung tightly to the hands of McDonald and Jones, who assisted me in maintaining my balance, as the logs threatened to turn at each step. Then we paid one dollar each to cross in a scow on which even F—'s horse was carried. We stopped a moment on reaching the other side to photograph a tavern, and were then off on a corduroy road which the miners had made, winding round beautiful mountains, looking down upon gorgeous scenery, over stones, through springy moss, then over more log bridges, deep bogs, precipices, until we reached Halfway House where we had supper of roast moose, mashed potatoes, corn, cabbage, delicious bread and butter, Spanish and apple-pie.

We next met a Mr. C—, who had just found some rich ground while prospecting, and told us where to stake; he also showed us a large piece of rock filled with gold, which he had taken from a mine near the Forks, and from which the owners were getting a thousand dollars a day, but being "Chee Charkers" (newcomers) and homesick, they wanted to "go out" and would sell for thirteen thousand dollars. A man from Illinois next joined us on the trail; said he was

EDITH ON HORSEBACK, OFF TO EL DORADO

78 working for wages, but had had time to do some prospecting and to stake out a number of claims for himself—some of them very rich—but he found it impossible to get into the Recorder's office to record them. He offered a third in each to anyone who could have it done for him. Our Illinois man said that he could conduct us through high dry ground on the other side of the river. Once there, he said that he should like to tramp with us, as it did him so much good "to hear the sound of a lady's voice."

At last came the "yodel," which meant that someone in our party was exhausted and wanted to pitch tent for the night. We joined forces at Gordon's Camp, where we were surrounded by tents. While Isaacs was pitching ours, McDonald took us to the cabin of Mr. and Mrs. — to pay a short visit. Their quarters were nice and comfortable, and even the baby had a modern cradle into which we peeped, but, as it was late, we bade them goodnight the moment Isaacs announced that all preparations had been made for us. Pine boughs had been spread on the ground, and our robes and blankets over them. After crawling in, McDonald and Jones lighted a bonfire at our door, and then sought the cabin in which they had been offered bunks.

No fear felt we, though surrounded on all sides by unknown men. One has but to know the honest miner to recognise that he is ever ready to assist woman, and that sad would be the fate and speedy the death of one who should offer her an insult. As the bonfire died out, we watched the new moon rising over the mountains opposite, and lighting the valley below, and felt that the wonderful and beautiful works of the dear Lord are everywhere present.

Tuesday, August 9th ☞ My ears were greeted on awakening with, "Flour's gone to hell! What fool tied this horse up here! We'll make McDonald give us another bag," and then came the folding of tents, the tramping of men and the departure of the prospectors for another day's work towards fortune or disappointment. As we continued our tramp, Edith's horse floundered and stumbled so in the mire and over the rocks that, after several hairbreadth escapes she also concluded to walk; so Isaacs was relieved of his pack and the horse received the burden. At 10 AM we reached a restaurant at the forks of the road. We four sat on a bench and, with Isaacs at our feet, devoured bread and butter and coffee. When the irrepressible [Isaacs] said, "Had no time to wash my face; is it dirty?" he was snubbed, if he could have been, by hearing, "No time to look at it." Another long tramp over rolling stones, mossy grounds, narrow ledges on the edge of a precipice from which a tiny rolling stone would have precipitated us to instant destruction, but the unvarying kindness and assistance of McDonald and Jones made us repress all signs of fear for very shame. We came to sluice boxes with signs prohibiting people to walk therein, but the owners of which invariably gave us the desired permission, which we enjoyed until we reached Bonanza, where we "panned out" and shouted with joy as the stones and gravel disappeared and we saw the rich gold gathering in the bottom.

We were promised another pan on our return, so, as the miners were just about to blast, we went on to Skookum Creek, in which McDonald had also a half-interest. Here we were filled with excitement and joy as our pans came to seven and ten dollars each, and we picked up a few nuggets besides. Then came the worst trip of all, to Grand Forks Hotel, which we reached about midday, ready to drop into the first seat that offered itself. A fee to the cook secured a tub of hot water, which was most soothing to my poor blistered foot. Here we met a large party of miners, owners of several mines. An agent from the Alaska Commercial Company, soliciting orders, had an excellent luncheon cooked by a Japanese, who confided to us that he had been nine years in the country and was now "going out" and that almost every customer had given him a nugget.

In the meantime Jones, instead of resting, had gone to the thirteen-thousand-dollar mine and brought me back some of the rock which he had hammered off; it showed gold in every part. McDonald said he would accompany us to pass judgment on the proposition, so we climbed up the steep hill where we broke off rock which McDonald pronounced of unusual richness, but said that the mine had been so thoroughly worked that there was little left. On we tramped, stopping at one claim after another, never knowing that the greater number of them belonged to modest McDonald, until some employee of his told us. We stopped at B—'s mine, where Edith was brave enough to go down the very steep incline to see the panning and was rewarded by the gift of a couple of nuggets as a souvenir of the occasion. My blistered foot kept me on the top of the hill with no nugget. A little farther on, a miner stopped to chat with me. Not having seen a woman for ages he was anxious to ask me about his sore throat for which I promised him a remedy on my return to the tent. He then told me of his son, who had met his death in one of the mines of S— of Colorado, and how the generous owner had educated his remaining son, who was prospecting nearby, but had had no luck as yet.

In the evening we reached McDonald's mines. In a comfortable, nicely floored cabin sat pretty, refined Mrs. M— at her sewing machine, with all about her as clean and attractive as though she had a dozen shops at hand upon which to call for supplies. There was but one room, according to the custom of the country, with the stove outside in a sheltered nook, and a cache like a closet adjoining. Mrs. M— welcomed us with her soft, pleasant voice, and cooked some ham, fried some real potatoes (which she told us were described in this part of the world as "human potatoes"), gave us some delicious bread with equally delicious butter and tea. After we had done full justice to these viands we were treated to something which made our mouths water—a light, feathery, cream layer cake. The repast finished, we sat outside in the two home chairs, the men on boxes, and enjoyed the grandeur of the scenery, with its magnificent mountains opposite, on which bench claims are already staked and giving forth good pay. At our feet was the El Dorado River, filled with sluice boxes through which the water flowed rapidly, while the piles of rock and stone on either side showed how quickly the ground was being dug out. The men who were introduced to us said it was not at all necessary for us to pitch our tent, as there was a vacant one nearby, which they could assure us was thoroughly clean as the boys who lived in it were most particular, and they were now on the trail. We found a bed inside, raised about one foot from the ground, made of evergreen boughs, boxed in by the tent on one side and a board on the other. It was wide enough to bunk four men. Our man Friday had thrown Edith's blankets across the boughs for us to sleep on, and my fur robe to cover us. Fortunately we had brought our down cushions which served as pillows.

WEDNESDAY, AUGUST 10TH ⇛ This morning my poor blistered heel was so inflamed and bleeding that I dared not put on a boot, so slipped into a wrapper, made my toilet, and decided, to my intense disappointment, that there was nothing for it but to give that foot at least a day's rest. So Edith went alone to McDonald's where we had been asked to breakfast. No sooner had the news of my crippled state reached them than our host and Mr. Jones immediately appeared at the door and agreed that it would be folly for me to move. McDonald had already visited one of his claims and had a bag of gold on his shoulder almost too heavy for even so large a man as he to stagger under. Jones and Edith went on to see a "clean-up" at No. — and were then going to No. — where the gold ran from two to three hundred dollars to the pail. This is so marvellous that they did not wish us to take it on faith, but to see for ourselves. How I groaned as they started off without me, and felt indignant that so small a thing as a pebble in the boot could have worked such damage.

Edith returned enthusiastic over her day's trip, though with lame and aching feet. "We went first to No. —, El Dorado," said she; "Mr. McDonald met us there and we watched the end of the clean-up of half a day's work, two men, and out came five thousand dollars, all washed through sluice boxes, then raked and spaded. From there to No. — and thirty feet down a perpendicular ladder; another clean-up, twelve thousand dollars in two days, seven men at work.

Gold fell out wherever I poked my umbrella, and, at the last moment, Jones knocked out a stone and right behind it shone a nugget weighing between seven and eight ounces. In the cabins were great pans of gold which I tried to photograph, one pan with six hundred and seventy-eight dollars. Next we went to McDonald's pet, No. — but I did not care so much for that, as the gold was finer and not so easily seen. Then back to No. — to see them sifting and drying gold, taking the black sand out with a common magnet such as children use."

THURSDAY, AUGUST 11TH ☞ Jones and Isaacs appeared to dress and bandage my wounds. Then came Mrs. M—, with such a nice breakfast. Finally, our guide, Mr. McDonald, appeared, to know if I should be able to go on, and said, "As Miss Van Buren panned out some nuggets yesterday, I thought it would be only fair to fetch a few for you," and he handed me four beauties. Isaacs admired them so loudly that he was handed a small one by McDonald for a scarf pin. "Now," said the latter, "if you feel equal to the walk, we'll go down to Skookum Gulch and you shall have your turn at panning out."

Our first stopping place, after bidding farewell to the hospitable M—s and inviting them to visit us in West Dawson, was at the B—s' comfortable cabin with its carpet, rocking chairs and homelike appearance. Mrs. B— showed us a tin box filled with hundreds of nuggets from their mine. She was able to tell them all apart, their weight, and when and where found. Her sister also had a fine collection, but said that panning was such hard work that she did not do it very often, even though it meant extra nuggets.

We next went on to Bonanza where Mr. McDonald told us we might have all the gold we could pan out; but as they had just had a clean-up and my first efforts were not successful, McDonald finished his business with the overseer and said, "Let us go over to Skookum Gulch and there we'll find some nuggets." So, leaving Edith and Jones digging, surrounded by the honest miners who were helping them in their search, we went over sluice boxes and crossed narrow ledges down into Skookum Gulch where F— welcomed us and said, "Had you only come yesterday I could have helped you to find some beauties." However we crawled under the sluice boxes, and on hands and knees we chipped away until two big nuggets fell into my hands; then we filled a pan, took it over to the water box, and the excitement began as the stones and gravel washed out and the colours began to show. More shaking of the pan, and the colours became clearer, until at length the small stones fell out and only nuggets remained. These were dropped into my handkerchief in accordance with the custom here, that the best the mine affords is scarcely sufficient to do honour to woman, so highly is she appreciated where she so rarely appears.

CLEAN-UP

We had sent Isaacs ahead with the horse and pack, telling him to meet us at the Halfway House, but, as that was eight miles distant and Edith had not much confidence in her ability to walk it, Isaacs was told to listen for our yodel and not to keep too far ahead of us, on the horse trail opposite. How the trail changed! Sometimes the ground was hard and dry, then suddenly would appear a marsh in which our feet would sink beyond the ankle, and so extensive that, peer as we would, not a sign could be seen of the trail beyond; we would wade through the marsh, carefully picking our steps for fear of disappearing entirely from view; then we would suddenly come upon one of those beautiful mossy, spongy carpets of such glorious colours of pale grey, green, and red that it looked as though prepared for a dance of the fairies. How we longed to get an adequate photograph of such exquisite beauty that no pen can picture! On we tramped over this most delicate of carpets, on which the foot rests but leaves no impress, and, just as we were in despair at the thought of having lost the trail, it would loom plainly and clearly before us again, well trodden and unmistakable.

About 8 PM we reached the junction of the two roads and gladly seated ourselves on the bench under the tent for supper. Two men stopped to have lemonade, and were charged fifty cents a glass. Before starting again Isaacs took off Edith's muck-a-lucks and filled them once more with fresh straw to protect the soles of her feet from being cut by the sharp stones which we sometimes encountered.

Finally, it became almost too dark to see the way, as, at this time of year, one has really a few hours without sun or moon. Now came the bridges; not wide ones with a railing, but a log of wood, which sometimes rolled over as we stepped upon it, laid across a dashing torrent without any support. Poor John Jones was obliged to cross it first with Edith, then return for me, and how we did cling to his hand! At last we were really off the trail, and, search as we would, no trace of it could be discovered. We were almost ready to weep with fatigue, but knew that we must keep up our spirits and not depress or discourage the man who, although so ill and faint himself that he could scarcely walk, still bravely led on. Finally we sat down to rest while honest John went on a voyage of discovery, but when he returned he had found no sign of a trail. Suddenly we heard a sound in the distance and walked towards it until we reached a mine where men were still working. They told us that we must either retrace our steps for a mile, or try the perilous task of climbing the rocks and stones that had been thrown up from the mine, leaving the deep cavern beneath. We decided upon the latter course, rather than go back. In fear and trembling we began to crawl over the pointed mass of rolling stones, carefully testing each step before daring to trust to it. Slipping, sliding, clutching for Jones's ever-ready hand, it seemed hours before we reached the bridge and tried the dashing water with our sticks to probe the depth before we dared put foot upon the log. During the entire trip we had said to each obstacle, "So long as we do not sink above the knee it doesn't matter," but here, although Jones did all in his power to steady us, the log rolled and the water rushed into our boots as we went up to our hips and were pulled out on shore. Poor John was in great distress at the accident, but we assured him that it had cooled our burning feet deliciously, and that, as no one ever takes cold in this country, there was no harm done. But still he worried, feeling himself to blame, and all we could say did not restore his spirits.

Then came a long stretch of woods and bog, and as there was nothing to light us on our way, I began to sing. Just then we stumbled over a sleeping man. As he sat up I began to apologise, whereupon he said, "Don't make no excuses, lady. I'd be willing to be woke up every night to hear *Lead Kindly Light* sung by a lady." Another mile of marsh brought us, thoroughly exhausted, to the small

84 hotel. All were sleeping, but "mine host" was soon aroused. There was accommodation for Jones in an eight-bunk hall. The proprietor placed his room at our disposal, while Isaacs had to put up the tent and sleep outside. We quickly turned in to beds almost as narrow as coffins, but we were thankful enough even for such accommodations.

Friday, August 12th ☞ In the morning Isaacs brought us big tubs of hot water and with it towels which we did not care to use. This reminds me to add the caution, that one should always travel with one's own linen, no matter what else has to be left behind. He also brought us the news that the horse for which we are paying from ten to fifteen dollars a day had strayed away during the night and wandered several miles on the homeward trail. He was told to go at once in search of it, but said he could not do so without his breakfast. Several hours later he tried to overtake the beast, but returned saying that it was not to be found. So Isaacs had to pack on his back the sixty or seventy pounds, and was told to start on the horse trail, transfer the pack to the horse's back and lead him into town, meeting us at the stores of the Alaska Commercial Company. We took a few pictures and then started off, Edith having changed muck-a-lucks with the cook, and I wearing one India-rubber boot and one muck-a-luck.

We started on the last stage of our journey at three sharp, and having been told that by climbing the mountain we could cut off two miles, we took that route, intending to do the eight miles leisurely—eight miles, possibly, as the crow flies, but, with all the circuitous windings of the trail, how many could it have been? The climb was one steady pull up—up—the mountain growing steeper and steeper. We rested many times, as Edith's feet were almost too sore to touch the ground, while mine felt as though there were mustard plasters on each sole. Up—up—and steeper and more steep became the mountain, until it was almost perpendicular. Had we seen a map or picture of it before starting, never should we have attempted the climb, but with patient Jones ready to tender assistance at any moment in spite of being still pale, ill, and faint, we were shamed into a courage we were far from feeling. Many men passed us on the trail; many we passed as they rested by the wayside, and from each one came pleasant greetings and compliments at our pluck and courage, praise which I little deserved, being such a coward at heart. At last we reached the summit, and the magnificent view was well worthy of the exertion. There was our tent in the distance; before us the Klondike River; on the right a beautiful island, and, just beyond, Dawson. We seated ourselves on the mossy carpet, and feasted our eyes while resting our weary limbs. Then came four miles down hill, through woods, then a marsh where the trail was lost again and again, but as there were so many passing in each direction, it was easily refound. Our way next led us through a town whose name I do not like to mention—"Lousetown."

We hastened through, nevertheless, and then found ourselves at the head of a perpendicular descent; after walking, sliding, and rolling down a long hill, which seemed so dangerous that we should have taken a picture of it had there been light enough, to enable us afterwards to realise our own bravery. Never should I have dared it had there been any other way of reaching home. Although the bank of the river was lined with boats and the place filled with men, it took nearly an hour to find one to row us, or rather to float with the strong current to West Dawson, not a mile distant. The first man wanted ten dollars, the second three, which we willingly gave, as, had we walked across the bridge, it would have cost one dollar each, and then we should have had the Main Street of Dawson to traverse before reaching the Alaska Commercial Company to take a boat. As we drifted downstream, we yodelled to Isaacs, and shortly after he appeared with his pack.

Bad news greeted us on our arrival. The neighbours' dogs had come into the tent during our absence and killed quite a number of the pigeons. It was eight o'clock and Isaacs, though exhausted, managed to prepare us a nice little supper. Dr. H— came to see if we required his services and then such a night's rest as we should have enjoyed had it not been for the incessant barking of the dogs just outside the tent; a noise which their owners do not seem at all to mind, but which awakened us again and again.

SATURDAY, AUGUST 13TH — We must get rid of the pigeons! They have become so tame that they not only fly all about the tent, but even light upon the bed; at half after five this morning I was up decoying them out by offering them food and drink outside the tent door, and then Poll had to be fed in order to quiet her scolding. The silence then was such an inducement that I began to write, and have been at it ever since. The pigeons, however, have come back through the air holes in the top of the tent, and are so saucy that they are sitting on the bench at my side, on the table at which I am writing, perching on cups and making them fall with a crash, dipping into our drinking water bucket, which our man-of-all-work was too weary to cover before going home last night, and even going into the barrel, which makes me feel like covering it up so that they may never come out. Moral—never open a pigeon box, after a voyage, in a place where you do not wish them to remain, for, fight them as you will, it is impossible to drive them out afterwards.

It was after ten, Isaacs had not yet appeared, and our feet were too swollen to permit of our taking the least liberty in using them. Edith, however, made some of her delicious biscuit, which the cook, sauntering in before eleven, enjoyed with great gusto. Then Edith, who now takes charge, kindly relieving me from all care, had her first unpleasant experience with Klondike housekeeping. The storm had been brewing for some time, and she felt it necessary to "have it out." M— had arranged with his unfortunate friend to come to us as cook, carpenter, boatman, etc., for one hundred and fifty dollars a month and his "grub." He had worked well, cooked well, made us tables, shelves, and stools from boxes, etc., was willing and obliging, and at first we were well pleased. Then he found our "grub" too dainty for a strong man, so we got M— to order just what miners used, and advanced him money to purchase a tent, blankets, and other necessary articles. His tent was pitched very near ours, and he was allowed the time to go back and forth for his meals. But this took so long that when we were in a hurry he remained, partaking of our food.

Next came a demand for fresh meat, and, as the regular price is one dollar a pound, and we found on inquiry that very few men got it, we refused this modest request. We also objected to his coming in and out of the front door before our guests with pipe in mouth, or to carrying in big boxes when the back door was quite as convenient. We had requested him to take his "grub" with him on the trail, but after the second day he informed us that he had lost it, and when his friends no longer lined the route, two dollars and fifty cents a meal was the price paid. We then asked him to bring his "grub" over to our tent, and use our stove, rather than spend so much time in making extra fires. There were also many other small causes of complaint, of which he could not be made to see the impropriety, but when Edith said, "I am not in the habit of having my servants" she got no further. "Servant, madam!" shouted Isaacs, snatching up his hat. "How dare you call me a servant! Do you know who I am?" From his tone it seemed as though Edith's end might be very near, and I prepared to go to her assistance, when suddenly his voice changed and he said, "I begs your pardon, marm, for anything I've said or done that's not right, but it's hard for me to be menial." Such a scene can only be done justice to on the stage.

Mr. Jones and Mr. O— soon came to inquire if they could do anything in town for us, and next Mrs. B—, to tell us of a miners' meeting, at which everyone expressed resentment at the conduct of the Canadian officials, and concluded to protest and to bring pressure to bear for a change.

Our Man Friday

SUNDAY, AUGUST 14TH &— We were up early—I to drive the pigeons out and feed the pets, Edith to make biscuit, as Isaacs had dipped into our bread, which we had bought for Sunday's dinner. He had gone off without washing the dishes or making the bread, leaving everything in the kitchen in the utmost disorder. We were so discouraged that it then devolved upon me to lecture. So, when Isaacs came in about 9 AM, I said, "You must listen to a few words from me, as you have paid no attention to Miss Van Buren, who is housekeeper." After a talk of half an hour, the sky was cleared, fine promises made, and Isaacs was working like a trooper. Soon from the different tents came the shouts of "Going to church?" "Going to wear your overalls or trousers?" "I say, Jim, have you got my shaving soap? I want to shave before going to that Big Tent." "Oh, those ladies said we might come just as we are." "So they did, but we can shave, at least" and so the preparations went on all about us. Dr. D—, unable to appear, sent a substitute. At eleven o'clock only three persons were present. Isaacs said they were all ready, but were waiting for the bell, so he was allowed to toll it. Then they came trooping in, sitting on rugs, boxes, and benches. I remained behind the screen for the music, the clergyman asking to have it alternate with songs of praise.

Mr. W— and son, of Colorado, came after luncheon to ask for a "lay" on one of the many claims we had staked during the week, but to which I have not referred specifically, as the "tips" where to stake were given us by Big Alex. The results will be seen after the spring "clean-up." The next visitor was Jones, who begged to hear the zither, offering to unpack it upon learning that it was in the bottom of a big box. So the zither was brought out and enjoyed until it was time to prepare the dinner, to which we had invited Big Alex. He arrived at six o'clock instead of seven, which we accepted as a pleasant compliment. Isaacs not only cooked, but served the meal as well as any one at home could

88 have done. Our menu consisted of our last tin of mock turtle soup, which was so greatly appreciated that we were fully repaid for having used it; lobster à la Newburg—the name of which Jones asked many times; Edith, who prepared it, was flattered by having each one ask for it twice, even though it was made of tinned lobster and California cooking sherry. Next came the leg of mutton which had been purchased the previous week, and had been hung so long that it was as sweet and tender as lamb, potato balls, made from desiccated potatoes, Edith's famous escalloped tomatoes, my asparagus salad, my peach ice cream and Edith's black coffee, with Cresta Bianca during the dinner, "topping off" with a glass of curaçao.

While we were still at table our consul arrived with a Mrs. B—, and they joined us in ice cream, cake, coffee, and wine. Mr. K— also called, saying, "Here are some nuggets for you." So you may imagine that we expressed our disgust when, instead of beautiful yellow souvenirs which are freely distributed in this country by the lucky owners of mines to their less fortunate friends, K— handed us some newspapers called *Klondike Nugget*. "Well, by Josh!" said McDonald, "I'm not a-going to see you disappointed like that," and he fished down deep in his pocket and handed me first a souvenir from "Hunker" and then one from "Dominion," and added, "When you go again on the trail you may pan out as much as you please from the mines on Hunker." "I like that," said Edith. "You never let me pan out a thing either on El Dorado or Dominion, and you saw me carefully put back the handfuls of nuggets I had dug out from behind the stones." "Well you never asked me," said McDonald.

DINNER WITH A KLONDIKE KING

MONDAY, AUGUST 15TH ☙ Cold, drizzling rain! And, although we have on heavy winter flannels and our warmest clothing, there is an icy chill in the air which makes us long for a nice warm room with a fire inside of this enormous tent. Our air mattresses have been worse than useless, heavy, and, although carefully cared for, the air escapes through a seam.

Then came Dr. H—, who carefully dressed and bandaged our feet. Someone asked M— if the ladies in the Big Tent had returned, to which he replied, "Oh yes, but they're in so many poultices and bandages that it's hard to get near them." Isaacs called out from behind the screen, "I say, 'ave you 'eard the latest? The people in Dawson want to know if you two ladies are missionaries, as they see as 'ow you have services hevery Sunday, an' I told 'em indeed you was. Then somebody said as I was a-waitin' on you, and they arsked me some questions, but I didn't let on a thing, just told 'em you were two princesses from India wanting to see the world."

2 PM. While at luncheon the irrepressible came in saying, "Now that you two ladies are at table and neither readin' nor writin', I've got a think or two I'd like to say; have I your permission?" Looking first at one and then the other, as he drew up an empty box and placed it at table between us. "You see," he whispered, with a mysterious air, "I've been a-digging about here and have found every symptom of quartz. Now what's the matter with looking nearer 'ome for someone to put you on to a good thing instead o' listening to your Mr. T— and all the other fellows who tries to do the 'owlin' swells in your heasy chairs, while I, as is worth twenty of them, slaves away be'ind that there screen. Now if you ladies will just fit me out all right with grub and money, and start me hoff on the trail, you'll see that Zeke can do even better for you there than in the kitchen. I'm not a-satisfyin' you because my heart's set on the trail, an' I can't give my mind to my work, an' as you two ladies don't like to 'ave me sit 'ere an' entertain you, why I thinks as 'ow, if we can square up accounts, we'd better give one more o' those big dinners. 'Ere's my account, marm, of what you've advanced me:

Tent fixings	$32.00
Fry pan and coffeepot	2.50
Tools	2.00
Shoes	2.00
Tobacco	1.50
Socks	0.30
Pencils	0.50
Medicine	1.00

The bill for Isaacs's meals and for the horse still to come! As it was payday, M— next submitted his account:

Oars	$6.00	2 assistants	$5.00
Oarlocks	2.00	Help in pulling tent	8.50
Salmon	1.00	Extra help	2.00
Salmon	.75	10 pounds rice	2.50
Veal	1.00	Tackle	4.00
Bread	1.00	Poles for tent	7.25
Two water buckets	4.00	Marketing	5.00
Bread	.50	Isaacs's grub for month	28.10
Dishes	1.50	Assistant	2.50
6 towels	3.75	Nails	1.50
Rope	6.75	Gallon coal oil	2.50

Dr. C— had kindly brought us over a 12 x 14 tent to erect inside of ours, in which to sleep and dress, that we might not only suffer less from the cold, but have more privacy than screens and curtains permitted. The ground inside was covered with evergreen boughs, while a mound of them was made in each corner, on which our hammocks, mattresses, and rugs were placed.

At 7:15 we sat down to dinner. We had airs from the music box, R— played the mandolin, and then they called for the zither. Finally, the graphophone was asked for, but as it had been put out of order the first night, Edith said it could not be used, and would not allow the "boys" to try and repair it; but they coaxed with such good effect, that they finally managed to gain her consent and shortly after we were listening to the *Ravings of John McCullough*, until our blood curdled and we shivered as we called for a xylophone solo and some lively quartettes.

Judge and Mrs. B—, of Santa Clara, had sent by us a bag of clothing and goodies to be delivered to their two sons in Dawson, but although they had left before our arrival, we were told that F— and C— were their heirs. We jokingly told the former that we had no written instructions to that effect, but would take his word for it, and the presentation was made with great ceremony. No sooner had the "boys" heard that there were three boxes of Maskey's chocolates in the bag, than they fell upon F— and forced him to open it. He immediately presented one box to me, but as we were soon to "go out" I preferred that it should be enjoyed by those who had another two years to remain. The chocolates were seized without further ceremony, and disappeared so rapidly that F— thought it necessary to sit on the bag for the remainder of the evening.

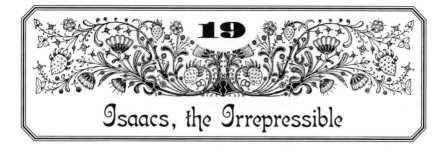

Isaacs, the Irrepressible

TUESDAY, AUGUST 16TH ☞ Such a night's rest in the little tent! My head kept sliding down hill, until I dreamed that H— was dying and my every energy was being expended on trying in vain to get to her. The air is now so cold and chill that we have on our sealskin wraps besides being heavily clad in winter flannels. Never before have we so longed for the intense rays of the sun. The heat from the stove on which our breakfast is being cooked makes no impression even on a corner of this immense tent. The irrepressible performs his morning tasks to a running accompaniment. "Parrot! You'd better get rid o' her—get someone to buy her, she requires too much care and attention. You'd better not present her to Miss E—; she'd have an apoplectic fit."

Edith had put some macaroni to soak, but when she looked for the large cheese it had disappeared. After a long search, it finally became evident that it was not in the tent. "Now, Isaacs," said Edith, "you know you said you loved cheese, and if ever you stole anything it would be that." "Guess the dog must 'a' taken it, marm," said Isaacs; "that macaroni's awful good, but just think 'ow good it would 'a' been with cheese. Mrs. Hitchcock, there's only one favour I'd ever ask of you, and that is, to send me a copy o' that book you're a writin'. I'll bet I'm getting a roasting in it! Why don't you write a book, Miss Van Buren? You don't seem to write much, but p'raps you make up for it when you do get started. Oh, you lazy old dog, just a layin' there enjoyin' of yourself, whiles everybody works 'ard."

5 PM. Return of Mr. Q—. "Why didn't you tell me I'd need a scow for your mail," said he, as he handed sixty letters to me and almost as many to Edith. Scarcely had we begun to read them when Mr. O— came with a friend from Dawson whom he wished to present. The former intended to have a grand opening of his new liquor saloon and begged us to sell to him our British and

American flags, but we could not spare them. However, we allowed him to have some small pictures of Dewey, Sampson, Sigsbee, and General Lee. Everyone is now anxious for the picture of the new hero, Schley,* but, unfortunately, it was not ready when we left San Francisco. Mr. O— next admired a beautiful calendar which Edith had given me for a Christmas gift and which was tied to the screen with blue ribbons. As Edith and I have both decided to "go out" light, that is, to take nothing unnecessary back with us over the trail, she nodded her assent to this disposition of the calendar, which O— carried off triumphantly. Just then two of our fellow passengers from San Francisco entered—the mother and daughter who had been so enterprising in buying out laundry, swimming-baths, and shop under one roof. They agreed to take our linen for two dollars a dozen, which was exceedingly reasonable compared with the six dollars asked in Dawson. They had been farther than we on the trail, had staked out some claims, and, in two months, intended to give up their establishment and begin working their mines.

WEDNESDAY, AUGUST 17TH ❧ We had requested our "help" to come at eight o'clock and have breakfast ready at nine, but it was after nine before he came sauntering in, and we two frightened women dared say nothing. On the previous day, when spoken to concerning a similar offence, he confided to the parrot in a stage whisper that "just because a fellow's watch was wrong, 'e must be jumped on for it." Edith told him what to prepare for luncheon, but he seemed to take great pleasure in acting contrary to her orders, and continued his arrangements as though she had not spoken. Finally I thought it necessary to interfere, saying, "I cannot allow you to disobey Miss Van Buren. Did you not hear her forbid you to do what you are now doing?" "Oh, I 'eard all right enough," said he, continuing to disobey; "but some'ow or hother horders hir-ritates me, an hi'd rather take the consequences than be bossed." "Then," said I, gathering courage, "the quicker you pack up and leave the better." "Yes'm," said he, smiling sardonically, "but I'll 'ave one good breakfast first." With that he seated himself, neglecting his own bacon, beans, and customary food, and helped himself to some of the few delicacies which we had brought to tide us over until the arrival of our stores.

Before leaving San Francisco, finding that we were allowed but a thousand pounds freight on the Alaska Commercial Company's steamer, and that our boxes weighed very nearly that, to say nothing of the tent, music box and other

---

* Winfield Scott Schley, a Rear Admiral in the U.S. Navy, played a key role in the defeat of the Spanish at the battle of Santiago de Cuba in July 1898.

═══ VAN BUREN (LEFT) AND HITCHCOCK IN THE TENT ═══

heavy articles, we decided to send our supplies, which we purchased for the winter in case of being accidentally frozen in, by another line. From one company to the other we went, but no one would guarantee sending freight up the river by the first steamer except the Johnson-Locke Company, of which M— wrote us that it was thoroughly reliable. The representative in their office assured us that not only should the goods start on the same day as we—June 11th—but also that they should go up the Yukon at once, with no detention at St. Michaels, adding that they would probably arrive in Dawson before us. Upon this we purchased so large a cargo that the freight alone cost us very nearly five hundred dollars, and took with us only enough delicacies and solid provisions to last a few weeks. We had also been informed that the Johnson-Locke Company and the Joseph Ladue Company were identical. The contract, however, has not yet been fulfilled, and we are impatiently awaiting the arrival of the much needed stores.

After Isaacs had finished his breakfast, his soliloquies recommenced. "Now I'll clean up heverythink, Polly, and let them see how nice heverythink looks when Isaacs goes away; hi've 'ad enough o' being bossed by women, an' I don't want any more of it." He smiled a smile of childlike innocence as he deliberately poured out the hot water which he had been told to prepare for my manicuring, and the smile broadened as he saw me search for a tin pan of cold water to be used in its place. He called Edith to go over the list and see that all was correct, making sarcastic little remarks as he did so. Edith said something

94 about servants, but before she could get any further he thundered, "Servant! Servant! Great Julius Caesar! 'Ow dare you call me a servant? 'Aven't I told you a 'undred times that I'm not a servant? I just—." "Isaacs, I cannot allow you to be impertinent to Miss Van Buren," said I, gathering courage to interfere, and walking to the tent door to let him see that, although we were only two lone women, there were plenty of neighbours on whom to call for assistance. Fortunately, the voice of Mr. Q— was heard at this point calling to know if we had any commissions for town. Isaacs was paid off, and left without so much as saying goodbye, after cutting a little wood and bringing water in accordance with Edith's request.

At 1 PM, while Mrs. T— was asking for contributions for the new hospital, which we most willingly promised, Jones rowed me over to the Recorder's office, where I went to record a bench claim on El Dorado and one on Bear Creek. Being a woman, I was at once admitted into the private office ahead of the long line of men, and, although I felt sorry for them, my feet were not yet in condition to stand and wait my turn, so I resolved to delay the line as short a time as possible. I then went to the Alaska Commercial Company and followed the Dawson habit of sitting on the counter and swinging my feet while giving orders. I next went to the consul's to deliver Edith's letters that were to go in the official mail; had a chat with my old fellow passenger, Mr. W—, who said that he arrived in Dawson while we were out on the trail. Asked the price of an acetylene bicycle lamp such as we had purchased in San Francisco, with fifteen pounds of calcium carbide for four dollars, the merchant wanted forty dollars—the best investment yet discovered in case they are really salable.

At last, all commissions finished, I crawled under wharves, over ropes, and through mud to reach good Jones's boat, which had been shut in by the *Ora*, and the peaceful row across the river was most grateful after the noise and bustle of the town.

At 6 PM the faithful Jones rowed Edith and me over to the Fairview Hotel, where McDonald had invited us to dine and the dinner made our poor attempts seem almost ludicrous. McDonald was awaiting us, and had a table in the corner of a goodly sized dining room. He had ordered a mandolinist, a guitarist, and a banjoist, and the proprietor, the proprietress, and manager came often to the table to inquire how we were pleased. The menu will probably be of interest to those who think of starvation and hardships at mention of the Klondike: Eastern oysters on ice; tomato soup in cups; salmon, sauce Hollandaise; sweetbreads and mushrooms; green peas, chops and mushrooms; chicken en casserole; lettuce salad; preserved pears, cheese, biscuit, nuts, raisins, café noir—washed down with German wine; even bonbons were passed.

After dinner we walked down to the *Ora* to view the accommodations in case we should decide to go out by her. Deck so narrow that one had to cling to the side to keep from falling overboard. There was one room with twelve bunks, one with two, one on either side with one. No linen or blankets were provided, and everything was filthy. We almost decided at once to return down the Yukon the same way by which we came. After travelling such a distance, however, it seems a great pity to miss the grandeur of the scenery over the Pass, and by thinking of Turkish and Russian baths and shampoo parlors to be found at the end of the journey, and an entire new outfit, we shall probably screw up our courage and take the plunge. A magnificent new steamer of the North American Transportation Company with electric lights and all the luxuries hitherto unknown in these regions, was lying at the dock and attracting general attention by throwing her searchlight in all directions.

We were next escorted to the private entrance of the theatre, where in a box from behind drawn curtains we watched the play, *Stillwater Willie,* * and heard some wretched singing from girls who were applauded to the echo by their admirers in the audience. A sign in the box read, "Gentlemen in private boxes are expected to order refreshments," so our entertainers sent for my usual beverage, lemonade, while the others enjoyed crème de menthe. No checks were given us, as McDonald was not present to "jolly" the waiter into doing so, and he did not dare offer them to "the grand ladies," as we are now known, owing to the size of our tent and the supposed depth and richness of our purses. M— told me that Isaacs had been to him for employment that afternoon, but that as he did not understand the situation he had put him off. We begged him to give him something to do at once, and as far away from Dawson as possible, as we feared that, his money once spent, we should have him hanging about. "Well, that's what I'll do, by gosh," said McDonald. "I'll give him something the first thing in the morning, so that ye ladies will have nothing further to bother ye." Before going into the theatre we were joined by Consul [James C.] McCook who told us of a grievance he had against the Collector of Customs, who was in the same building, but refused to serve where the American flag was allowed to fly. The papers were full of the case, and boys were crying in the street, "Full account of the row in the American Consul's office." At 11 PM McDonald and Jones escorted us to the small boat where the former bade us goodnight and the latter rowed us across.

---

* A satirical play about the misadventures of William C. "Swiftwater Bill" Gates, the much-married Klondike miner.

96   **Thursday, August 18th** ☞ A visit from Isaacs this morning, who came to return a candlestick, and to tell us that if we wanted to give our regular dinner he would be happy to come and cook it for us. He asked if we had said anything against him to McDonald as he was hoping to get work from him, having known him many years, and if we blocked him, he'd hate to do it, but—here he stopped as he caught my severe glance, and Edith said, "On the contrary, when McDonald spoke to Mrs. Hitchcock last night about you, she begged him by all means to give you work, and he said you should certainly have it the first thing this morning, so I advise you to go at once."

"I've brought you a Jap cook," called the cheery voice of John Jones, from outside the tent, after the departure of Isaacs, and in he came, followed by "Frank," who surveyed the Big Tent with much pleasure, saying, "Very nice, very nice; very fine ice cream freezer." After hearing what duties he was expected to perform, he decided to go back at once, bring his household goods to this side, and put them in the tent which Mr. Jones kindly offered to loan him. Poor John was then called upon to row him back and help him over with his stores as soon as possible. We protested against taking such advantage of so much kindness, but John silenced us by saying, "Why, I never enjoyed myself so much in my life as by being allowed to help wait on you ladies. I've got nothing to do until I go out to my mines, and might just as well be doing this as anything else; besides, it keeps John out o' mischief." 1 PM no cook; 2 PM no cook. At 2:30 Mr. Jones

THE LADIES AND A GUEST

returned saying that the Jap weakened on his return to Dawson at the thought of having to cross the river each time he wanted to meet his compatriots, and decided that it would be too lonely for him, so our kind neighbour had brought us back bread and cake in order to tide us over while another cook was being searched for. He lit the fire for us, went to the spring for a bucket of water, and did any number of chores besides.

The bill came for the horse which Edith had ordered to ride to El Dorado—sixty dollars, which meant thirty dollars from 4 PM Monday to midnight Tuesday, and ten dollars a day until the horse roamed into town of his own free will and accord, and we never yet have learned how he crossed the ferry.

We managed a cold dinner, Edith as usual insisting upon doing more than her share of the work, saying that she loved camping out, and the culinary department in particular. John Jones, who had returned empty-handed from the post office, as it was closed when he reached there, said, "Yes, if you didn't do the cooking and I didn't bring the water and even fill her glass for her, Mrs. Hitchcock would die of starvation and thirst, as she never seems to have time to do nawthin' but write, write, write." This shows me up as a very lazy member of the party, who only reconciled that quality to her conscience by Edith's apparent enjoyment in making certain dainty dishes, and her pleasure in the appreciation which was manifested.

Scarcely had we finished dinner when Mr. M—, Mr. R—, and Mr. W—, the handsome blond Englishman, and Judge— appeared. M— brought a big bag of ice to make ice cream, so one of the "boys" got the tin of condensed cream and opened it, another whipped it, another got the sugar, another found the tin of peaches we had sent for, which proved to be a tin of pears, so we had to substitute strawberry jam. After thoroughly mixing and pouring this preparation in the can, the boys stood in line to turn the crank, the lazy ones being relieved from duty sooner than the bashful ones, who waited for volunteer relief which failed to materialise. Such constant opening and tasting! We first discovered that it tasted too much of the cream so added water, as condensed milk made it worse; then it was too weak, and Kirschwasser was found to be just the thing for it. At last it was ready, and I said jokingly, "Now boys, pack it down for our luncheon and dinner tomorrow." "No, madam," replied M—. "Women have special privileges in this country and are always waited upon and treated with most distinguished consideration, but when it's a question of grub, the man is bound to have it every time," and with that off came the lid of the can. There was a scramble between two of the boys for the paddle which they called the wishbone, as they wanted to show us how clean it could be licked by a "Siwash," as they called themselves for the moment. Each fellow provided himself with a tin cup, M— with a tin plate; the one supposed to have the keenest sense of justice was deputised to ladle it out, and the spoonfuls were carefully counted so that no one should get a feather's weight more than another. Then came the groans and grunts of satisfaction, as some of the boys said "the first I've tasted since leaving home. Wouldn't 'a' missed it for the world. Ah, it's necessary to come to this country to enjoy everything!" Then each fellow was told to hold on to his cup while we had some music.

R— played the mandolin, and the Judge the guitar better than I have ever heard, and we listened with keenest enjoyment as they rendered *Cavalleria Rusticana, Abendstern, Traviata, Lucia,* and many other airs. A second round of ice cream and cake was next in order, and M— was accused of getting more on his plate than anyone else could put in a cup, against which assertion he protested in his ludicrous way, saying, "I'll bet I've lifted down less than any other fellow here."

It began to get so cold that we put on our sealskins while M— and R— rolled themselves up in fur robes and looked like bears. Our illumination consisted of three candles and a lantern.

At half-past ten it was still colder, so the boys bade us goodnight and started for their canoes which speedily took them to Dawson and their warm little cabins. Then came the voice of Jones saying, "I waited up until your guests had left, to see if I couldn't fetch you some water or do something for you. Well, if you don't want nothing, I'll be saying goodnight." How we congratulated ourselves that Dr. C— had loaned us the nice little tent into which we crawled to our beds, only to find that Ivan, also feeling the cold, had snuggled himself in among the rugs on my air mattress from which the air had entirely escaped, owing to the crack in the seam and his weight combined. We shivered and shook as we undressed and wrapped ourselves in our fur robes, and thought of the comforts of the homes we had left behind us, but never once did we dream of regretting having taken the trip, of which each new experience added to its interest. We also felt that upon returning to luxurious civilisation it would seem hard to breathe the stifling air of a city.

Our Helpful Neighbours

FRIDAY, **A**UGUST 19TH ❧ At 9 AM Jones came bringing us a bucket of fresh water from the spring; then offered to cut some wood, and light our fire for us, and also to do our shopping in Dawson, objecting to our going, on account of the typhoid fever. So off the good fellow went with our list of commissions, saying in answer to my protests, "It's no use; I shall never be able to do enough for you after your kindness to me, when you'd only heard of me as the 'sick boy.'" Next came Mr. Q—, who also said, "If there are any commissions for town this morning, you must give them to me and not show your faces on the other side of the river; two thousand are down with typhoid fever, and I saw a poor girl carried in a chair to the hospital yesterday. It's a lucky thing you're on this side of the Yukon. The 'old girl' wants to be rowed over, and asked me to take her, but she's not yet ready." "Who is it you call the 'old girl'?" said I. "Oh, that woman who always goes about in men's clothing. She went to the post office and walked into the ladies' entrance, when they called out to her, 'The other door, sir, the other door; can't you hear? That door is only for ladies.' 'But I am a lady,' she answered. 'Well, you don't look it,' was the reply." We laughed at Q—'s story, but declared that it must have been manufactured on the spur of the moment, as the Canadian officials are noted for their kindness and courtesy to those of our sex.

J—, K—, Dr. H—, and Jones spent the evening. K— said he had just been making a batch of bread, and Edith exclaimed, "Oh, do show me how you make it up here, and I'll do some myself, for goodness knows whether we'll ever get another cook. The men are all so wild to go on the trail that they turn up their noses at five dollars a day and grub; besides, I love to cook, and Mrs. Hitchcock is most appreciative and never finds fault if things don't come out right." "That's the way we all have to be up here," said J—. "We can only say in the most polite manner possible, 'This bread is awfully good, but don't you think it would be

100 better for a little more salt? But it's delicious all the same!' or 'This pie is as heavy as lead, but I couldn't begin to make anything so nice myself' and then we must find lots to praise about it or straightway the messmate throws up the job and one has to cook for himself, and you know there are some lazy fellows who hate to do anything."

"So you're going over to town tomorrow, Mrs. Hitchcock, to record claims," said the doctor. "Well, don't touch a drop of water while you're there, because the water even from the creek flows first over the bones of a tribe of dead Indians." "What a yarn!" "No, it's an honest fact. Don't you see that steep embankment over there? That was formed by a slide which buried an entire Indian village." "How long ago?" "Oh, about a hundred years or so."

"I saw two bears on top of that embankment yesterday." "Now, Mrs. Hitchcock, that's a yarn! You mean horses, although I don't see how they could have climbed there." "No, they weren't horses," I stoutly protested; "they were bears, real, live bears, on the very steepest part, and I watched them from this side for some time." As the incredulous ones laughed, good John came to my rescue, saying, "Yes, I seen 'em, too, and would 'a' gone for 'em if I'd 'a' had my rifle." Then the little company really became excited and begged me to call them the very next time these animals made their appearance, promising me some of the finest bear meat ever tasted. "Now, little one, what can I do for you next before saying goodnight, for I'm off to my tent?" I gasped in astonishment at the new appellation, but dared not quarrel with so kind a friend and assistant, so begged him to go to the spring and get us some freshwater. In passing, he whispered to me, "I seen them little fists o' yours clench when I said 'little one.' They couldn't hurt a flea, an' I ain't afraid o' them, an' don't you be afraid o' John, 'cause he wouldn't touch a hair o' your head, but somehow or other I have a kind o' weakness for you what makes me always want to speak kinder tender-like to you, but it don't mean nothin' for you to take offence at. You just tell me what you don't want me to say and don't you never be afraid o' John. Goodnight."

Sunday, August 21st ☜ A cold, chilly morning, but we were up early and had breakfast before we heard any signs of life from the other side of the tent. Then there was a yawn, and a shout of "What! You folks up already? Just wait a moment, an' I'll be dressed and round to chop wood and make the fire before you kin say Jack Robinson." "Mrs. Hitchcock has built three fires," called Edith, "and they've all gone out, so I've made the coffee on the oil stove." "Oh, them little hands o' hers can't make nothin'—she's gotter wait fer John. Now don't you do no more work, little one," said he; "John's all ready for to set the table, do the cookin, an' everything else. Here's your hot water for to manicure them little hands o' yourn, so you just sit down an' be quiet an' happy, coz I knows you're always happy when yer gits them little fins o' yourn in water."

As he was working over the stove, and Edith was dishing up the oatmeal, a strong gust of wind blew the tent flap into the fire. In a moment it was in a blaze, and, as the others caught sight of it, before they could move I had a large bag of salt on the fire, pounded the rest out with my fists too rapidly to burn them, and then threw a bucket of water over the smouldering embers. "Bravo, little one! Didn't she do that well? Did you ever see the likes o' that? Well, upon my word! She had it out before we could move, and me thinking them little fins couldn't do nothing. Well, I take it all back." But, notwithstanding all his praise, it never equalled that I was showering on myself, as it was the first time I had ever shown any presence of mind in danger, having been paralysed with fright on many another occasion.

"Here's a note for Mrs. Hitchcock from M—. Says you want a cook," said a young man outside the tent door. I'm cook on one of the North American Transportation Company's steamers, but want to stay in Dawson this winter, so should like to cook for you two ladies, as I hear you give five dollars a day and grub, and that's much more than I'm getting now." "But you are giving up a permanent position for something which may not last more than a fortnight, and you ought to take that into consideration." "Oh, I didn't know that; then perhaps you'll let me think it over." Breakfast finished, the dishes washed and put away, then John helped prepare the pulpit, benches, and rugs for the minister and congregation, but no amount of persuasion could induce him to remain through the service. "No, ma'am, I'll do anything you like to ask me to, but no church for John; howsomever, here's the brush and I'm going to brush my children good, 'cause I'm proud o' them and want to see them look nice."

Rev. Dr. D— arrived with two friends from Dawson. I tolled the bell, and the little congregation soon assembled. Service over, we had a little chat with Mrs. W—, the lady who had been told to go to the other door of the post office. She also was anxious to meet Mr. M—, and wanted us to introduce him. We said that he had invited us to go on the trail to Sulphur the following morning, but that we should not be able to, and she quickly replied that she would be very glad to act as substitute.

The last member had gone, the tent flap was drawn down, when M— and R— called out, "Open the door, we've come to church. What! Over already! We heard you ladies needed a cook, so we've come to get up a nice dinner for you. You show us what you've got and we'll do the rest, but we must start the music box first and work to slow music. Oh! By Jingo! Isn't it nice to come to a place where a fellow feels as he would at home! If you only knew what an unusual thing it is out here." While talking they rolled up their sleeves and went to work. M— made the most delicious English muffins I ever tasted. R— chopped wood and heated the tomato soup; Edith broiled a beefsteak, fried potatoes, and heated some corn. I prepared the table; the easiest lot always falls to me as, luckily, no one will have me "fussing round in the kitchen." We finally seated ourselves, Edith and R— on one bench, M— and I opposite. Such funny stories, such laughter, such Klondike expressions as "Please give me another throw at the potatoes," etc. "I say, are you going to have ice cream tonight? I thought so, for the boys are all hunting up their fur coats to wear. Now you ladies sit perfectly still, as we're going to clear the table and wipe the dishes." We took them at their word and played ladies while they hustled about until M— came back and said, "Please, ma'am, the work's all finished. May we have an afternoon off, as we're invited to get a dinner for another party at five?" Off they rushed full of animal life and spirits, enjoying every moment of their stay in the Klondike, and helping others to do the same.

We were interrupted by the arrival of our fellow passenger S—, who had left us at Circle. He was accompanied by another passenger, P—, who was out for the first time after quite an attack of illness. They were quickly followed by Von M—, R—, D—, Edith, and K—. "I say," said one, "have you heard that peace has been declared?" "Oh, yes," said Von M—. "America's suing for peace, and Spain has been rather noble in granting most advantageous terms." Here, on the 22nd of August it is quite impossible for us to tell whether our dear ones are still in the thick of the fight or at home once more. We were also told of the death of Bismarck but it is as likely as not to be untrue. After the "boys" had washed the dishes and put everything in order, and two of them had gone to get us buckets of water, the "sour dough" bringing his from the spring, the "Chee Charker" his from the Yukon River, and being heartily laughed at for his pains, we all gathered around on the benches, with our elbows on the table; someone called, "Douse the glim," in response to which elegant language the candles were blown out, the lanterns turned down, and many stories were told. K— who had slipped away during the latter part of a ghost story, out of sight but not out of hearing, appeared with a shovelful of fire on which he had put salt, alcohol, and other ingredients, which cast such a ghastly glow over each member of the party that we shouted for the lights to be turned up, and were so nervous that as we said goodnight we longed for Mr. Jones to stand guard again.

Monday, August 22nd ☞ "Why didn't you come to church yesterday, Dr. H—?" said we, as he appeared at the door. "Oh, I'm awfully busy now; had all my washing to do yesterday, and then I've bought out half-interest in the brewery. Studied that for three months before going to Japan. Awfully paying thing; pays much better than medicine. Plenty of illness in Dawson, but the patients are all too poor to pay anything. Most of them get ill because they've not enough money to pay for food. One doesn't come out here for philanthropy, nor for one's health, and one can't get more than five dollars a visit at the hospital. Surprising one can make such good beer out of rice! We just put it in bottles and let it ferment for a day or two. I'm going to make my fortune now, and give up medicine for a while. If there's nothing I can do for you, I'll go home and wash dishes. J— says you gave them a fine ice cream supper last night; wish you had asked me. Let me know when you give another, won't you?"

Some Indians passed and peeped in at the door. A tramp looked in at the front door and disappeared. I went behind the screen and into the kitchen and found him at the entrance of the back door, but he beat a retreat with never a word. Truly the place is changing! Even the miners acknowledge that they can no longer leave their gold dust out in tomato cans. Things disappear mysteriously. The boats are bringing in too many "Chee Charkers" and there is talk of a miners' meeting. If we were to air one or two grievances over missing articles the storm might burst, and we be allowed to see a lifeless body dangling from a tree, or a solitary man put on a raft and set afloat downstream with the swift current to carry him to an unknown destination to begin life once more.

8 PM. I was expecting Von M— to teach me to develop photographs, so gave Edith a policeman's whistle with which to call me when he came, carrying one myself to answer her call. The night was perfect, the stars shining, and had it not been for the strong current a daily boat ride would have been blissful, but contending against a current of six or seven miles an hour made the exertion of rowing so great that accepting an invitation seemed too much of an imposition.

Scarcely had we reached the raft when the whistle sounded and we floated downstream to the landing, where Mr. W— was waiting to assist me in scrambling up the steep embankment. This gymnastic performance would be more easily accomplished were it not for the impediment of skirts. Society is not educated up to it, nor is the writer, but really the only way of getting about in this part of the world, sensibly and without accident, is garbed in bloomers. We developed no photographs nor did we make the attempt, as we became wildly excited over the possibilities of a business scheme.

A New Scheme

ON THE PREVIOUS DAY, we had mentioned before Von M— and a number of the "boys" that, in accordance with a request from M—, we had brought a bowling alley and an animatoscope with which he declared he could make his fortune and our own within six months, as neither had yet been seen in Dawson. It was distinctly understood, however, that they were not to be placed in his hands until after certain inquiries had been made at the end of our journey. W— had decided not to turn over to him the many articles purchased, but to make some other disposition of them. Immediately, several of the "boys" had expressed a strong desire to take the matter in hand, and we agreed to consider their propositions.

Von M— had been to town early in the morning, had visited the few halls there, and had numerous plans to lay before us. "We're not any of us up here for our health," said he, "and there are several who would be glad to go into this thing, and push it, on a business-like basis." W— also became intensely interested as we looked over the magic lantern slides, and made out the list of moving pictures which all pronounced wonderfully good. Von M— was to be manager, W— to take tickets and weigh the gold dust.

TUESDAY, AUGUST 23RD ☞ Four steamers are in together. The harbour is becoming very gay, and the "Chee Charkers" numerous. We went to the office of the Johnson-Locke Company to see if we could get news of the *Tillamook* and our stores. They knew nothing of the *Tillamook*, but said that the *Rideout*, the Company's riverboat, was reported at Circle City three days ago, and was likely to be here in forty-eight hours. Our hopes are now high that we will soon be off short rations and living in luxury. "What day for the big dinner?" asked M— and R— as we met them and told them the good news. Mr. L— S— then joined us; he had been "in" for ten days, and advised us not to remain later than the middle of September if we did not wish to be frozen in. He opened a fine illustrated paper, *Klondike Edition*, with pictures of the Bonanza Kings, and as we looked over his shoulders and criticised, a crowd soon formed in a semicircle close behind us, for the sheet cost one dollar, and many had not that amount to pay.

One o'clock, and time for the Record Office to open, so W— accompanied me there. Being a woman, I had the privilege of entering the little side door into the small anteroom, where my escort and I seated ourselves on a bench, and waited for the window to open. Just then a nice young boy who had been particularly courteous to me on a previous visit, came in my direction and I said to him, "Why can't you record my claim for me?"—"Because the fellow who does that is bigger than I and might put me out. You just go right in and tell him what you want. Don't be afraid. He's ill, but he's all right." So I summoned my courage and timidly approached his desk, saying meekly, "Won't you please record my claim?" "I'm not ready for business yet," he replied, not gruffly, but in such a tired manner that I felt sorry for him at once, and said, "When you are, please let me know. I shall be sitting on the bench back of you."

A few minutes later he opened the window, and began taking papers from the men outside, apparently oblivious of my presence. My escort glanced at me as though we were two naughty school children being punished for too much presumption, and whispered, "Why don't you go? Don't you dare?" The young woman at the desk motioned "Now's your chance"; the nice young boy beckoned, but still I was afraid, and said, "He told me he would let me know when business was about to begin." "You'll have to wait all day, if you don't stand right up to him," so with a mighty effort I once more approached the great man, who did look so ill, writing with one hand and supporting his head by the other; I felt that I might be contrary, too, shut up in that office with a throbbing head. "Well," said he, turning to me as he finished with Number One on the line. "I want to record No. —, Quartz Creek, Indian River District, please." "There are four contestants for that claim already," said he, referring to his book, "four Swedes." "But if they have not had it recorded, why can't I?" "How can I do it for you, if I can't for them?" snapped he. "It's got to be resurveyed. You'd only lose your fifteen dollars, as well as your rights in that district." "Oh I'm not going to fight four poor miners, so let it go, and record No.—, Bear Creek."—"Which side? Upper or lower? Next Gulch?" Having answered all these questions satisfactorily I was just congratulating myself that at last I was to receive the bit of paper entitling me to another claim in the Klondike, when he said, "Where's your miner's certificate?" "It is No. —," said I, pleasantly. "But where is it?" "Why, I didn't bring it with me I got it only a few weeks ago from the young man at that window; he can tell you that it's all right." "But I must have it to record this deed." Then in despair I cried out, "How can I tell all that you want in this office? You should publish a set of rules and regulations. I took the trouble to come all the way from West Dawson last week and after losing a whole afternoon and answering a thousand and one questions, because I couldn't tell you on which tier I had staked, you sent me back to get my lesson over again, and now you want me to go all the way back to get my certificate, when I bought it right here in this very office from that young man, who can tell you so."

This outburst completely astonished his royal highness, and evidently fearing that I was about to burst into tears, he said quickly, "All right, all right; here's your paper, and you can send your certificate tomorrow." I breathed a sigh of relief, clutched the slip, and presented my fifteen dollars. "Thank the Lord it's all over, and now I'm a millionaire claim owner, but poor Miss Van Buren will have to go through with this ordeal tomorrow."

We found Edith being entertained by Mr. T—, whom she left to prepare luncheon for the weary tramps from town. Hardly were we seated ere Mr. H— arrived, followed by Dr. C— and W—, who all remained to prepare dinner for us. Each one had a special dish to cook, while I, as usual, prepared the table. Our *pièce de résistance* was kidneys stewed with sherry, over which great satisfaction was expressed.

After our guests had washed the dishes and put the kitchen in fine order we settled in steamer chairs and on boxes, warmly wrapped, to relate startling tales. Just then Von M— appeared, saying, "I've got lots to tell you, but I'm starving and must first go and get supper; just thought I'd stop at your tent to say I'm coming back." "Nonsense!" we cried. "We've finished dinner and there's nothing left but some bread and butter; how would sardines and a cup of coffee go with that?" "Fine! What luck! You're sure you don't mind?" "Sit down and stop talking and you'll have all you can eat in a jiffy!" So he was handed a tin of sardines with half a dozen slices of bread and butter.

"I've been to every hall in town. I've talked to every proprietor, and have just finished a conversation of two hours with —. I asked him how much he would pay me to bring such an attraction to his theatre; he said he would furnish hall and lights, and expect fifty percent of the net proceeds. We can get the Pioneer Hall for fifty dollars a night and probably for less if we take it for any length of time, but that's off the Main Street. It would be better to pay twice as much on the principal street where crowds congregate. We can have Pioneer Hall from 2 PM to 2 AM, whereas the man who wants half-profits can let us have the theatre only from 2 to 6 PM." "Oh, that's absurd," we cried; "we to bring out the most expensive outfit to be had in San Francisco, to have all the trouble of selecting, learning to run it, learning to prepare limelight, paying freight, duty, etc., and he to have fifty percent. Shouldn't dream of it for an instant," and so we discussed the matter and looked over the magic lantern slides.

"I shall be a thousand times more proud of going back with an inexhaustible sack of gold earned by my own efforts than if the winter had been passed in idleness in New York, Paris, or London. I'm ready to work in such good company, and I'm proud of it. Besides, the poor fellows who are shut up here and have had no chance to see and scarcely to read anything of the war, ought to be able to see the processions of soldiers on the way to Manila, the funeral of the Maine victims, the pictures of our heroes—and it will be a great pleasure to show an animatoscope to them." "I want to work, too," said Edith. "I just want to show my family that I know how to do something and it would be a proud moment for me to carry home a bag of my own earnings—and I want it all in gold dust, too." As we talked and discussed, the time passed so rapidly that midnight came before we were aware, and there was a general stampede to boats by those who lived in Dawson, and to cabins by their fashionable occupants in West Dawson.

Wednesday, August 24th ☙ Luncheon finished, Mr. T— arrived with a Mr. B—, who was anxious to have our bowling alley and animatoscope, and wanted to know what terms we would make. I said we were not making terms, but were willing to consider all bids placed before us during the week, with the intention of accepting the most advantageous. Mr. B— requested permission to be allowed to put in his bid.

"What do you think of it, Mrs. Hitchcock?" said K—. "I think it is a matter not to be decided upon before the end of the week. What do you say, Edith?" "Quite agree with you. We'll wait for all the propositions, which are to be submitted to us this week." "They can't be better than B—'s," said K—, "as he expects to turn in to you at least from eight thousand to twelve thousand dollars a month, and you'll not have a penny of expense." "We cannot decide before Saturday," we replied, and so the interview ended. It was after four when Edith returned. She had recorded her first claim, had been invited to luncheon at the Regina Café by Dr. C—, had held a reception all along Main Street, being stopped at every corner, and was glad to get back to our easy chairs and to the quiet of our tent.

Our next visitors were J— and L—, the latter having just arrived from Circle City for a day or two in Dawson. Ivan welcomed him gladly, and we were pleased to see the fellow passenger who had given us our first oranges and lemons and loaned us a fur robe, which he said again he should not need or want us to return until we were quite ready to depart. He tried to persuade us to

108 move to the American side and settle in Circle or at Eagle City, promising that we should be well looked out for; but our interests are growing here, in many directions, and to leave at all will be difficult.

Supper was soon on the table, consisting of beef soup, chops, and desiccated potatoes, rice cakes, macaroni and cheese, and prunes. Von M— came in and we settled down to business and talked over the big scheme which we expect to coin money for us. We asked Von M— to read over B—'s proposition and advise us from an unprejudiced standpoint, but he was square and honest and said, "I can't do it, don't you see, because I want it so much myself and have such a nice staff of assistants selected; we are not only intending to work for ourselves, but to advance your interests, so that it seems to me that no one else could make so much of a success of it. Although I've never done anything of this kind in my life, I shall devote every moment to it, and feel that no one else could do more." The fellow had shown so much energy, and spent so much time over it, that we felt he really deserved the position. He had secured the option on the Oatley Sisters' Theatre from 2 to 6 PM daily for ten dollars a day, and was to find out about getting it after the play in the evening. He had seen many others and placed the proposition before them, and was expecting answers from all sides. He had also seen the men who owned the raft and found that lumber could be purchased at one dollar a log, and that the boys were all willing to give us a "building bee," so that it now looks as though we should soon be able to move from this enormous tent with its damp ground to a house of our own.

THURSDAY, AUGUST 25TH ❧ Von M— came to find out what we would contribute towards the hall in case he engaged it. He received the following list:

One animatoscope, gas bags, and all appurtenances;
two dozen films of various subjects, ranging from the *Maine* funeral
   procession to the Corbett fight;
one magic lantern, with views of naval heroes, battle scenes.

The Rideout at Last

FRIDAY, AUGUST 26TH ☞ A cold, sunless morning. The hundreds of dogs that have been barking all night at the sound of each passing footstep are now enjoying a well-earned rest, as are others who have been kept awake by their combined howls which make a veritable pandemonium.

2 PM. Our first visitor this morning was Von M—, who returned too late from Dawson to call on us last night. He had not yet decided on anything, as he was expecting answers from many to whom he had applied. Everyone is eager to have the animatoscope, but not so anxious for the bowling alley, as it takes so much space, where land is extremely valuable.

Dr. C— and John cooked and prepared the dinner of soup, fresh salmon, potatoes, macaroni and cheese, and evaporated peaches, but all had to be taken as usual on one plate, owing to the scarcity of dishes, and to the fact that the bread was rising in the dishpan.

After dinner, as we were sitting before our tent wrapped in furs and robes, a screeching of whistles, and crowded docks, announced to us the approach of a steamer. We walked to the water's edge, accompanied by our neighbours with their field glasses, and strained our eyes for the name of the steamer, which was towing a new barge. The *Rideout*! The *Rideout*, at last! After a whole month of waiting! Of purchasing stores at Dawson prices! And now, as we are ready to leave for home, she comes, bringing the table linen, bed linen, kitchen utensils, luxuries and delicacies for which we have been longing, and which it is now too late for us to enjoy.

SATURDAY, AUGUST 27TH ☞ Two men called to ask if we were the ladies about to build a house. If so, they desired to be engaged as assistants. H— called again to see if we had decided to let his capitalist B— have bowling alley and animatoscope, but Von M— is so hard at work, so nearly ready to begin, and we have such a high opinion of his honour and integrity, that, although H— raised his offer from sixty-five to seventy percent of the net receipts, we decided to allow the property in question to remain in the hands of Von M—.

Jones assisted in preparing dimmer, which consisted only of beans, muffins, and stewed apricots, as our rations have about come to an end.

After dinner I went for a short walk with Ivan. Mr. K— stood outside of his tent blacking his boots, and I cried, "Oh! For a Kodak, that your people might see something of the details of life on the Yukon." He laughed, saying, "I was just dressing up for a visit to the 'Big Tent.'" "It's freezing there," said I, "so that most of our friends have deserted us, while those who do come run the risk of pneumonia or rheumatism." "Yes, it's the coldest place in Alaska," replied K—.

SUNDAY, AUGUST 28TH ☞ We held our last church service this morning, as it is not only too cold, but the building of the house will block the entrance to the tent. After service an informal, friendly meeting was held, when the parson (substitute sent by Dr. D—), who had come into Dawson to seek his fortune as a photographer, bemoaned his fate, saying that he was now almost too poverty-stricken to leave, although very anxious to do so. "How can that be," we queried, "with prices at one dollar each for developing photographs?" "That's all well enough," said he, "until one runs out of material it is then that the expense and difficulty begin. Never in all my life have I required so much patience and faith as during my stay on the Yukon." So we came to the conclusion that his stores had also been sent through the company we had chosen, and that he had been obliged to purchase at Dawson prices as had we.

One of our neighbours came to the tent door saying, "Won't you ladies accept a pair of ducks? My partner and I have just come in from Ottawa, and have shot so much game during the trip that we have more than we want," and so the beauties were turned over to us, and we congratulated ourselves that such generous neighbours were about to set up a cabin next door but one.

MONDAY, AUGUST 29TH ☞ We went on board the steamer *Rideout*, where H— was checking off freight, but got someone else to take his place while he accompanied us to the Pavilion to show the rooms on which he and B— had the option—only fifty feet long, and the bowling alley is just that length, and requires at least seventy. "Oh, we'll manage." "But how? There's not another foot of ground to be obtained here." "We can fix it somehow." But it was quite useless we found, as we examined; so we left for another consultation with Edith and H— with his backer.

At last, the commissions finished, we started for the boat, only to find that Dr. C—, who had borrowed it at eleven o'clock to pay an hour's visit to Edith, had failed to return, so we all seated ourselves on the platform outside the Alaska Commercial Company, and waited and watched the shore near the Big Tent to see when the doctor should push off. Jones appeared at last ready to take Ivan and me home. I begged passage also for W— and Von M—.

W—, who was carrying under his arm our four loaves of bread, which we had purchased for a dollar, let one of them slip from the paper to the ground. "Bread is too precious to be thrown away for a little thing like that," cried the "boys," and immediately commenced giving it a thorough dusting. On reaching the Big Tent we were met by half a dozen men who had heard of our strike on Bear Creek, and were ready to start out staking in case we would give them a few details. "There are five of us," said they, "and we'll all give you an interest." "Ah! In case your claims turn out well I shall expect a million from each one," and so saying, I spread the map out before F—, explaining to him carefully the entire ground, but without exacting the usual bargain of half-interest in each claim. Off they all started with heavy packs on their backs, and a strange sight it seemed! These society men, who are dined and wined in New York, who lead cotillions and attend teas, cheerfully making beasts of burden of themselves, by strapping anywhere from thirty to eighty pounds on the back, bending under the burden, tramping miles daily, with perspiration rolling from the brow, yet making no complaint.

Seven o'clock came and no dinner guests: eight, ditto, so we sat down with W— and Von M—, enjoyed our stewed clams, delicious roast of beef, potatoes, scalloped tomatoes, asparagus salad, etc., which they had assisted in preparing, and discussed whether we should waste a bottle of champagne upon these two "boys." They overruled us by saying that once it had been iced it had to be used, so the contents of the bottle were carefully divided into four parts. We drank success to the animatoscope. The tent door was wide open, and the table was lighted by the soft rays of the moon.

After dinner a man came to see about moving the logs for our cabin. All our neighbours pay twenty dollars a day for horse and man, but for the Big Tent twenty-five dollars is the lowest price. So Big Alex and I walked along the riverbank to a place where we were told we should find a man who owned a very strong horse. We found him, and tried to strike a bargain, but the horse's master recognised the owner of the "Big Tent" as well as the Klondike King, so bargaining was more than useless, and, finally, ten hours' work was arranged for on the morrow, to begin at 8 AM. We seated ourselves on a log, where the moonlight shone softly over the Yukon and the mountains back of Dawson, and there McDonald told me the history of his life. Although he had started with only three dollars and a half, he had always been so sure of success that his dreams were ever of how to invest the coming millions. He told of his plans for "going out," for visiting Seattle, San Francisco, Colorado, where he had worked for years, New York, and even London, and kindly offered to escort us over the Pass, and help us in the difficult places which we should be sure to encounter, as well as to show us the famous Alaska-Treadwell mines.

He also promised that in case of our return to Dawson, he would take us to virgin ground and tell us where to stake, and a promise of that kind from Alex McDonald is worth more than a promise of millions from anyone else.

The next afternoon an Indian came to the tent and, in a most imperious manner, asked if we wished to purchase fish. As we had a roast of beef on hand, and W— and I sat plucking feathers from ducks, a first experience for each of us and one which amused us hugely, we thought we had too much fresh food, but when he said only "four bits each" the temptation was too great, and we accompanied him down to the boat to select our salmon. We told him to bring it to the tent and receive the pay; this he declined to do in a most stately manner, handing the fish to W—, who accepted it as naturally as he carries bread and washes dishes, with never a thought as to what the members of the crack regiment to which he so lately belonged would say. The Indian followed us with great dignity, holding the hand of a small child of three years of age. After receiving payment, he stood calmly surveying the decorations. I started the music box, to which the child listened with awe; then took her hand to show her the parrot. The father objected, however, saying, "got no time." But the child had caught sight of the strange bird and was so eager to make its acquaintance that it was some time before he succeeded in leading her away. I asked if they would like their pictures taken to which he replied, "Got no good clothes." The picture taken, however, the Indian said with an air of command, "Picture finish very quick and then you give me." "What a haughty manner!" said I, as he disappeared from view. "No wonder; that's the chief of the tribe, and the kid is a princess," said one of my neighbours.

The Trials of Building

TUESDAY, AUGUST 30TH ☞ At 9 AM Jones came with a man to dig the foundation. At ten the man with the horse appeared, but after viewing the heavy logs said he must have an assistant, so he went off and finally secured one at eight dollars a day. Work commenced after ten, nearer eleven. I got our tape measure and gave it to Jones to stake off ground, after the return of which he disappeared.

Before leaving, Colonel Q— said, "Now that you are not to have service here again, don't make any engagement for next Sunday, as I'm to have a steam yacht (?) at my disposal, and am going to give a picnic only to members of the 'four hundred.' So I want you two ladies as leaders of it. Then there is to be the daughter of Senator —. I tell you I'm going to be in the very choicest society on that day." "Is 'Windy' going?" said one of the "boys." "Who is 'Windy?'" we asked. "Oh, she's the lady that comes to all our tents and talks so much." "Not very kind of you to speak in that disrespectful manner, and you a *Virginia* gentleman." "Yes, I know; but I just can't help it. I like ladies as is ladies, like you two that all your neighbours are proud of. It's a fine thing for us to have such ladies around, and it keeps us from getting demoralised; but how can we have the same respect for women who dress like men, and live like men, and talk like men, and act like men?"

Now to return to our house building. While the owner of the horse and his assistant were hauling up logs from the raft, I superintended them, Edith overseeing the man who was digging the foundation. From nine to twelve he dug the south and east sides, then saying, "I think I can work better for a little luncheon," left for the other side of the river. Work being stopped also on the log hauling, more as a joke than anything else, I said, "See how much I can dig while the men are at luncheon," and immediately began overturning the earth on the north side. Edith seized the Kodak and caught me in the act, with the perspiration rolling down my brow. "Let me show you how to hold a shovel, if you won't allow me to dig for you," called another neighbour. "I hate to see a woman working, but then you can't make much impression; it's only play for you." This put me on my mettle, and caused me to work with such determination that I had soon dug the entire thirty feet necessary to hold the first log, but as different ones came in and refused to believe it the work of my hands, I realised more and more that those at home would be equally incredulous.

Down to the raft again, while Edith continued the housework, which to me is most obnoxious. The two men had done so little that I began to fear their task would not be finished by night, so questioned them. They could not tell! Thirty-three dollars a day and only half a dozen logs hauled up. At that rate they might spin out their job indefinitely. Neighbour E— came and kindly brought us a bucket of water. We consulted him and others, but although they knew we were paying steep prices, they saw no way of our getting better terms, for, as one of the "boys" said, "They've all heard that you're very wealthy, and there are only three horses on this side."

While we had been waiting for our stores from the *Rideout* another animatoscope had arrived in town, and had forestalled us, and this was their opening night. Crowds were hanging about the door awaiting admission. We were told that as the "lightning express" appeared, dashed on, and disappeared, the miners howled with delight, and that one of them stood up and shouted, "Run her through again! Run her through again! I ain't seen a locomotive for nigh on ten years." To think what we have lost by the detention of our cargo! Our "lightning express" will be old when it is finally turned over to us.

On reaching the Alaska Commercial Company's platform, we found the Salvation Army holding its meeting, surrounded by miners and idle men. Jones found me a vacant seat, which I took, attracting no attention, and told him to hurry off on his errand. One or two dogs came to be petted, then a young man approached, raised his hat, saying, "Is this Mrs. Hitchcock? I am Mr. —, and learning that you brought in a great many novels, magazines, and illustrated weeklies for winter reading, which you are not to remain and enjoy, thought that you might be willing to dispose of them. If so, I should be very glad to take the lot," he added, with the air of a millionaire, "and I won't be greedy about the price, am willing to make just a small percentage." "Do you purchase for cash?" said I. "Well, no," he reluctantly admitted; "I'm sorry to say I have no cash whatever, and thought perhaps you'd just let me take them on commission, as I'm very much in need of money."

WEDNESDAY, AUGUST 31ST ☞ Such a downpour of rain! It starts the canary singing at the top of his voice, as he hears the patter on the tent top. How grateful we are to Dr. C— for his little tent within the big one; it at least keeps us dry and away from the rivulets and rills which are beginning to form in various directions. At 8 AM the man with the horse and his assistant appeared. An overseer was absolutely necessary, as some neighbours had told us that they could spin out the job for any length of time otherwise; so, buckled into rubber boots, bloomers, and a jersey, with the mercury at fifty degrees, I went out into the rain and down to the riverfront to count how many logs had been hauled up after a thirty-three-dollar day's work.

I then returned to the Big Tent, where Edith, most patient of cooks and housekeepers, insisted upon my partaking of the breakfast she had kept warm for me. She had placed all the buckets outside of the tent in order to catch the raindrops, as our kind neighbours, who generally keep us supplied from the spring, and with wood, had not yet opened their doors and seemed to be sleeping the sleep of the just.

A messenger from W— brought the following note, addressed, "Mrs. Hitchcock, The Big Tent," "I saw the animatoscope last night; it was a very poor show, but evoked great applause. We must get ours started at once before people tire of it, as it would be, at the present moment, a great success, for the other show has not the funeral of the *Maine* victims nor many other processions which the 'boys' are anxious to see. Von M— has done all in his power, but it is impossible to obtain from the *Rideout* your cargo which was promised you a month ago. Somebody ought to make the loss good."

Shortly after, W— himself arrived, and said, "I've only five minutes to spare, but couldn't resist the temptation of running over to tell you about the show last night. They hadn't the funeral of the *Maine* victims, nor the troops and patriotic scenes which we have, but the audience howled all the same, so it appears to me that we shall simply coin money, once we can get hold of that cargo."

Von M— soon came also, quite enthusiastic for him. "Well! I've got permission to show it on Sunday, as I promised to give twenty-five percent of the receipts to the hospitals, which need money very badly. As there is nothing in the world for the people to do on that day, everything in town being closed, we ought to have the hall packed. As you took some lessons in San Francisco in order to teach your protégé how to run it, Mrs. Hitchcock, you'd better come over tomorrow; we'll go with you to get the cargo, and then you can teach us how to run the machine, and make the limelight, and we'll start ahead at once."

We objected to a Sunday performance, but were overruled by our staff, who argued, "You've done a lot of good with your church services here; now why shouldn't you take the people from the streets and temptation? For you know how true it is that Satan finds mischief for idle hands, and you'll be keeping them out of mischief while they're looking at our naval heroes, and learning what they have done during the war; and then think of the big sum that will go towards the hospital; and last, but not least, of how we shall coin money!"

"Have you heard the news?" called out one of the "boys" at the tent door after dinner. We thought from his tone that our army or navy had again been successful, and eagerly questioned him. "Why, there's been an explosion at the the-*a*-tre, an' Arizona Charlie's show of moving pictures is bust up, so he had to return all the money. He couldn't get the right kind o' oil or kerosene or something, an' so used the only thing he could buy—a cheap stuff which exploded and burned his man terrible bad all over the face and hands and everywhere."

THURSDAY, SEPTEMBER 1ST &- At 10 AM Jones and Von M— turned up, each one with an invitation to go in his boat to Dawson. Ivan accompanied us, wearing his fine new collar for the first time. As we were now preparing to leave for the "outside," and could not take our pets with us, we had accepted Jones's offer to raffle the parrot, which he took in his canoe. On nearing the banks of Dawson, there was the usual difficulty in working one's way through the rafts, which crowded the waterfront to the obstruction and annoyance of all boat owners. My first visit was to the post office; Ivan alone accompanied me, as Von M— and Jones were fully occupied in carrying the heavy boxes to the Oatley Sisters' Theatre where our performance was to take place. "The mail arrived yesterday, but will not be ready for distribution until the second or third of September," was the answer to my question. "How soon will you send a mail to the United States?" "We closed one yesterday at five o'clock." "Oh, what hard luck! Is there no way of overtaking it?" I asked. "Just a chance, madam; it was sent on board the *Ora*, which may not have sailed yet, so if. . ." But off I dashed to catch the *Ora*, which had blown her last whistle a few moments previously. Down the wharf I rushed, with Ivan at my side, for whom an admiring crowd made ready space. Many willing hands were extended as I jumped on board the steamer, and the purser kindly accepted my batch of letters.

FRIDAY, SEPTEMBER 2ND &- At 10 AM, as neither Jones nor Von M— had put in an appearance, Ivan accompanied me to the water's edge, to see if there was a chance of getting across to attend to the necessary commissions. Two of our neighbours from Ottawa, the ones who had presented us with the ducks, had started, but on seeing me called out to know if I wanted to go to Dawson, and not only returned, but went to their cabin for a tiny camp stool to put in the bottom of the canoe. We were soon in town, and as usual my first visit was to the Alaska Commercial Company, where M— met me, to assist in getting the cargo through the Custom House.

The agent shortly after made his appearance. One of his bills was forty dollars for transporting the bowling alley from the steamer to the warehouse, a distance of not more than two blocks, but I was grateful to him for having paid the bill instead of leaving it in the street, and found him a most courteous man to deal with. Von M— and the others soon found the boxes containing the manganese, the chloride, and the gasoline, and took out enough to generate gas.

As we were about to start for the hall, Mr. H— appeared, saying, "I have just been to West Dawson to see about the books, and as I have an offer for the entire lot at twenty-five cents each—books, newspapers, weeklies, etc. Miss Van Buren considers that it would be preferable to distributing them between dozens who may leave many on your hands, particularly as a man is expected in at any moment with five thousand." "And your commission?" "Two cents a book." It was hard to think of some of them going for that price, but time is growing short, so I went with H— and his backer to have the bags opened, and they were delighted with the appearance of our winter library. Down I sat on

ERECTION OF TAMMANY HALL, DAWSON

the floor, checking off as H— counted. It was slow work but, when finished, I was given $153.25 in gold dust for what had cost us $49.78.

We entered the theatre through the side door, and went behind the scenes. Dr. C— studied the instructions carefully, and in a few moments was making the limelight as though he had been in the business for years. Under my instructions Von M—, aided by W—, soon had the machine in position, and all was working beautifully, when we discovered a leak in the bags. The members of the staff here assured me that as they now thoroughly understood the principle of the thing, it would not be necessary for me to wait, so W— escorted me back to the Alaska Commercial Company to keep my appointment with M—, who was to have crossed the river with me at 4 PM. As the rain was then coming down in torrents, we sought shelter in a warehouse near the boat and seated ourselves on a couple of boxes.

As we were planning to have our cargo moved from the warehouse to our new cabin, which is to be finished in a few days, Colonel Q— advised us strongly not on any account to do so, saying, "Never mind how strong the lock, should the winter be a hard one, people knowing of the comforts and luxuries not being used, and thinking you enormously wealthy, would be too greatly tempted to help themselves." The other men in the party all agreed with him, and advised us strongly to dispose at once of everything which we cannot use, and which we do not care to pay heavy freight upon. Jones came in and announced that the parrot, which was being raffled for fifty dollars, had dropped from its perch and died shortly after.

Business Propositions

SATURDAY, **S**EPTEMBER **3**RD ❧ Up at half-past five to write yesterday's experiences before the arrival of the men and the interruptions consequent thereon. Mercury thirty-nine degrees! Almost too cold to hold a pen. Never before have I so appreciated sunshine nor so longed for the gorgeous orb to make its appearance. At seven, one of the men gathered wood and started a fire, which scarcely made any difference in the atmosphere. A man appeared asking for work, saying that he and his partners were in great need of money. On learning the terms, he went back to inform them, and returned, saying, "We don't care to take it for so little as seven dollars and a half a day." As we sit in steamer chairs shivering with the cold, while watching the slow work on our new cabin, how incongruous seems the note just written to the postmaster to change our address from Dawson, Yukon Territory, to Palace Hotel, San Francisco! How impossible seems the thought of being in the midst of luxuries once more, of having a nice warm room in which to dress, and to choose just what one likes to eat. We shall have to live on the American plan this time, as the European would cost us a small fortune with the appetites we now have in reserve. Yet how often shall we find the rooms overheated, the atmosphere that of a conservatory, the life limited and restrained, and long for the wilderness and the freedom thereof. A taste of such liberty as this must finally spoil one for civilisation.

Breakfast over, Von M— came to inquire if I would be ready to go to town by ten o'clock, so off I went to the Alaska Commercial Company, meeting Miss —, who said, "I was just watching for you. You must let us have some of those articles which you expected to use this winter had you remained. Papa wants to see you also, for you have many things which we need, and shall not be able to have sent in until next spring or summer. Won't you come with me? Papa's just gone up the street, and we'll overtake him in a moment," and the

120   attractive young girl waited for me while my commissions were attended to at the Alaska Commercial Company.

As we started back I was stopped by the proprietor of — Hotel, who, introducing himself, said, "They tell me that you and Miss Van Buren have been waiting here all summer for your winter's supplies, and that now just as they've come you're both 'going out.' Everybody supposes as how the grub that you have got is such stuff as one can't buy here, and as it wouldn't be safe to lock it up for the winter with a lot o' starvin' men about, I'm ready to take the whole lot of it off your hands; and if you don't sell it to me, I'll have to go out over the Pass an' then like as not, be kept out until it's too late."

"Excuse me," said a man, raising his hat, "but can't I interrupt for just one moment? Hearing that you ladies had just received your winter's supplies, as you were going back home, I made so bold as to go over to the Big Tent, where I saw Miss Van Buren, and told her I'd take the entire cargo, which she said would be much better than dividing it up among all who are trying to get it." "Good morning, Mrs. Hitchcock," said H—. "My friend, the stationer, is about out of stock and wants to know if you won't let him have your winter's supply instead of locking it up; and as for groceries, there's a corner in the market and you can make a very handsome profit, if you will dispose of yours."

I was joined by R—, who said that he had engaged the only cabin on the *Ora* for Edith and me, and advised us to take our robes and pillows, as the bunks were not furnished, and we should be obliged to "turn in" on a piece of stretched canvas. Then came M—, who said, "Had such fun at the masquerade ball last night! I went as a giddy blonde, dressed décolleté with short skirts and stockings filled with chips, and wore long golden curls."

"Have been looking for you everywhere. Alex's ready and waiting," interrupted the cheery voice of Jones. So with two escorts down the bank, into the canoe I went, and was speedily rowed across by the stout arms of good old Jones. In landing, McDonald attempted to assist me up a bank much steeper than the place where we generally landed. Jones, who was tying the boat called out, "She can't do that; go around the other way," to which Alex replied, "If she's going over the summit, the quicker she learns the better," and with the aid of his strong hand, I sprang lightly over ground from which I should have shrunk in fear and trembling only a few months ago. "Is the summit very much more difficult than this?" I asked anxiously. "You bet!" replied Big Alex with such an air of conviction that my heart sank, and doubts began to arise as to whether I should dare attempt so perilous a trip.

Edith had a nice dinner ready for us—her fish with sauce hollandaise being delicious. McDonald was preoccupied, and had little to say, but, in walking out before the tent, he confided to me that he felt heavily the responsibility of having offered to escort us over the Pass, as business was still pressing on all sides, and so much remained to be done that he greatly feared not being able to leave by the fifteenth even, in which case there was danger of the river freezing us in, so that we might be obliged to spend the winter on the tiny steamer, with scant provisions and perhaps not fuel enough to keep warm.

The rain is again coming down in torrents. We are worried beyond measure that the house, which we had been told would be finished by Saturday night, is still far from completion, and that the cost is to be nearly eight times the estimated price; that the principal part of the animatoscope is missing; and that we may be "frozen in" before we can get everything arranged satisfactorily. All this, combined with the rain, the general dampness of everything belonging to us, the impossibility of making a fire burn with wet wood, and the chilliness of the air, had such a depressing effect upon our spirits, that for the first time we felt thoroughly inhospitable, so shut up the tent, put out the lights, and crawled into our beds without receiving any visitors after dinner. As may readily be imagined the thought of the possibility of a winter in these icy regions was far from cheering, and as a result we both had very little sleep.

SUNDAY, SEPTEMBER 4TH ☞ Rain still falling in torrents. Ground so damp that the water oozes out wherever our feet touch the earth, even in our living part of the tent. Mercury thirty-eight degrees. Camping out is no longer a pleasure, and we glance at our roofless home, so near and so inviting, wondering when we shall be able to move in. Oh, if the sun only would come out now that we need it so much! After breakfast Von M— appeared to ask if we had any commissions for town, as he was going over and expected to be able to give the show. While Edith prepared the breakfast, I was engaged in the dignified task of gathering wood, being protected from the rain by rubber boots and mackintosh. We were in a half-frozen condition, and I was scarcely able to hold a pen, when I attempted my daily record. At ten, Jones arrived, and, by saturating the green wood with coal oil, he soon had a brilliant flame, which was the most cheerful event of the morning.

2:30 PM. Arrival of some of the "boys" from the — Company. After a visit of half an hour M— exclaimed, "Don't you want me to make some muffins for luncheon?" In a few moments, this society boy from home had a pan of flour, cornmeal, and butter, and was deep in the mysteries of the kitchen. Such delicious muffins!

Just then a little field mouse ran near the stove, picking up the crumbs that had fallen. With a shriek I jumped up on the bench, calling, "Kill it! Kill it quick!

122   Don't let it get away," while Edith was equally vociferous, begging that its life might be spared, as it was "a dear little thing, and so tame," but my terror caused the "boys" to put an end to the existence and future unhappiness of the rodent, particularly after Edith said, "Why I watched him playing on your mattress this morning but never told you for fear you'd make just such a scene."

As we gathered around the stove in which the "boys" had succeeded in building a magnificent fire, K— said, "The *May West* is in with a cargo of one hundred marriageable widows. I'd like to cut the rope and let her go out with them all, and the boys are very much inclined to do the same, and if you were to see them you'd think us quite right. Such a lot of frights the eyes of man never beheld! Now, Mrs. Hitchcock, if you really do come in next year, and bring some pretty girls with you, think what a blessing it will be for the 'boys' who cannot get on the 'outside' without imperilling their millions; and how fine it would be for the girls also, for you can answer for us, and know what a splendid lot of husbands we would make." I was not surprised to learn later that the story about the widows was a hoax.*

Edith had a long search for the meat for dinner, but the box in which it had been placed was empty, and the bread near it had also disappeared. Not a nook or cranny was left without thorough investigation. At last Ivan, who had been soundly sleeping all day, rolled over and revealed to us half a loaf of bread, giving us a decided clue to the culprit, who was quite unconscious of the betrayal of his secret. "How could he have found it?" said Edith; "I not only hid it deep in the box, but covered it with dozens of papers." After the departure of McDonald and his friend, the fire began to die out again, and we were in despair, when good Jones arrived.

Everything was soon in apple-pie order, the fire blazing, and as we heartily thanked our kind neighbour, he said, "I don't want no thanks, but I just want you to notice the difference between me and them there dudes o' yourn, who wouldn't give you a hand to cross the summit, I'll be bound. I dined with Alex tonight and he says he'd start out tomorrow with you two ladies, for he just thinks you're the nicest things on earth, and he's so afraid you might get frozen in he can't sleep nights. It's worryin' him almost to death. What are you writin', Mrs. Hitchcock? You're allus writin', no matter how early I comes in the morning nor how late at night, you're as busy as a cat with two tails. You still too busy to talk, Mrs. Hitchcock? I believe it's jest as Isaacs sez—you're haughty. Why should you have such haughty ways about you? Now Miss Van Buren, she's always ready to talk to a fellow, and she's so nice to me that it almost emboldens

---

* See *Klondike Nugget*, September 7, 1898.

me to ask her to be my wife. I say, can't you git Miss Van Buren to have me? Has she had many other offers durin' this trip with you? Hard to count? Bet your life I kin count 'em if you'll jest tell me where you've been. One in Colorado Springs," repeated John, as he told it off on his thumb. "Two in Denver," marking off forefinger and another; "two at Coronado," and down went the fingers of one hand; "one at Los Angeles," and the second hand was brought into requisition. "One at San Diego, five in San Francisco." Here Jones suddenly bent double and put his hand on the toe of his boot, calling out, "Hold on a bit, I ain't got fingers enough; they've run out; got to start in on my toes. Well, it's no use; if she wouldn't have any o' them dudes, she ain't got no use for John."

A little later Von M—, K—, and W— arrived. The former was in a high state of indignation as he held out the retort belonging to the animatoscope and showed it with two big holes. "The most outrageous thing that ever happened! Just see how they have 'done you.' We had the animatoscope in perfect condition and were just ready to open the doors and take in hundreds of dollars, for every one in town is wild to see the war scenes and the Corbett fight. Crowds were asking when we should open up. We were trying it for the last time, when we suddenly discovered that the gas was leaking frightfully, and, upon examination, we saw the rottenness of this retort. A slight pressure of the hand and you could put your thumb right through it." The others were equally indignant that we should have been allowed to come this distance with such an article, and said, "That's just it. You were women, and they knew you were coming to the Klondike, from which you might never return, and so they didn't care. I hope you will write them up and fully advertise them for doing so dishonourable a thing."

MONDAY, SEPTEMBER 5TH ☞ While we were at breakfast, the invalid's partner came in saying, "He's almost gone, and he sent me to thank you ladies for all your kindness." "What can we do for him? We've been so busy for the last few days that we've scarcely had time to be of assistance." "Oh, but he's grateful and your air pillow was such a comfort to him and made his poor head so easy. There's nothing can be done now, unless you might have a little brandy to keep him on a bit longer.'" The stimulant was given instantly. "It's very dear here, and I wouldn't like to take it without paying for it, you've given him so much already." "Don't mention it; he's more than welcome to all that we have." And here the poor fellow broke down as he thought of his comrade's approaching end.

John rowed us over to town, Edith promising to go the following day, if I would only attend to the business once more. W— and Ivan accompanied me to the Oatley Sisters', where we found Von M— in despair. "It simply means a

124 fortune lost," he said; "not a soul in town can make a retort for love or money. It was a despicable act for your merchant to have started you off with such a thing as this, and you really ought either to bring a big suit against him or show him up so that no one will ever trust him again. Such a small saving to him means such enormous loss to us."

Next stopped at the office of the *Ora*, to arrange about passage. They promised to reserve the only cabin on board holding two bunks; no mattress, no bed linen, blankets, or furniture of any kind. It will be necessary to carry even our pillows with us. Price, one hundred and twenty dollars to Lake Bennett, and no food supplied. Meals, two dollars each. Steamer to sail on the fourteenth. "Can she surely make it as late as that, and not be shut in the ice?" I queried anxiously. "We think so," replied the agent. "Oh yes! Mrs. Hitchcock," said a man, raising his hat. "I went out early in October last year and there was only a thin sheet of ice through which we cut our way without difficulty." "But it is much colder this year everyone tells me, and the winter will begin earlier." "So they say, but there's not much doubt of your being able to make it. Don't you worry. Take all the blankets you can carry, though, and the warmest of wraps. You can sell them all at Bennett, and for better prices than here, as you won't want them after you reach civilisation again."

At last my good boatman Jones appeared, and glad I was to return once more to the quiet of West Dawson. Edith had a nice hot dinner all ready and promised to attend to the business the following day. In the midst of dinner the invalid's partner arrived, saying, "It's all over. Mr. Jones has been in and washed him and done everything that could be done for him, an' I've brought you back your pillow an' your chair, which he enjoyed so much; seems like they made him more comfortable than anything else," and his lip quivered. We saw that he was about to break down completely, so made him join us, insisted upon his taking food, and tried to divert his mind, but it was all in vain. "His wife's the nicest woman that ever walked the face of the earth, and here's his little girl—she's only ten years old, but there ain't a finer elocutionist in all Kansas." Here he opened a watch and showed us the picture of the fatherless child. "I want you to take care of this watch and chain," said he, handing them to me; "there ain't no one I'd rather trust than you two ladies, and if I don't go out, I want you to take these trinkets to her. It's goin' to be a terrible blow, coz last time he wrote he wuz in as good health as any of us. I can't write. I've hed many a partner in the past fifteen years but no one I thought so much of as him, an' in his mind there warn't no one like Jerry, an' all during his sickness he was the most uncomplainin' man you ever did see. I've been over to try and get him a coffin an' there wasn't one to be had for less than seventy dollars, an' that the most ordinary, common wood. At last, ez I wuz feelin' pretty discouraged, I met a fellow as wuz on the trail with us, an' when he heard the coffin was for poor —, sez he, 'You can take it for forty dollars, and that's just what it cost me,' an' it ain't got no handles neither." "I just been up with J— for to find a place where to bury him," said Jones; "we had to choose the new cemetery coz his is the first grave we've ever had on this side of the river." "Where can we have the service?" said the bereaved partner, looking around the Big Tent. "You might have this in a moment," we responded in answer to his glance, "but, as you see, the cabin is rapidly going up in front of our doorway and the stove is before the other entrance, so that there's no possible place of exit for an occasion of this kind." "You'd better have it right in his own tent," said Jones; "the parson can stay inside with him, and we can all remain outside," and thus it was arranged.

The poor fellow then talked of sitting up all night with the remains of his friend, but he was in no condition to do so and good Jones promised to do it himself or to secure someone else. His grief was great, and we tried to console him with the thought of the devotion he had shown in tender care and nursing. "Yes," said he. "I've done everything. I stopped work and run myself in debt to get him what he needed, and only last week, when someone offered me seven thousand dollars to go out and stake a claim on Dominion, I wuz a-goin' coz you ladies said you would take care o' him, but my heart failed me at the last moment, and I sez, 'No, I'll lose the seven thousand dollars rather than desert him,' an' I with only ten dollars left an' no grub. I wuz feelin' pretty down about it, but I never let on to him, and I thank the Lord now for it. He only had a little while when he could talk to me before he went, but he sez, 'I ain't a-goin' to tell you what to do, coz I know you'll do what's right,'" and here the poor fellow gave way again. "I want to thank you, Mr. Jones, for washin' him an' bein' so good to him, an' if you'd only cut a little lock of his hair for his wife. I can't do it. She expectin' him back hale and hearty as when he went away, and waiting for a letter, an' he under the ground when she gets it."

TUESDAY, SEPTEMBER 6TH ☛ One o'clock came, and I went to see if anything could be done for the departed neighbour before he should be laid away. Not a flower of any kind to be had. A little before two the clergyman arrived, but was told that the men had dug twice and, although high upon the hillside, had been unable to get below four feet, as they strike ice.

Just then the clergyman returned, saying it would take another hour to dig the grave. "I wonder who we can get to put him in his coffin," said his partner, the tears rolling down his cheeks. "We'll help you," said D—. "John and I'll do it." The hour passed, and a dozen of us stood in solemn silence before the door of the cabin in which the remains had been laid. A sled was brought out and on it was placed the coffin neatly covered with black cloth. Two ladies offered wildflowers which they had gathered on the hills, miles from Dawson. The grave diggers returned and joined the throng of mourners, as did my dozen workmen, whom I had told to stop work for the service. As we gathered around the box and sang, *Jesus, Lover of My Soul,* our voices faltered as we thought of the poor fellow who had left home, wife, and child, buoyed up with the hope of returning to provide them with comfort and luxury; of his weary tramp over the trail; of trials, vexations, and disappointments as illness came on, and funds became low, until the last days when he called for his loved ones who were far away. The service was most impressive, the silence broken by the sobs of the bereaved partner, and all eyes were filled with tears of sympathy. The ceremony ended by the broken voices taking up the strain, *Shall We Meet Beyond the River.* Heads were bowed for a blessing, and then the pallbearers took up their precious burden and carried it to its last resting place in the lonely grave on the hillside.

A short visit from J—, and then Edith returned and was greatly surprised to find that I, the lazy one, had washed all the dishes and laid the table for dinner with clean tablecloths (newspapers). Her trusty boatman, Jones, followed with a box of groceries, which he almost dropped as he caught sight of the table, saying, "Well, well, well! Who ever would 'a' thought them little fins o' hern could 'a' done all that." "Miss Van Buren is the only one for whom I would have done it; but I couldn't bear to think of her returning after a tiresome day and finding things in confusion. But before I forget it let me ask, Did you cut a lock of that poor fellow's hair before you left? For his partner is waiting to send it in a letter to his wife." Jones dropped. "Well, now, if that ain't awful! I clean forgot! Oh! I know"; and before we could divine what he intended to do he had seized the scissors and cut off one of his own curly locks. "She'll never know the difference," said he; "me and him had hair about the same colour, and if it ain't just the same, she'll think it changed up here, or after death." Horrified, Edith and I protested, but in vain. Jones was sometimes obstinate, and this was one of the occasions. The partner came in and received the precious treasure, while our lips were sealed. "What must I pay the grave diggers?" said he. "Oh, not much," Jones replied; "an' as for me, many's the corpse I've washed and dressed, an' never asked nothin' for such services yet, an' don't intend to begin now."

After dinner Edith related her experiences of the day. M— R— had selected over a hundred dollars' worth of goods from our boxes of groceries, D— had done the same, also G—, giving her checks which covered the entire amount we had paid for said articles in San Francisco, and leaving us still two-thirds of the stock. "What a pity we never thought to bring in brooms," said Edith.

"They are selling at seventeen dollars apiece in Dawson, the commonest kind, and very few to be had." She had disposed of a tin of evaporated tomatoes for seventeen dollars, when D— saw it and said, "You must let me have that. I've sent orders for them all over the country and never have had one filled since coming here. It makes my mouth water just to think of them. I'll take it right now and carry it home." "Can't do it," replied Edith; "it's sold." "Doesn't matter. You can say it was stolen," and off he walked with it, before her very eyes, calling back, "This stuff is too delicious to give up. I've been longing for it for ages." Listen to his punishment! That very evening, as he prepared his first dish, he found the tomatoes full of tiny white worms, and rushed into the Big Tent, exclaiming, "Well, if you oughtn't to give Goldberg and Bowen a piece of your mind! To think that you should be 'done' even by a firm like that." [Let me state here, however, that on our return to San Francisco, this same firm returned, not only the price we had paid for the tomatoes, but also the freight to Dawson.]

WEDNESDAY, SEPTEMBER 7TH 🙂 Hardly were we dressed when two men arrived, announcing themselves as grocers from Dawson who were just about to start in business. They wanted to purchase our entire stock of winter's supplies in that line, but finally asked if we would be willing to accept one hundred dollars down, and let them sell the remainder for ten percent commission. Edith promised to give them an answer after a day in town. Examining our lists carefully they offered cash for the entire lot of stationery. Next came the dead man's partner, saying that one of his friends was going home, and had offered to take the watch to the widow, whose address he gave, begging me to add my letter to his. A tremendous gale is blowing, shaking the tent to such a degree that its collapse or inflation seems imminent. The builders have come to tighten all the ropes. We are grateful for the sunshine and a temperature of seventy degrees, which allows the fire to be extinguished, as the stovepipe was long ago blown off.

25

A New Experience

THURSDAY, SEPTEMBER 8TH ☙ Thank the Lord for a warm day and sunshine. It takes a little from the dampness which strikes a chill to the marrow. Jones took Edith to town with Ivan, while I remained to fill a trunk with all the finery I had brought, expecting to dress daily for dinner; but life in the tent makes such garb an impossibility, and silken hose are not exactly appropriate in rubber boots or muck-a-lucks, which we now take off only at bedtime. Nothing but heavy flannel, such as one rarely wears at home, is comfortable. A skirt is decidedly in the way in gathering wood for the stove, washing dishes, cooking, etc. Edith has tried it on several occasions and has succeeded in burning three of them, consequently we put them on now only when we are on our way to town. So, as our merchants told us that they had many calls for finery and that it would pay us much better to leave all such articles here to be sold by them, asking ten percent commission, we gladly decided to rid ourselves of all that we do not need, and thus save fifteen cents a pound freight. Not until 6 PM was the list finished, the articles marked and packed, and the little eight-dollar steamer trunk labelled twenty-five dollars.

About two o'clock, as I saw how much there remained to be done, and looked at the kitchen with its unclean pots, pans, and kettles, I called George and asked him to find me a man to wash dishes and put the place in fine order. The assistant soon appeared and worked steadily for three hours at seventy-five cents an hour, and what a transformation I beheld! Everything shone as cooking utensils do at home, new tablecloths (newspapers) were on all the tables, etc. I complimented him, adding, "Your three hours will expire in five minutes, but come tomorrow and there will still be work for you." "Oh, I don't mind working overtime," he replied; "it 'most kills me to loaf, I get so lonesome." He continued to talk, telling me of a claim he had staked on Bonanza, which he went to the office to record. After having waited in line for ages, he finally reached the desk, but to his great disappointment was told to return in two or three days, as there was some surveying to be done.

At last Edith returned, saying, "I have some bad news for you; some of our things are missing, and the man who took all the stationery for two hundred and thirty-five dollars and paid me in gold dust, must have it back, as we haven't the things to deliver. Between the cheating of the people from whom we bought goods, the spoiling and detention of our boxes by the steamship companies, and the non-responsibility of the warehouse owners, it is enough to drive one crazy. The purchasers might have held us responsible for the missing articles, but they were awfully nice about it. They asked me to go with them to their new store and check off as they took the things out of the boxes, and see for myself just how they looked and what was missing; so round I went, sat in the rear of the shop with my back to the door, and checked off as fast as I could write. They were so delighted with the groceries that they wanted them all, and as they placed them on the shelves, the people, seeing luxuries such as have never before been brought here, commenced crowding in and wanting to buy, and I know they think the store belongs to you and me, as the boxes were marked with our names. A dear old lady said to me, 'Have you any sewing silk?' so I just said in my sweetest tones, 'Oh! I'm awfully sorry, but we haven't opened the box containing it yet. Couldn't you wait till tomorrow?' and she said, 'Certainly, dear.'"

"Those jars of orange marmalade that we bought at Goldberg's, three for sixty-seven cents, I had put aside to bring home, as we have none and that is all there is in town; well, a man came in and saw them and exclaimed, 'Orange marmalade! How fine! How much is it?' I said one dollar and fifty cents, and would you believe it, he took it instantly! Oh, it's such a lark! I never had so much fun in all my life; how I do wish that we could open a shop of our own. Won't you? I'll do it in a minute if you will, and we'll not only make our everlasting fortunes, but we'll have great fun besides!" "You'd just oughter 'a' seen her," said Jones, gazing at her admiringly; "I'll be durned if everyone in town didn't want to come and buy of her just for the honour of speaking to her."

"You should have seen how everyone admired Ivan," said Edith. "He is really the best-trained dog I have ever known—was not a bit of trouble, followed me everywhere, and I should not have known he was there, so unobtrusive was he." "Well, he ett with me," chimed in Jones. "Miss Van Buren she wouldn't, and so I said, 'Ivan, you want to go to the restaurant?' An' he never so much as looked at Miss Van Buren to say by your leave. He knowed that restaurant and how everybody stuffs and feeds him there, and he just made one dash for it, an' you never seen the likes o' it in all your life."

Miss Van Buren in travelling costume

Friday, September 9th ☞ At 4 PM as I was going over accounts, Von M— appeared in utter despair. "The man who sold you that animatoscope outfit ought really to be killed," said he. "After great expense and endless trials we have succeeded in getting a retort made that will do. Then I filled the bags with gas, but in one hour it had all gone, and I found, not only that the bags were leaking, but also that they had already been mended in several places, and if we use them we are liable to have an explosion. I can't imagine a man low enough to send two women this distance with such a rotten lot of stuff. Merchants seem to think that when they outfit you for the Klondike they can put upon you all the stuff that no one else will take and that they never will hear from you again. I hope you won't lose patience, for I'm working at the thing night and day, hoping my best to bring it out. A lot of my friends who were wild to see it and also to chaff me for running a show have all gone 'out.' That alone means hundreds of dollars, and the amount we are losing daily from men who would gladly pay a dollar or more to see the Corbett fight, is incalculable. I'm doing my very best, but as soon as we get one part straight another gives out." "Patience! You are the one who is showing that quality beyond all others," said I; "for you are devoting your entire time and attention to it, simply in the hope of what may come." So off the poor fellow went to continue his hard work against obstacles which should never have arisen.

At 6:30 Edith returned, the faithful Jones carrying meat and provisions. "How's the house gettin' on?" said John. "You don't know! Been a-writin' all day as usual, I suppose, but by Jove, everything does look nice and clean, and no mistake, though of course you didn't do it yourself." We went out to see George, who pointed out with great pride the solidity and substantial character of his work. "It's all arranged so's you can put another story on next year, if you want to, and here are some poles for the awning over your balcony." From the doorway a most glorious view was obtained of Dawson, the hills, and the full sweep of the Yukon River—a view from a second story would mean something not to be surpassed in Switzerland. The resemblance to Lucerne is great.

Saturday, September 10th ☞ Up at 6:30, and thankful for mercury at fifty degrees instead of forty.

Four o'clock, and Edith came in, looking ready to drop. "It's all off, all off," said she. "We've everything back on our hands again." I was alarmed and perplexed, and, fearing that something dreadful had occurred, questioned her anxiously concerning the result of her interview with the merchants. "Oh, I've had the most awful two hours of my life. Now that the grocers, M— and S—, have all our boxes there and all our things displayed, instead of giving us a thousand dollars down and good security, they want to send us out of the country without a penny; said they would be willing to sell on commission for us, but wouldn't put down a sou. They know we are leaving on Wednesday, that we have not the time to do all our own packing, collect our goods (which make a fine show on their shelves) from them, and transfer them to someone else; they have heard we are building a house which is to cost several times more than we were led to believe; that we have grub-staked men liberally, and spent so much ready cash that they think they have us in a tight place and are taking advantage of it. M— said, 'I will not give you one penny down and no security of any kind, and would rather you would take your goods away.'"

"That was because she intimated that she could not trust him to render a true accounting," interrupted Jones, "and you can't talk to men like that in this part of the world." "I beg your pardon, Mr. Jones," said Edith in her most dignified manner, which completely crushed poor John; "I said it would not be business-like to trust them without security, nor would it." The talk continued for some time until finally I said, "You are perfectly fine at business, but you are tired now and this, naturally, has upset you; shall I see what I can do?" "You can't do a thing with them," cried Edith. "Yes, do go," said John; "coz she was so excited, she wouldn't let them talk and say what they would do. You'll see they wants to do wot's right an' the likes o' that, only they got hot, and didn't care then what they said." "Here I've wasted a whole week, and when I told M— that his partner S— had offered me five hundred dollars down only yesterday, he said he didn't believe it. I simply opened the door and said, 'Will you come here a moment, Mr. S—? Did you not ask me yesterday if I would accept five hundred dollars?' 'I did, Miss Van Buren,' he replied. M— was furious, but could not go back of that; so the situation now is five hundred dollars down, which M— doesn't want to give, or selling our goods on commission of ten percent and no security of any kind. That doesn't seem right or business-like to me, and I don't see how we can safely trust them with our goods."

"Do come an' see what you can do with 'em, Mrs. Hitchcock," said John. "I'll row you across now—I think they'll come round all right when they've cooled down. They're friends o' mine, an' I introduced them to yer so as to do all I could to help yer, but if you come back next year I'll never introduce a livin' soul, not even if you never has nobody to speak to," and Jones looked also as though he had lost his last friend.

"Don't be discouraged, Edith," said I, ready to start; "I'll arrange something."

While crossing the Yukon Jones said he thought that Edith had taken offence where none was intended, and hurt the *amour propre* of the two men. In a few moments we had reached the store. Jones then said, "Mr. S—, I've brought the partner of Miss Van Buren, who has come to have a fuss with you." "Oh, I hope not," said Mr. S—, with a sigh. Mr. M— asked me into the office, and I asked him to lay all the facts before me. In a quiet, dignified manner he explained that as a commission merchant he thought that five hundred dollars down was sufficient guarantee of good faith, and that his books would be open weekly to the inspection of our agent, to whom he would pay over all monies; but that, owing to some expression of doubt as to his good faith he had requested Edith to remove her goods, preferring to fill his shelves with other articles of his own, from which he would obtain much more profit than the ten percent commission. As for security, he could give references from reliable persons here and on the outside if we wished, and should be glad to keep our goods on these terms if we saw fit to accept them. After thoroughly discussing the matter, I promised to give a decision the following day, and was referred to Colonel K—.

I went to his office, but he was not in. I waited for a short talk with the gold weigher, who had been very kind to us, and asked his advice. "Commission merchants are not supposed to give security," said he, "particularly in this town where money brings ten percent a month, and I think their offer of five hundred dollars, with a decision to report to your agent weekly, a very good one." Colonel K— returned, greeted me most cordially, and said, "I'm very glad to meet you, Mrs. Hitchcock and have long wanted to know you, but am the busiest man in Dawson, with never a moment to myself night or day. What can I do for you?" He listened carefully to my case and said, "I think, if you have your own agent to collect weekly, that M— and S— might do very well by you, and I'll be very glad to superintend or do anything in my power." With such advice from so responsible a man my mind was relieved, and I went down quite content to wait on the platform of the Alaska Commercial Company for Jones.

Good, kind Jones here made his appearance to row me back. "Well, did yer fix it?" said he, as soon as we were floating down the Yukon, with Monsieur L—, the brewer, as passenger. "I hoped yer would. It don't do no good to lay down the law to them people up here; they won't stand it." Von M— spent the evening. Said the animatoscope was working beautifully, except for the leak in the bags, which could not be discovered. He had engaged a man who thoroughly understood acetylene lights at two dollars an hour, and they were to practise at one o'clock the following day.

SUNDAY, SEPTEMBER 11TH &- Our watches and clock were not wound last night, so excited were we over the events of the day; consequently there was no way of telling the time. I had written several pages, and Edith had the breakfast almost ready, when, glancing at one of the watches, she exclaimed,

134   "Why, it's going! And it's only half after four! Well, if that's not a good joke on us! I thought it strange that I did not feel hungry, and it's as silent as the grave; even the dogs are quiet after a hard night of barking." Shortly after came the sound of a gong from one of the river steamers at Dawson. "That may mean anything from six to seven," continued Edith.

10:30. Jones sleepily appears, only to hear that we have no wood and have not been able to hire anyone to fetch us some, as there have been no passersby. He kindly skirmished about West Dawson, but not a man would chop fuel on Sunday.

It was quite eleven before I could reach Dawson to keep my appointment with M— and S—. "Only an hour late," said they, as I entered the little establishment to check off the goods on the only day when we could not be interrupted by customers. We worked steadily until one, when Mr. M— invited me to the restaurant opposite for luncheon. The cheapest thing on the bill of fare was "lamb chops, one dollar and fifty cents." This I immediately selected. It was served with very good bread, butter, and pickles. M— told me of many interesting experiences in Alaska. After luncheon I finished checking off the list of "personal effects" that I did not wish to take back. M— had written them all down, and the sum amounted to between seven and eight hundred dollars. "Well, I guess I won't get married," said he, "if ladies have to travel with so much stuff that they don't want, besides all the beautiful things that you ladies are taking back."

Von M— escorted me down to the waterfront, where I met C—, who inquired if the bowling alley had yet been disposed of and, if not, whether he could get at it after our departure in case he should find a good customer, his intention being to try and float a small company with the idea of gaining a ten percent commission on its sale.

Before pushing off, a man, catching sight of Ivan, said, "What a beauty! I say, partner, I'll give you five dollars spot cash for that dog." "Don't you think four would be quite enough?" retorted Von M—. "Oh, you're joshing; but honour bright, I'll give you seventy-five dollars," he shouted, as we got farther away from the shore. To relieve his mind, I called out, "A thousand down would not buy him; he'll earn that in prizes next year, and be known as the great Klondike traveller." We were soon at the tent, where Edith had been holding a reception the entire day, every one of our Dawson friends and acquaintances having turned up. Nevertheless she had a dinner of corned beef, potato balls, and asparagus salad prepared.

Von M— and Edith washed dishes, and, as we gathered around the stove for pleasant converse, a sudden gale of wind sprang up, shaking the tent as a dog would a rag. In a few minutes shelves were all thrown down with a crash. Fortunately, that very day the glass had all been removed. The tent next became inflated, and was raised so high that all the side poles were lifted out; papers whirled about; the stovepipe bowed first in one direction, then in another. Edith looked outside and said, "It's a hurricane sky, as black as ink; the tent will surely fall tonight, and I don't want to remain. Oh! If those men had only sent the lumber as agreed, we should now be under a solid roof." Good John came to the rescue again. "Take my tent, ladies, I'm going to sleep over in town tonight any way, an' you might, just as well as not. It ain't for the likes o' you to be skeered all night when John's got a nice little tent as tight as a drum, what no gale can harm." Edith was decidedly inclined to accept this offer, saying, "We'll be crushed to death if this does come down, and you'll be responsible." But the workmen had assured me that, although the tent had been badly put up, at the same time there were so many ropes and they were so tightly fastened that we had no real cause for alarm. Towards midnight the gale abated, our fears were quieted, and we crawled into our smaller habitation and slept the sleep of the just.

MONDAY, SEPTEMBER 12TH ☞ Up at 5:30. Wrote steadily for two hours. At 9 AM Jones arrived, saying, "Unless you ladies want the frost to draw the nails out and the rain and snow to leak through your house, you'll have to buy some tar paper to put between the lumber and the slabs. It's an awful price, but it's the only thing to do; only costs three dollars a roll in the States, but there's a corner on it here and so it is selling for thirty dollars each, and almost impossible to get at that." George came to confirm this statement as to the absolute necessity of this extra expense, saying that had the lumber and slabs been according to order it would have been all right, but, owing to the fact that a different lot had been sent, tar paper must go in; that perhaps a roll and a half might do, which Jones hoped to get for forty-five dollars. Extra nails, door, hinges, and hasps were also wanted at once, so over I went with Jones to the North American Transportation Company to cash a check for one hundred dollars. Only ninety-five dollars was handed me in return. "What does this mean?" "Five dollars for commission; that's what we have to pay at the bank." "Very well, then, you may close my account at once. I refused to go to the other company because they charged me two dollars and fifty cents a hundred on notes that would be sold at a premium to miners going home who cannot carry so much gold dust, and opened an account here owing to the fact that you cashed at par." "Well," said the clerk, "we will do so this time, but hereafter must charge the percentage." Jones was then given seventy dollars with which to purchase the necessary articles, and went off on another mission, for which as usual he would accept nothing but thanks.

The work ended, I went to pay Mr. W— for the lumber with which our house was built, but his office was closed and padlocked. On my way back through Main Street, I stopped to inquire of real estate men if there was any demand for houses in West Dawson. They said that there was none, but that they were ready and willing to take charge of the cabin at once, and see what could be done. Met Mr. W— talking to our consul, and stopped to tell him that as we were going out on Wednesday, I must pay dues "then or never." "I'll go back with you," said he. "Tell him, Mr. Consul, please, that although I do live in the 'Big Tent,' which has created an erroneous impression in the minds of the people here, that I am only a poor widow, and must not be imposed upon." "On the contrary," said M—, "widows are dangerous, and should be doubly taxed."

Mr. W— then escorted me to the office, and made out the forms, which I signed on four different papers, paying thirteen dollars. On handing me the receipt, he said, "The government has decided to recognise 'squatters' rights' in 'Dawson Annex,' so this bit of paper shows that you have paid your dues, and prevents your land from being jumped."

"So it is not 'West Dawson,' but 'Dawson Annex?'" questioned I. "That's the official name for it," he replied.

Back to M— and S— I went, only to learn that Von M— had called for me and concluded that someone else must have rowed me across the river. Down to the usual rendezvous, to see if perchance good Jones might be there. Not a sign of him, and six o'clock struck. A long day from 5:30 AM.

After waiting half an hour Neighbour E— passed on his way home, and kindly rowed me over. He spent the evening, while a few of our neighbours "looked in" long enough to exchange a yarn or two. "Here's the first letter I've received for months," said one, and before reading it aloud he made the following explanation: "You see, I struck it pretty rich last year, and a reporter happening to meet me when I came back from one of my mines on Dominion with a big bag of nuggets, took a snapshot and wrote me up. The picture and the story found their way up into a corner of New England where I used to live, and the next mail from there into Dawson brought me letters by the dozen from people I'd never seen or heard of, but who'd all developed an enormous lot of friendship for, and interest in me, since hearing that I'd probably struck millions. The only one I answered was from a young girl who wanted me to look out for her brother, and here's what she says in reply:"

My dear Sir: Your kind and much appreciated letter came to hand several days ago. It may surprise you to hear that my brother returned home, after getting as far as Lake Linderman. He, with many others, lost his outfit and all provisions and turned homeward, reaching here about —. His tales concerning the Klondike were thrilling indeed and we are heartily glad to have him return with good health. He brought with him a handful of nuggets and a ring which is quite a curiosity. These he will keep to remind him of those miserable days. I can never thank you enough for the kindness you show in your letter. I feel assured that you would have done anything in your power for my brother, and in return, let me say that if I can in any way return the kindness, I shall be happy to do so. Though poor in this world's goods, we should rather have brother at home with us than running such risks. I have no sweetheart to go to the gold mines. As you say of yourself I have never been a favourite, but that does not make me miserable. I have my father and mother to think of, and their comfort ought to be considered. You see my brother did not have very much "New England grit," or he would have pushed on while so near. Now with many, many thanks, for the kindly and generous manner with which you have treated me, I am ever your true friend, D— J—.

P. S. Many wishes for good health and success.

The reader of this epistle was so unmercifully chaffed that the party soon broke up. Edith then confided to me that when Jones took her across he had as passenger the bartender of C—'s saloon, who said, "I ain't seen the parrot for a day or two. It made such a lot o' noise that I kinder miss it. What's become of it?" "Why, it died the first day it went over," responded Jones. "Not much," said the barkeeper. "I tell you it did," said Jones, "the very first day, as I told these ladies."

"Well, it's a pretty lively bird for a dead bird, then," said the barkeeper. After he left Jones said, "That there barkeeper was just a-joshin' yer ter try and make you hot." What is the mystery?

In the New Home at Last

TUESDAY, SEPTEMBER 13TH ❧ Edith was rowed across by Jones early in the morning. She was to finish lists and attend to commissions; I to remain and do the packing. At noon, George brought five men in to be paid off and laid off. One was paid a dollar too much, and not having the change offered to work it out in chores, an offer gladly accepted. He got some kindlings, but when we asked him to clean and hang up some pans, he said he wasn't accustomed to such work and couldn't do it. "Neither are we accustomed to it." "Well, it's woman's work, anyhow." "Won't you clean this coat outside for me, then? It's too heavy for me to brush." "I don't know as I care to do that, either," said he, stepping outside the tent; "when you want wood chopped you can send for me."

At two o'clock George announced that he could give me a couple of men to lend a hand at moving into the house if I were ready. In one corner in the back of the house we placed the stove, put up shelves, I driving in nails, having plenty of them for the first time. In another corner was an enormous supply of wood, all the ends left from the house, and shavings. The two other corners were reserved for our beds, which were boards, placed on four short logs of wood, covered by canvas tightly stretched, our hammocks were laid on top of that, then our air mattresses minus the air. Blankets and comfortables were covered by the fur robes so kindly loaned by Mr. L—, and by the one recently purchased for one hundred and thirty-five dollars, for which a generous man has just offered me seventy-five dollars.

At 5 PM everything was in order, and I enjoyed receiving my first visitors, Von M— and W—, who brought me fine news—that the animatoscope had been tried and was running so perfectly that they thought of giving an exhibition the following day. But their hopes were again dashed when they discovered another serious obstacle, viz., that the one hundred pounds of carbide for generating the gas, and for which we hold the receipts from the Johnson-Locke Company, have never arrived. This necessitates the purchase of the only fifty pounds of carbide in town at a price twenty times higher than that which we paid in San Francisco. Their next information was that "Arizona Charlie's" show had shut down again, as he could get no more 86° gasoline.

It was after seven when Edith returned in high spirits, after a most successful day. She was delighted with the house, the arrangements, and everything in general. Many heads stopped at the door to see the largest house in Dawson Annex. Many compliments were passed and we were feeling most happy over the change until Jones came with a bill for lumber almost one hundred dollars greater than the price contracted for. We became decidedly annoyed over the discussion that followed. Jones declared that lumber at one hundred and twenty-five dollars a thousand was marvellously cheap, and that we had all that the bill called for; we, on the other hand, could not understand why the lumber merchant had failed to keep to his contract. Jones said that he had sent much extra wood that was not included in the bargain, while George declared that it was not extra, but short. Jones concluded that there was no pleasure in doing favours and commissions for two such ladies, who thought more of twenty dollars "than a poor man like me of a hundred."

═══ Our new house finished at last ═══

Von M— came back from Dawson quite elated at the thought of the speedy opening of the show and pleased with his aristocratic staff of assistants to which is now added R—, of Victoria, B.C. Mrs. T— looked in to say, "You are never intending to sleep in this damp cabin tonight!" "Damp! Why we've taken off rubber boots and muck-a-lucks for the first time, and are now enjoying shoes and a floor, instead of sinking in muddy ground." How we did enjoy our beds!

Wednesday, September 14th ☞ Such a splendid night's rest! It was nearly seven when I got up, quickly dressed, and opened the door facing the Yukon River, as the windowless mansion was in total darkness. What a glorious view! The sun was just peeping through the mist that covered the mountains.

Two steamers have left this morning, of which I have taken views while wondering whether their passengers will reach the outside or be shut in by the ice. Quite a gale is blowing, and my soul is filled with gratitude at being under this solid roof instead of in the Big Tent. Several neighbours called to admire the new house, which they said could easily swallow any four of the cabins of Dawson Annex. Towards dusk a young man approached the door saying, "Have you any bread for sale?" "Not this evening," I replied. On seeing my quizzical look, he took off his hat, saying, "This house is so big I thought it must be a store, excuse me for the mistake."

Jones has been feeling sore for some time, and speaking of Big Alex, said, "I told him Miss Van Buren said me and him wasn't no gentlemen for coming two hours late to dinner. I think you're both o' you grand ladies givin' us the laugh anyway, an' don't believe you'd recognise us on the 'outside' even at a dog fight; anyway, you've learned a lot o' Klondike expressions an' knows how to talk language that me an' Alex understand, and don't put on no airs, nor talk highfalutin' like them there dudes o' yourn. By gosh! Wouldn't I like to be at a dinner in New York and hear Mrs. Hitchcock say to Miss Van Buren, 'You bet,' and hear Miss Van Buren call back, 'That's what.' I guess the folks would all drop their knives and forks and stare at you both like you was crazy." Edith brought some lamb chops, and that with potatoes constituted our dinner. As we were at table a neighbour called with his wife. They pictured the horrors of the Chilkoot in such a way that we shuddered and began to think of trying the White Pass instead. We were awakened at eleven by a knock at the door, then a voice called out, "Oh, I beg your pardon, have you already retired? Just came to report about the show; the advertisement across the street worked beautifully and attracted hundreds and thousands. Will tell you all about it in the morning. Goodnight."

Thursday, September 15th ☞ Opened the front and only door at half after six. Such a glorious day! The sun already shining on the beautiful hills opposite, dressed in yellow autumn garb. Edith then told me of her trip to the steamship office the previous day, where she had been able to change the cabins from the *Ora* to the *Columbian*, as it would have been impossible for us to be ready in time for the former, but when she visited the *Ora*, and saw C—, F—, M—, K—, and others all going out and informed them of our change of plans, their regrets were loud and long, as they said they had arranged such a charming party to go over the Pass together. Pass goes in capital letters as we have not yet crossed it and treat it with great respect and awe even in writing. Edith also told me of having disposed of the soda machine, until the purchaser found that the man who sold it had failed to enclose directions as promised, so that the deal was off and the article left on our hands.

Von M— appeared at 9:30 most enthusiastic over the show of the previous evening. He is now to employ his evenings, from eight to eleven, throwing advertisements on a sheet across the Main Street, he to have fifty percent of the profits, the man who makes the slides twenty-five, while twenty-five percent is to be divided between Edith and me for furnishing the machine and light; so we felt very proud of having introduced a novelty into Dawson. Von M— explained that they first threw artistic pictures until they had a large crowd gathered together, then advertised the animatoscope with the Corbett fight to take place the following day: "Go and see the Corbett fight," etc., etc., and wound up by saying, "Those who wish to advertise may leave orders at the Oatley Sisters.'" After the show was over, they were delighted to learn that many had made inquiries in regard to subscribing. We purchased in San Francisco one hundred pounds of carbide with which to run the acetylene light that illuminates this show, but although we have the receipt from the *Tillamook* or Johnson-Locke Company, and their promise that it should be sent by the first boat up the river, the barrel was left at St. Michaels and we are paying one dollar a pound for that which cost seven cents in California. The experience, however, is valuable, though costly, and we shall know what to do next time.

I locked the cabin and went with George to select a site for the new house. We went on the hill, questioned the neighbours as to where the land had been staked out, and where the street would probably run, and took 50 x 100 on a small elevation quite close to the creek. There I left George building the cache and returned to my journal. Dave soon came to see if he could assist me. He chopped wood and brought water, then was paid eighty-odd dollars for his twelve days' work, and said goodbye, as he was going up "to work for wages" on Bonanza this winter. As he wished me a safe trip home, he said, "In going out, I hope you won't have luck like ours, for when we came in we first struck a rock, and then an iceberg, after which the captain told us for to get out the lifeboats, as we hadn't much time, as the ship was about to sink, an' then, would you believe it, I missed that landslide just as narrowly as I missed the shipwreck, an' my family in Los Angeles knowing nothing about it. I dunno what my wife would say to see me up here washing dishes for two ladies and doing kitchen work, when she thinks I'm panning out nuggets and coming back with millions."

Jones has not yet made his appearance and it is now after one. "Our show" is to commence at two o'clock. Edith is going, but it would make me nervous if things went wrong. "Arizona Charlie's" show has shut down, not to reopen, and he has applied to Von M— to take up his contract at the Combination Theatre, as he finds it impossible to continue without gasoline. Another neighbour has just called to tell me that he is to build between two cabins as the commissioners say cabins can be five feet apart. Am thankful that there is no room on either side of our big house for more than a garden. A man who has an invalid wife at home and is wild to get to her, called to offer me a half interest in his richest claim for two hundred dollars—just the amount necessary to reach home, as he has no other way of raising it. Another neighbour stopped to tell me that he had a fine chance of buying a claim from a man just sent to the hospital. What opportunities for magnificent investments, besides ten percent a month on all money lent on A1 securities! Still another neighbour stopped to say that Mr. O— has promised to pay a visit to "Dawson Annex" on either Saturday or Monday to take the lay of the land preparatory to a survey.

Edith refused invitations to dinner and returned shortly after seven, Jones rowing her back and remaining to dine and wash dishes. After dinner Mr. S— and Mr. F— of the Alaska Commercial Company spent the evening, bringing the unheard-of luxury of a box of chocolates. Just as he left, Von M— rushed in, saying, "The animatoscope is such a success that the manager of the Combination Company wants to hire it, and has sent to know our terms, and as for the magic lantern show in the street, we have three advertisements already at thirty dollars a week each, and are likely to have so many more that we shall probably soon be able to advance the price." Well-deserved success for Von M— after so much hard work!

FRIDAY, SEPTEMBER 16TH ☞ My turn to do commissions in Dawson today. Von M— rowed me across, Jones carrying my packages to the boat. My first trip was to the Alaska Commercial Company, as a Mr. Q— had expressed a desire for my beautiful fur robe. Knowing that I was so soon to leave, could not take it out with me, and had no other opportunity for disposing of it, he made me an offer of one hundred dollars, though aware that it cost one hundred and thirty-five, and that its mate had been sold for two hundred and fifty. To M— and S—'s, where the latter said, "Oh, Mrs. Hitchcock, you are just in time; there's a lady in the little room who's going wild over the pretty things you and Miss Van Buren are leaving here. I couldn't show them or explain to her satisfaction; would you mind seeing her?" In I went and found "playing saleslady" so amusing and pleasant that I disposed of eighty dollars' worth in half an hour. Back to W—'s office, where, finding that I could not sign for Edith I was obliged to put in an application for the lot on which our house now stands, and proud I was to learn that my name heads the list and my receipt is number one in the Dawson Annex or West Dawson book. "Land will be very valuable there next year," said the Crown Agent, "as Dawson is crowded, and filled with typhoid fever and dysentery, so that those who can get no land here, or who wish better sanitary arrangements will turn to the other side."

On leaving the office, Captain B— joined me, presenting two other officials, who posed before the government quarters in compliance with my request. Met Mr. W— just returning from his claim on Bear Creek which adjoins mine. He stopped and triumphantly displayed some of the most beautiful gold I have ever seen, which he obtained at a depth of only two feet. From that time on, applications for a "lay" on our claims began to come in, until it is now *embarras de richesses*. W— said, as he left, "I'm sure of one thing, and that is, there's enough gold in my Bear Creek claim to keep my family in luxury for the remainder of their lives." Passing M— and S—'s store again, they begged me to come in and see two ladies who were anxious to get some of our fine laces, so in I went and explained and showed to their heart's content. After they had decked themselves in our laces and ribbons and flowers, etc., I said, "Have you ever tasted any of Van Camp's tomato soup? It's the most delicious thing we brought in." "Oh, we must try it then, if you think so," and presently their order ran up into the hundreds and our commission merchants wanted to engage me as well as Edith for a partner. I found it quite as much of a lark as she had done.

A storm was brewing, and we gained the shore just as the gale sprang up in all its force and tried to blow the canoe out to sea. Von M— and Jones dined with us. We were thankful at being out of the tent and in high and dry quarters, as the floodgates were let loose and the rain came down in such torrents that it seemed as though Biblical history were about to repeat itself and we to be prisoners in the ark. We gathered around the table to read the latest paper from

Seattle, dated August 26th, which I had been induced to buy for fifty cents, as the young rascal who was selling them like hot cakes had called out, "War still going on in the United States. War begun between England and Roosh-er."

SATURDAY, SEPTEMBER 17TH ☞ Jones and I are decidedly at cross-purposes. He does not like my "dude" friends and "haughty" ways, and is becoming very sulky to me while still devoted to Edith. There was no water in the bucket, and the spring is a block off. I spoke of it once or twice to Edith but Jones made no move to get any. I took the bucket and started for the spring; he never moved, and allowed me to go. He looked very sullen when I returned, and soon after disappeared. Edith said, "I told him he ought to be ashamed of himself," to which he replied, "Well, she's nicer to them there dudes an' the likes o' that than she is to me, and if she wants me to do anything for her she's just got ter ask me."

Edith left at ten to be rowed across the river by Jones. I had just begun to wash the breakfast dishes when she entered, dripping. "Fell into the Yukon and was up to my neck when Jones pulled me out." "Don't stop to talk, but come to the fire and get into dry clothing as soon as possible," said I, hastily preparing a hot drink and warm flannels. "The rock from which I stepped was very slippery, and as I was about to get into the canoe I lost my footing and was in the Yukon before I could realise what had happened. Had Jones not caught my hand I should have been carried down by the current; even as it was, it seemed an impossibility for him to lift such a weight as mine into the canoe, which tipped as he leaned over. I could get no hold on the rock, so simply threw myself on my back to float, and that was the only thing that saved me. How I got on shore is a mystery to me, for you know the river is very deep there. I did not think of myself at all, but only of what a terrible thing it would be for you to go home and tell my mother of my drowning. Oh, but the water was cold!" An hour after, Edith had quite recovered and insisted upon carrying out her original plan of rowing to Dawson, leaving me to finish packing. She is in for another ducking, unfortunately, as the rain is now coming down "in sheets."

Jones then arrived, saying, "Miss Van Buren has just sent this bag to you, and says, will you sell one of your hats, as you are 'going out' where you can get plenty, an' the likes o' that, and some ladies over in town ain't got none and wants to have one o' yours." Five minutes after, my two city hats were packed and Jones was taking them down to his canoe. Jones also told me that the *Columbian* is not in yet, and should she come tonight she cannot leave before Monday or Tuesday, which is rather alarming, as yesterday we had the first frost and the ice is ready to form at any moment. What should we do if shut in for

the winter? Just then we heard a loud whistle and blowing off of steam, and a
steamer passed. "What is her name? She's flying the British flag."

"The *Domville*, I think," and down to the bank I rushed. Twilight was coming
on, but glad indeed was I to see *Columbian* in big letters, which means that
by this time next week we shall be well on our way towards home and friends
once more.

Edith returned at six after a most unsuccessful day. Her bath in the Yukon
had delayed her so that she was too late for her appointments. She had found
the streets too slippery and muddy for words, and said that she might just as
well have remained at home. Jones chopped wood, brought water, cleaned the
fish, washed the dishes, and made himself so helpful that I forgave him for let-
ting me get the pail of water in the morning, and pretended to have forgotten it.
I also bound up his finger when he cut it during the wood chopping. We were
all tired, so he left at nine in such a rainstorm that, feeling certain no one would
venture out, we retired early.

Sunday, September 18th ☞ We slept soundly until after six when, by
the dim light of the candle, I saw a mouse running across my bed and into
the blankets. There was no stopping then to yawn or to turn over for an extra
snooze. Out of bed I bounded with a shriek that must have aroused every
neighbour, while Edith shouted with laughter, saying, "How can you be afraid
of a dear little thing like that? It seems impossible." After dressing, on opening
the door, the first sight that met my eyes was the mountain opposite covered
with snow. Our hearts sank. What will it be on the summit? What shall we do?
We never can cross with a light snow hiding the bad places, and not sufficiently
packed for a sled. And we both marvelled at our daring to wait until so late in
the season. The rain was still pouring down, everything muddy and slippery,
and only a little wood remaining that was fit to burn, although many cords are
stacked in one corner of the house, but they are too green for this year's use.
Not a man in sight who could be hired. All our kind neighbours would gladly
work as a favour, but this pride forbids our asking.

"Jones says he'll never cut another stick for you nor bring you a drop of water
unless you ask him; that you're 'that haughty to him now you treat him like the
dirt beneath your feet.'" At this moment he entered, and Edith said, "We are
almost frozen to death." "That so? Well, I ain't goin' to have it said that two ladies
froze to death while John was here to make a fire for 'em an' the likes o' that,"
and with these words he took the green wood and wielded the axe with such
force that he soon had the stove filled with shavings and small bits that crack-
led and warmed that corner most beautifully; then we had to choose between

two evils, keeping warm and sitting where it was too dark to read or write, or remaining near the door through which came our only light and being too cold to hold the pen.

Jones finished chopping, eyed the wood and said, "Well, Miss Van Buren, if I'm to row you over to town at ten o'clock, I think there's enough wood to keep you warm until then, an' I'm glad to have chopped it for yer, coz yer asked me so perlite like," and he seated himself on a box and looked at me maliciously as much as to say, "an' if you don't do the same, yer kin stay here an' freeze to death." I went several times to the door to see if there might be a passerby who could be hired, but although the rain had at last ceased no one was in sight. Finally, as Edith's preparations for town were almost completed, I humbly said, "I'm sorry to trouble you, Mr. Jones, but would you be so kind as to chop enough wood to keep the fire until Miss Van Buren's return?" "Certainly, with great pleasure," said John, as he caught the axe and swung it high in air and rapidly packed the wood, as one having had years of experience.

"You'd oughter 'a' seen Miss Van Buren yesterday morning though, Mrs. Hitchcock," said Jones suddenly; "if it'd been you, you'd 'a' drowned sure; but she never said a word and never shrieked as you'd 'a' done, nor clutched at the canoe to tip it over. She didn't lose her head a little bit, but when I reached her, she just kep' a-holt o' my hand and turned over on her back and floated without making any fuss at all. And then you oughter 'a' seen the clever way in which she gradually worked one foot into the canoe quiet-like, and that too with the Yukon thirty feet deep right where she was. I didn't know for a minit what I should do. I knowed I couldn't get no grip only holding her by the hand, and that I must get her arms, so I dropped her hand sudden-like and caught her right under the arms, where I cud lift her good, an' you know she ain't no light weight, so it shows how strong I am, to 'a' been able to 'ave saved her," concluded Jones proudly.

"What's this?" exclaimed Edith, as she raised a cover from a saucepan, "and this?" raising another, "and this?" looking at a platter containing a white pyramid. Meekly I confessed, "I wanted to cook something before your return, so thought I'd try a risotto. I filled a saucepan with rice, covered the rice with water, and while writing happened to glance up to find the rice swelling so fast that the overflow filled that first pan; a few moments later, it did the same thing again, and so I had to fill one dish after another until there was nothing left to put the surplus in, and the remainder in the bottom was cooked to death and there was no multitude to be fed, for even the Siwash dogs refused to eat it." "Why, that's just like the miracle what I heard about in church one time when I was a kid," said Jones; "only them was bread an' fishes." Edith said she had once

read of someone's having a similar rice-cooking experience, but thought it a **147**
fable, never dreaming that anyone could be such a "ninny." She begged me to
leave the culinary department to her for the remainder of our stay.

W— then appeared, saying, "Well, ladies, I've something pretty to show
you," as he carefully unfolded a paper and showed us another lot of gold from
his claim which adjoins ours on Bear Creek. "Oh, how beautiful! Won't you sell
me just a little of it to take home?" "Would you say it came from your claim?"
"Certainly not," I replied in righteous indignation. "I have not lived here long
enough to have learned to tell Yukon lies, and shall only represent absolute
facts." "Well, if I don't go out on the *Columbian* tomorrow to sell my claim, I'll
present you with this," replied W—, "because I can go back there and get plenty
more. I saw a lady up there yesterday who pulled out a poor fellow's stakes and
put hers in, and when I told her he might call me for a witness, she said, 'Well,
he hadn't oughter 'a' staked here when he knew I was a-comin'; he only got two
hours ahead o' me an' that don't count.'"

Edith finally started for Dawson to get the steamer tickets. Sunday or no
Sunday, it had to be done, as they refused to sell them before the arrival of
the boat.

A sudden booming as of hundreds of rifles. The dogs run in all directions.
Ivan comes and seeks protection at my side. Bang! Bang! Bang! I go to the door
to discover the cause of all this commotion in Dawson and see an enormous
flock of wild geese flying across the town. Not one seems to fall; they are high
in air; but Dawson covers a long extent of ground, the geese do not change their
course, and the shots continue for some time. "Don't believe they've hit a single
one," calls out a neighbour. He joins me as we walk down to the waterfront to
see the result, when down comes the rain again and we rush back to cover.

"What you goin' to do with your mandolin? I wouldn't mind taking care
o' it myself till you come back. Dunno how to play, but I might learn long
winter evenings." "No one ever had a better lot of neighbours," said I. "They're
all making such kind offers. One is willing to take care of my beautiful dog,
another of my fur robe, still another of my zither, and even half a dozen have
offered to live in and protect the house for us during our absence." "Well?" said
the man, grinning expectantly. "So we have talked it over and decided that we
cannot impose upon such kindness and good nature and have appointed an
agent who will devote his entire time to caring for our interests, as this property
will be valuable next year. Already every lot on the waterfront has been taken,
and even on the hill very few bits of land remain, so what will it be next year,
should there be another influx? In Dawson, cabins of one and two rooms rent
for from one hundred to five hundred dollars a month, so a house with four

148   rooms and a wide mess hall should bring a handsome rental, particularly as it will soon be too cold for the hundreds who are now living in tents to occupy them much longer."

Mr. T— next appeared with a beautiful big fish cleaned and prepared for cooking. "Won't you and Miss Van Buren accept this for your dinner?" "How very kind! Just what we were wishing for, and not a shop open in Dawson!" said I. "Won't you please deliver a letter in person to my dear old mother? It would be such a gratification for her to see someone who can give her particulars impossible to write." And upon receiving my promise to look up the mother immediately upon arrival, and taking a last look at the sparkling, crackling fire, he left to attend to the haul of hundreds of fish from his net, which he intends to dry and keep for the winter's dog food. And thus is the time frequently passed instead of in the alluring search for gold with pick and shovel. Next visitor, Colonel Q— who said that he had come all the way down from Bonanza to bid us goodbye and asked if we had finished all that we had to do before starting. "Yes, we've given 'lays' on all our claims except the Bear Creek, and shall sign papers tomorrow for that." "Bear Creek! Why, that's the coming El Dorado! Why Big Alex has bought all around there, which shows what it must be. Don't give the lay to any ordinary miner. Let me put my men on both claims—yours and Miss Van Buren's, for this year's work; unprospected as they are, I'll gladly take an option on them for fifteen thousand dollars each for only half-interest, and will pay you in the spring out of my part of the pannings. I can show you all sorts of references from people whom you probably know, and letters from the syndicate that is backing me." After some further conversation on the subject, I promised to talk it over with Edith, Colonel Q— to come in the morning with papers drawn up, in case we should both be ready to sign.

Next visitor was Mr. E—, of the North American Transportation Company, who has been most courteous in cashing checks for us. "When do you go out?" "On the *Columbian* tomorrow." "But haven't you heard the news? She has just come in, and as the ice has already begun to form in the Yukon, she will not make another trip, but goes to her winter quarters at Fort Selkirk." "Oh, impossible!" I cried in alarm, at the thought of being shut in for the winter without proper stores and heavy clothing. "Why, Miss Van Buren and I have already engaged our passage." "All I know," said Mr. E—, "is that a friend of mine who was going out on her has just had his money refunded." At this moment one of my new neighbours entered and said, "Do you know that we are all shut in for the winter and cannot get out, as the *Columbian* is now going into winter quarters?" "Oh what shall we do? It would be delightful if we had come with comforts and luxuries, prepared to remain, but as it is, we have disposed of everything and have not even a good stove, as this one does not keep us warm enough even at this season."

Then came Edith, looking the picture of despair. "Well, I suppose you have heard the news! We are shut in for the winter. The *Columbian* has made her last trip, and now it only remains for us to freeze to death, and I should prefer blowing my brains out. I knew something terrible was going to happen. Why did we wait?" Von M— and Jones, who followed, tried their best to console us by painting the pleasures of a winter in Dawson in most glowing colours; but nothing could rouse us from the fit of despair into which we had been thrown.

Although it was 6 PM, and I had not dined, I persuaded Von M— to row me across to Dawson in search of better news. We went first to the agent of the *Columbian*, who said we might go as far as Fort Selkirk, where we would have at least a chance of being picked up by some small steamer and taken on to Bennett, but that he could give no guarantee that we would not be left at Selkirk the entire winter. He said, further, that he was going on the *Columbian*, and would do all in his power to assist us in every way, but thought it more than likely that we would run great risks, and he could not avoid the responsibility of telling us so. From there to the office of the small steamer *Willie Irving*. Her agent thought she would be able to make another trip, but she would not be ready to start for several days; thence to the office of the *Flora*. Her agent had not yet returned, but I would not go back without some encouraging news for Edith. We walked through the Main Street, meeting many acquaintances, some of whom said, "It is all nonsense worrying about ice in the Yukon. Why, the steamers can run until October 1st. The only trouble with the *Columbian* is that she has received a large contract for a cargo of cattle, which will pay her much better than taking the one hundred and fifty passengers, and so she gives them the 'go-by.'"

This was encouraging, but not sufficiently so, and we wandered on until, as good luck would have it, we came face to face with Mr. F—, the courteous manager of whom we were in search, and received from him the glad tidings that the *Flora* would leave on Tuesday or Wednesday and that, although her accommodations could not compare with those on the *Columbian*, the best cabin on board should be reserved for us. I was in a great hurry to take back this good news, but Von M— had a positive engagement at eight, so Mr. F—'s brother very kindly offered to row me back.

As we landed, F— said he must hurry back, then asked again how far upstream he must row before attempting to cross? There was that in his tone which made me quite certain that he was making game of me, so I was not at all surprised when Von M— returned at nine o'clock and said, "F— was delighted at fooling you so, and told me all about it. Why he's one of the best oarsmen of London. Couldn't you tell that by his stroke? Since Mrs. Hitchcock has told you that you'll not be troubled by the ice but can get out easily on the *Flora*, I suppose you're all right now, Miss Van Buren?" "No, I'm not," said Edith. "I don't like going in a tiny little cabin on the *Flora*, where there's scarcely room to move, no bedding and no comforts, when I had expected splendid accommodations on the *Columbian*." At this we all taxed poor Edith with being most ungrateful, forgetting how her nerves had been tried by two narrow escapes from death in the same week.

Monday, September 19th ☞ Edith's turn to remain at home and pack; mine to attend to the errands, so she coaxed Jones to row me across and bring back several articles which she needed at once. Scarcely were we well out in the stream when he unbosomed himself. "Well, I suppose you're satisfied with the way in which you and Miss Van Buren are leaving your affairs, but I kin tell you, you'll never git nothin' out o' them, from them there dudes. Now me and A— would 'a' taken charge an' 'a' done everything an' the likes o' that, but when I found you was a-askin' them dudes, then I just dropped out, an' told A— to, too."

On leaving West Dawson the sun was shining brilliantly, and the canary was singing with a heart of joy at the unusual sight, but an hour later the rain was coming down again in torrents, the streets were ankle-deep in mud, and too slippery for easy walking. A man stopped me and said, "Lady, will you do me a favour? My sister-in-law has just died of typhoid fever. I want to close my shop and put a notice on the door, but cannot write." So down I sat on a box just inside the door of his shop and wrote down as he dictated in broken tones, "Closed for today. Death in the family." As I heard the sounds of grief from the other side of the board wall I inquired if I could be of assistance. "No, lady, thank you kindly; it's all over now." I met Mr. A—, who said, "I've tried many times to cross the river to see you but have never been able to hire a boat, and then as time passed I was ashamed to go lest you might not receive me for being so rude." Had a pleasant chat with "Arizona Charlie," who inquired, as they all do, if Edith and I intend to spend the winter here.

I had been in almost every shop in town for butter, but there was a corner in it, and none was to be had except at exorbitant rates. One thing may be said to the credit of the Alaska Commercial Company that, corner or no corner, prices remain the same. I asked for butter there—none was to be had. Knowing that a plentiful supply of everything is always reserved for the employees of the company, I appealed to Mr. H—. "Couldn't you order your clerk to sell me just one two-pound tin of butter?" "It's against the rules, Mrs. Hitchcock," said this most obliging of men. "But if you are in great need of it, it will have to be done." "Need of it! Why we even ate toast without butter for breakfast this morning." Immediately the order was given, and a two-pound tin of the precious article was speedily handed to me at the old price of one dollar a pound, which obtained before the corner.

Stopped to get the heaviest, warmest mittens in town for Edith and for me, as we are told that we shall certainly need them in going over the Pass. Was passing the *Columbian* as the last whistle blew and saw a lot of fellows leave the steamer. They had been on board to see us off and were amused to find me talking quietly with Dr. C— on shore. "When do you leave, Mrs. Hitchcock?" said they. "On the *Flora*; am just going to her office to get my tickets," so they accompanied me. The second-best cabin was reserved for Edith and for me, as the first best is taken by the manager and wife. Back to the Alaska Commercial Company, to collect my parcels and then to wait for a neighbour obliging enough to give me a "lift" over. So off we went down the muddy banks, slipping, sliding, sinking, until we reached the boat, which contained so much water that I drew back in alarm. "Widow of a naval officer and afraid of the water!" they laughed. "Naval officers are those who really know the dangers of the deep," I replied.

Edith had finished packing, and was engaged in preparations for dinner, but gladly welcomed my addition of moose steak, fish, jam, bread, etc. I triumphantly showed her three loaves of bread "for fifty cents." She held them up laughingly, and said, "Look at Mrs. Hitchcock's bargain! It takes all three to make one ordinary-sized loaf." M—, as usual, prepared his pan of delicious muffins. After dinner Edith, who was anxious to see the advertisements which Von M— was throwing from our magic lantern on four sheets sewed together and hung in the middle of the road high in air, went across the river with Jones to sit in a nearby shop.

A Series of Disappointments

TUESDAY, **SEPTEMBER 20TH** ☞ On opening the door, I was horrified at the sight of ice and looked anxiously at the river, inwardly thanking the Lord that the stream was still flowing. No sign of our steamer, however, which is beginning to be overdue. Edith called out, "Any sign of the *Flora*?" and groaned at my reply in the negative. "We shall certainly be snowed and frozen in," sighed she. "If we were only safely at home again! We shall never be able to get out this winter. Why doesn't the steamer come?" We spent the morning packing, and were quite ready at twelve, when Mr. Jones came to row us across to Colonel K—'s for luncheon. It was most refreshing to see a house with carpets, windows, curtains, beds, easy chairs—even stairs to a second story, where we went to lay aside our wraps. Life in the Yukon would be delightful could one live in such luxury, but when small windows with four tiny panes of glass cost from seventeen to fifty dollars each, an ordinary broom between ten and twenty, but nearer the latter price than the former, a tub and washboard such rarities that there is only one in all West Dawson, and the happy possessor has so many friends that he is obliged to lend them on certain days at fixed intervals—then people become accustomed to doing without all luxuries, many comforts, and even necessities. The luncheon of "human potatoes," and real underdone roast beef was delicious, and we asked permission to go into the kitchen to see a real stove once more, instead of the small Yukon makeshift. Colonel K— had invited to meet us our fellow passenger Mr. R—, and a Dr. R—, who has been attending a poor young girl who came here on our steamer expecting to make her fortune as trained nurse, as she had certificates from three different countries. She had, however, immediately fallen a victim to that dread disease, typhoid, which is creating such havoc here, and Colonel K— and Mr. R— have combined with Dr. R— in their efforts to care for this poor, homeless wanderer. The Doctor offered his cabin and treatment free, the others paying for nurse and all the expenses incurred, not only because she had come here in the care of the Alaska Commercial Company, but because of their great, warm, tender hearts.

As we finished luncheon word came by telephone (there are a few in Dawson) that our steamer *Flora* was on a sandbar and that a drop of ten degrees in the mercury would freeze the river and arrest all further navigation. "Is there no possible way of getting out, then?" we cried. "Yes," replied Colonel K—, "the *Domville* sails in an hour, and I advise you to try and catch her, as it may be your last chance. I can let you have a boat and men to go across and get all your luggage." We hastily decided that I should go at once on board the *Domville*, see the purser, look at a cabin, and find out the latest possible moment for sailing, thence to the steamship office to pay for tickets, while Edith purchased eatables and a few necessary things for the trip, and by that time the boat and men would be ready to take us over for our luggage. We met McDonald taking unusually long strides, and he shouted, "Yeze had better hurry and get out by the *Domville*; the *Flora*'s on a sandbar."

On board I dashed, with Mr. R— helping me across a gangplank, and ran up the steps to the purser's office. A crowd thronged around the door, but, with the usual deference shown to women by the rough diamonds who handle pick and shovel in Alaska, way was made for me. The purser replied in answer to my question, "Nothing can be had except at the office." The ship was so terribly crowded that there was scarcely standing room. Off to the office we rushed, I, far ahead, turned to see if Mr. R— had been lost. "I'm following," he cried. "Your excitement means single file!" The office was not only packed to repletion, but there was also a long line of men waiting in the streets, hoping for the best. As I approached the desk, the clerk said, "Give Alex McDonald and his partner two bunks in the six-roomed cabin." The Klondike King, who could have chartered a thousand such steamers! I first asked for a cabin for two. "Cabin! Why, my dear madam, there is not even a berth! The men who are now buying tickets are to sleep on floors, tables, or anywhere else." "When will the *Willie Irving* go?" "Thursday, if she gets in on time." "Then put Miss Van Buren and me down for a cabin on her, please." "There are no cabins, but we can curtain off a place for you." "Anything—rather than be frozen in."

I then went in search of Edith, and we gazed at each other in despair, which became deeper as we saw the *Domville* push out on her homeward trip. Kind friends insisted upon our remaining over for dinner in order to try and cheer our drooping spirits.

We were invited to go to the theatre after the dinner, but thought of poor Jones waiting to row us back and so went to Mrs. T—'s, where he had promised to meet us. Her rooms are over the big saloon of C—, who, although he runs bar and gambling tables, is one of the biggest-hearted men in town.

We found our boatman awaiting us, but looking very serious as he said, "It's the blackest night we've ever had; there's a strong wind blowing, an' it's dangerous to cross the river, but I'm ready to row you over if you're willin' to take the risk." Mrs. T— interposed, saying, "I wouldn't cross tonight for a thousand dollars down; one of you could take my room." Here C— entered, and, hearing the discussion, said, "It's too big a risk; you take your lives in your hand, and could go to the bottom without anyone's being able to find your boat, even, in this darkness. Take my room, and I'll wrap up in blankets and sleep on the floor, just as I've done for years previous to putting up this building," and, in spite of all our protests, orders were given, his nice big room prepared for us, and we were duly installed. To think of it! A four-poster, regular mattress, sheets, pillows, and pillowcases. How curious it all seemed, after having rolled up in furs and blankets for two months! We could see through the cracks in the floor, however, down into the barroom below, and could hear the gamblers calling at the roulette table, red or black, triumphantly or despairingly as they won or lost.

WEDNESDAY, SEPTEMBER 21ST ☞ We were up and dressed before nine o'clock, and went to thank Mrs. T— and say goodbye, but saw through the crack in her board door that she was still soundly sleeping. We stopped at the grocer's to make some purchases and learned that our second box of drugs had arrived by the *Rideout* with the others, but that it had been stored in another warehouse from which he had just received it. This careless mode of delivering goods makes one feel a strong desire to intrust one's valuables only to the Alaska Commercial Company or North American Transportation Company.

Ivan, who had been a solitary prisoner during our absence, greeted us with wild bounds of joy. Our house seemed like a barn after the civilisation on the other side.

Edith returned from Dawson (whither she had gone again to see about the possibilities of "getting out") in a most excited state. "Neither the *Willie Irving* nor the *Flora* is in yet, and there is no news of them, so I went on board the new steamer of M— and S—, the *Clara*, which they will send up the river tomorrow. They have offered us the best cabins on board if we decide tonight that we will go with them, but we must let them know *at once*, as everyone who wants to go out is frightened, and their office is crowded with applicants. Even Mr. and Mrs. F— do not dare to wait for their own steamer, the *Flora*. I stopped to consult with Colonel K—, and he said, 'Go by all means, if you want to get out. If you want to stay all winter, we will give you the most charming one you have ever had, but if you are determined to run for home this may be your last chance." We must hurry and have dinner, so I can go back and tell M— of our decision." "Oh, don't go back tonight, Edith; it is darker than last night, and the cabin will surely be reserved until morning." "No, M— said I must come myself or else we could not have it; he has promised me the whole ship, and he means what he says."

Just as we were dining, who should enter but our former jack-of-all-trades, looking as though he had tramped many a mile. His beard had grown. He said he had been chopping trees where fire had been before him and blackened trunks and boughs, so that he felt too unclean for the presence of ladies, but could go no farther. "Shall I ask him to sit down and eat with us?" said Edith in French. "It is inhuman not to do so." Isaacs understood French, and looked such an object of pity that my sympathies were aroused as well as Edith's, so that the cordiality of our invitation soon overcame his scruples, and he thoroughly enjoyed the beefsteak, which he said was the first he had tasted in weeks. He was too fatigued to remain long after dinner, but begged to be allowed to come and assist us in the morning. Jones rowed Edith across the river to secure our cabin, and pay a deposit of twenty dollars. Edith and Von M— spent the evening with me. The latter having secured another "ad" at thirty dollars a week, felt that the magic lantern was more than paying for itself. He strongly advised our leaving at once by the *Clara*, as the *Flora*, if on a sandbar, might not be able to make another trip, adding that Mr. F—, the owner, feared to wait longer, and intended to take his wife on the *Clara*. When Edith returned the die was cast, our deposit made, and we were to be ready to sail the following day at noon on the *Clara*.

Thursday, September 22nd → On opening the cabin door early this morning, what was my surprise to see the ground all white and the snow falling heavily. A groan from Edith informed me that from her cot she also had caught a glimpse of the white mantle. "Now it *is* hopeless," she cried, "and we shall not be able to get out this winter. A direful death was predicted for me, and the prophecy will surely be fulfilled if the ice shuts us in." "We have received assurances, however, from different ones," said I, "that the river will flow for several weeks yet. We had better make an early start, and be on the Dawson side in plenty of time to attend to last commissions."

Ivan, who had heard many offers from those who wished to care for him during the winter, and an offer of a thousand dollars cash for him, seemed to realise that we were about to depart. The intelligent beast began dragging his blankets across the floor and, as we watched him, put them in a large telescope bag, then got into the bag and seated himself upon the blankets, seemingly content that his preparations were made. It was such an unusual thing for a dog to do that I immediately got my Kodak and took a picture of him, in order to have proof that my story was not a Yukon fable.

The neighbours came in to lend a hand, and consoled Edith by assuring her that the mercury would have to be ten degrees lower than at present before the river would freeze over. K— and Von M— had the honour of rowing us across, while two other neighbours took over our boxes and bags in their big boat. We boarded the *Clara* and asked if we had a few moments to spare. "Oh, she may not go out until four or five o'clock," said the captain, "and then it will be so late that we had better wait until morning." Edith started off to the office of the owner to discover the cause of the delay, while I went to Colonel K—'s to deliver to him the keys of the house and written instructions concerning everything left therein. Just then we saw the *Flora*, which has made the trip safely many times, coming in, and we were advised by several to change to her, in preference to going on a steamer that has never been to White Horse, with a captain who has the channel yet to learn, particularly as the river is very low—many rafts, even, being on sandbars. Some old captains, however, prefer low water, saying that the channel shows so much more distinctly.

After luncheon the colonel invited me back to the office, sent for M—, and interviewed him in regard to the *Clara*. "I had an engineer last night," said M—, "and we were all ready to start, but the man got drunk, so I discharged him on the spot, as I would not risk the lives of passengers and crew by taking out a fellow who drinks. However, I have many applicants for the position, and shall surely have a good man in a few hours." "And your captain, has he ever made the trip before?" "No," said M—, "but we have the best pilot who ever navigated, and with our strong engines are sure to reach White Horse before any other steamer." "Well, when you get your engineer, come back and let me know who he is." As M— left I thanked the good Colonel most heartily, and told him that as there was evidently no chance of our getting away until the following day, he must come and dine with us at the Fairview, where we should spend the night, and then went off followed by Ivan, to attend to final commissions.

Soon there came a message from Colonel K—, saying, "Have made inquiries, and find that the *Flora* has more chances of accomplishing the trip than has the *Clara*, so better change at once." Edith and I divided duties—I to purchase tickets, go to steamer and select room, and see that our satchels were placed as we wanted them, she to go to the office of the *Clara* to have deposit refunded, as they had not kept their contract of sailing on the 22nd. I saw the wife of the captain of the *Flora*, who showed me a small cabin with two berths, but the best on board. The door was of boards nailed together, the hook a twisted screw, the bunks of tightly stretched canvas, of canvas also the wall which separated us from the extremely narrow deck; the only article of furniture was a box standing on end holding a tin basin. There was no pitcher, no glass, no mirror, neither soap nor towels—absolutely nothing but the tin basin and the places in which to throw our blankets and pillows. Comfortless, to be sure, but safe—the one steamer which is now to be depended upon. Fare one hundred and twenty dollars to the end of the route, and all meals two dollars extra, while upon the *Clara* the fare was one hundred dollars, and meals one dollar each.

Edith manifested the most lively gratitude, and the deepest regret that she was dining out and could not join us. I thoroughly enjoyed listening to the colonel's wonderful experiences. The grandest courage in trying moments was manifested last year when famine stared the many in the face, and he alone quelled the riot when no one else dared to face the anger of the mob. Filled with a keen sense of justice, the men knew that he would patiently listen to their grievances, and that their wrongs would be righted.

The colonel would accept no praise for the wonderful way in which he has developed the interests of the Alaska Commercial Company in Dawson; said he was but an instrument in the hands of men who are at the head of a grand scheme, and told of their deeds of generosity and kindness until I confessed shame at the criticisms with which the first part of my journal was filled. "Yes,"

THE *FLORA*

said he, "you should be ashamed. Can you not recognise the grandeur of the pioneers? Their schemes to develop new countries, to aid the miner, to provide him with food even when a corner in the market would allow them to ask enormous prices? Their charges never vary, so that the miners feel that they are to be depended upon under any and all circumstances." "You make me feel like wiping out many pages," said I, "but still, mine is only a journal of daily events, faithfully and truly recorded." "Yes, but should you not regret it if your statements caused others to doubt the efficiency of so noble a company? And now, madam," said the colonel, "it is ten o'clock. I must work all night, and see the *Sarah* started for St. Michaels early tomorrow morning. I shall be too busy for words, so it is better to say goodbye now and wish you bon voyage." With this the noble fellow departed, and I saw him no more.

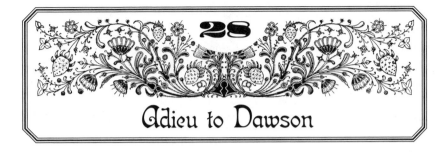

Adieu to Dawson

Friday, September 23rd ☞ Called at seven, and after dressing went into Edith's room to make plans for the day and we divided duties as usual. I went to the warehouse at the other end of town, and found not only all our goods and chattels, but also the protégé of Colonel K— with the list for me to examine. Nothing was missing, so with a line of thanks to our good friend, whom I would not disturb, as he was still engrossed in trying to clear the *Sarah*, I started for the office of the Crown Agent, who, fortunately, had arrived at an early hour. When he heard that our land had not only been "jumped" but the cache torn down, he said, "Don't you worry. I'll go tomorrow and find out all about it, and you may rest assured that your rights will be protected."

Having had some friendly hints, I purchased bread, butter, sardines, and jam, and other delicacies. The flannels which we had brought with us were not nearly heavy enough for a climb over the Pass. The articles desired had been received by the Alaska Commercial Company, but as so many of their steamers had come into port with heavy cargoes, the warehouses had been filled to overflowing. For three days the obliging men had been searching for the box containing the goods we were in need of, but, as the last moments drew near and we dared not wait longer, we bought men's flannels instead.

Down on the dock we were joined by neighbours, acquaintances, and friends, all but the busy Colonel K—, we who had arrived strangers and friendless, with only one to meet us. Mr. W— was among the many who turned up to see us off. I immediately began another attack. "If you would sell me just a little of that beautiful Bear Creek gold." "Why can't you let her have a little?" said Von M—. "Because I may go out by the next steamer myself if I can make it, and should then need it; there's nobody else I'd rather give it to. Captain B— has been begging for it for a week, as he has a claim on the other side." Others crowded in with their good wishes. The last moment had come, when

160 W— appeared, saying, "Well, I've concluded to let you have it upon condition that you'll advertise half my interest for sale, so that I can get money enough to work it in fine style." "Gladly, and send you and your wife each a copy of the paper or papers," and with a sigh of pleasure I accepted the small paper of the prettiest gold I have ever seen—but perhaps I am prejudiced.

W—, Jones, and other friends raised their hats as the whistle blew for the last time, the steamer slowly moved from her wharf, and this was the last of Dawson and of some of the most unusual experiences women could have. There were tears in Edith's eyes, and my own felt misty as I thought of the kind, good fellows obliged to remain through the winter, shut in by ice and snow from all communication with home and loved ones, though longing to be on the homeward-bound steamer. Some had to stay to protect their interests, others to work their claims, many were ashamed to leave without having made their pile, and were daily growing poorer, and so we were carrying back letters for them filled with hope of what another year might bring, and hiding from their families their trials and privations. Dawson was soon far in the distance, although the usual late passenger had called us back that he might scramble on board. It took us a long while to stow three telescope bags into a place where there was scarcely space for one, and to spread out our blankets on the narrow bunks. Finally we were at liberty to sit on the bench outside the door and watch the magnificent scenery with mountains on either side. The captain very kindly asked us into the pilothouse, where we enjoyed the superb view until dinner-time. We went down with Mr. F— and his fascinating little wife. Hash was the only hot dish; there were one or two kinds of tinned meats, stewed apples, and a dry cake. Two dollars each! Edith and I concluded that the box of delicacies we had with us would provide food quite as nourishing, and more palatable— so decided not to patronise the table again.

After dinner I had an interesting conversation with a fellow passenger, who, after a thorough survey of this part of the world, has concluded that the mines in Australia are far superior. While admiring Ivan he inquired if I had ever seen the Australian dog. "You would like him, as you care for big dogs; he is larger than the Great Dane, in shape like a greyhound, and is trained to kill the kanga-roo. He always springs at the throat."

Saturday, September 24th ☙ What luck that we did not go on the *Clara*! She is now far behind us on a sandbar, and we are mentally thanking good Colonel K— for his advice. Our captain is chuckling over having passed her, and told the story in this way: "I saw the *Clara* in shoal water, moving slowly and evidently waiting for me to pass so as to follow in my wake, so what did I do but go round the island and take another channel, and she, in trying to get out, went high and dry on the bar." "Do you never stop to tow off a boat in that condition?" "Not much! That belongs to a rival firm and our business is to beat her by just as many hours as possible." The next event was being signalled for, by a large scow. As we approached we saw nine bunks in rows of three on a side, a long table, at which sat at least a dozen men at dinner, of which the most prominent dish was one of beans. "What do you want?" shouted the captain. "Want to give you a passenger," so we tied up alongside. A man scrambled on board, and off we started again, leaving behind us this scow belonging to the Arctic Express Company. This company, we learned from the *Klondike Nugget*, "is a British one with President Battenbury of the *Ora*, *Flora*, and *Nora* line of steamboats at its head. It is engaged in perfecting a plan of building provision cabins all along the Yukon River and upper lakes, with relays of dog teams all the way. It is also planned to provide a mail service twice a month." If this plan is carried out, it will be of inestimable benefit to the Klondike region during the coming winter.

Towards evening a scow passed and was stopped in order to send off one of our passengers in her. The story told was that he had come on board intoxicated, thinking that he was bound for St. Michaels. When he recovered and found himself going in the opposite direction there was a scene and he wanted to get off at the first landing place, but his story was regarded as a Yukon fable, and rather than give him a lift of forty or fifty miles, and land him at the station which he was desirous of reaching, they decided to insure his return to Dawson by placing him in special charge of the captain of the scow. We also stopped twice during the day to land passengers on shores which looked most forbidding and inhospitable. There was the most magnificent of pyrotechnical effects, which would have been beautiful to watch had it not been so dangerous as to drive us all into our cabins at 8 PM. The cinders from the funnel fell in showers. Poor Ivan, who had been lifted by four men onto the upper deck (as he seemed to me so much in the way on the narrow corridor where we all sat) had trembled all day at the rifle shots, as the passengers aimed at ducks that were to be seen in great numbers; had started at the sound of the whistle; had shivered with the cold, and now presented a pitiable appearance as many of the sparks fell upon him, so the men were called and he was lifted down again.

SUNDAY, SEPTEMBER 25TH ☞ We peeped out this morning, but finding the decks covered thickly with cinders, and sparks flying in all directions, decided that it was much better to lie in our bunks and write, as there was not room to sit in the cabin and do so. The door was left slightly ajar, so that we

162 might get the magnificent view yet not be seen. The mountains became more grand, the banks more brilliant. Here and there patches of red mingled with green and made the scene variegated and a delight to the eye. We heard the whistle of a steamer, which was high and dry on a sandbar. The passengers said that they were from Vancouver with a cargo of cattle and sheep which they declared had been turned ashore to graze for a while—a story which seemed to us most highly improbable. Shortly after we heard talk of the *Willie Irving* in the distance, so concluded to dress and get pictures of her, and were just in time for a couple of shots; she was pushing a scow and had been on a sandbar for two days.

The next point of interest was a sailboat stranded on the beach and abandoned. We also passed a good-sized steam launch, and although the only sign of habitation on shore was a tent, we saw two women, nattily garbed in golf costume, tramping along the bank. The mountains on either side are becoming higher, some of them snow-topped. Now that we have grown accustomed to such close quarters, and such tiny rooms, the trip would be ideal were it not for the constant shower of cinders which penetrate even the cabins. A carpenter has been in and put up three small shelves for us and taken out the box, which was only large enough to hold the basin and a tin cup of water. After dinner a kind fellow passenger loaned us the canvas from his bunk to put up over our heads as an awning. This protected us from cinders, and we were joined by Mr. and Mrs. F— and one or two others, who sat spinning yarns until quite late.

Monday, September 26th ☙ At seven we tied up to a bank for wood, but our stay there was short, as the wood was all green. At 8:30 tied up again, and I took a number of snapshots of some of the passengers as they felled trees to supply us with fuel for the remainder of the trip to Fort Selkirk, which is less than forty miles distant. The passengers returned, bringing beautiful leaves of variegated colours that grow along the edge of the bank. Poplar trees are very abundant; also birch. The felled trees soon covered the lower deck, the whistle blew "all aboard," and we were off. The men then began sawing the wood into proper lengths for the mouth of the ever yawning furnace. The purser kindly offered Edith his room and a desk at which to write. After a while she came to me saying, "Read this letter; it will explain itself. I found out about it last night. It really ought to be headed the 'Parrot Mystery.'"

> Dear Colonel K—,
>
> I have just discovered something in connection with our affairs which I think you would like to know. About a fortnight before our departure from Dawson

Mr. — took our parrot, to have it raffled. The following day, he told me the parrot had died. Both he and — related how they had taken it out of the cage and nursed and petted it until it breathed its last. I asked to see the bird, but was told it had been thrown away. A week later, as — started to row me across the Yukon, he was hailed by a man who asked for "a lift." This passenger asked what had become of the parrot, saying that he missed it. — assured him that it had died within twenty-four hours of its removal from West Dawson. The man denied this, saying it was the liveliest bird for a dead bird he had ever seen. One of the passengers on this boat now tells me that the parrot did not die; that it was a put-up job between — and —, who wished to have the bird for Mrs. —. Our fellow passenger overheard a conversation between these two men and insisted upon an explanation. The parrot was perfectly well when it left our tent and undoubtedly is now in the land of the living. We valued him at fifty dollars. It seems incredible that —, who was always so kind, would have attempted to cheat us in such a manner, but here are the proofs, and if you can find out anything about it, we should be greatly indebted. The empty cage was taken to M— and S—'s store a couple of days before we left.

Very sincerely,
Edith Van Buren

The next steamer passed was the *John C. Barr*, tied up some miles below Fort Selkirk, taking on board cattle. On we went, admiring the beautiful rocks, the walls of volcanic formation, the red patches which we were told was very fine moss; at length a promontory of rocks came into view, with a head of the same material so clearly defined that general attention was at once attracted to it. It had been reclining there for ages, and will probably be visible to future generations who may make this trip when all on board this little steamer shall have passed away. Before dinner we saw the *Ora* in the distance tied to a bank and evidently awaiting us. We were soon alongside only to hear the sad news that our captain, purser, and the most obliging of stewards had orders to exchange with those on the *Ora*. Our second captain was much disgruntled at having his crew broken up and his plans changed, and expressed himself accordingly.

We had news that the *Domville* was "stuck on a bar" fifteen miles beyond Selkirk. Great was the rejoicing, not because she was in hard luck, but that we should pass her in all probability. Towards dusk, we tied up at the famous Fort Selkirk, too late for photographing, and the banks were so steep that climbing them was an obstacle we did not care to surmount, although sorely tempted to do so, when we saw the good missionary and his wife, who had been our fellow passengers from San Francisco. Their invitation to land was most cordial, but the time was so short that we contented ourselves with chatting from steamer deck to shore. The moon, which we had heretofore seen only peeping

164   for a short while nightly above the mountaintops, now came forth in full glory and presented a view of what appeared to be most perfect silhouettes of the hundred or more inhabitants on the banks, mingled with some fine specimens of Canadian officials and soldiers; but the aurora borealis, which was so often visible from our home in West Dawson, has not during this trip favoured us with its beautiful light. Great flocks of crane flew high above our heads, southward bound.

The Race with the Domville

TUESDAY, **S**EPTEMBER 27TH ☞ Very early in the morning we were hailed by the *Columbian*, which has gone into winter quarters. Thirty passengers were to be taken from her. The tramping on deck and noise of many voices prevented sleep after 6 AM; bits of conversation drifted through the canvas walls into our cabin.

As I stepped on to the crowded deck, plenty of room was made for me, and loud songs of praise were sounded for Ivan. All admired his size, his beauty, and his training. "Whose dog is that?" "Gad, what a noble beast!"

The smoke from the *Domville* was just ahead but around a turn in the river. She had been pulled free from the sandbar and was apparently tied to a bank. We tried to reach her, but not only was the current unusually strong just there, a headwind was also blowing such a gale that, work their best, the engines could not force the *Flora* a foot ahead; on the contrary, she was slowly but surely drifting back. A Mississippi River captain, who was one of the passengers, said, "Captain, there is only one thing to do—order all the men on shore; tell them to climb this hill, and you'll pick them up around the corner where the current is not so strong." The captain hesitated between his reluctance to accept advice, and his knowledge that lightening the load would be of great benefit. Finally his good sense gained the mastery, and the order was given. Nearly fifty men jumped from the deck onto the narrow, rocky bank; one fell into the water, but his wet, pitiable state elicited no sympathy, only evoked shouts of laughter in which he thought it wise to join as he scrambled up the slippery surface. As the passengers scrambled and pulled themselves up the steep hillside, a rope was thrown out from the *Flora* far in advance of the *Domville* (which was still helplessly hugging the bank) and made fast to a tree. The engines were hard at work, but the steamer was only holding her own. No sooner had the line been attached to the capstan than we began creeping, first neck and neck with the

166 *Domville*, then a length ahead, and finally there was a shout of triumph as we showed her our stern wheel and rounded the point. Just as we were about to take on our passengers and start ahead, the tree was uprooted. The *Domville* by the same tactics was soon able to follow us, but not for long.

The next object of interest was a rudely constructed scow going to pieces, of which we were told the following story. A widow with her son and daughter had invested all the money they possessed in a cargo of livestock. They were on the scow and were being towed by a steamer to Dawson, when an accident took place and the scow was broken. The livestock floated for a while down the river, but finally drowned, and the owners, sad and penniless, passed us on the *Ora* yesterday. I forgot to mention that last evening a man came on board with newspapers from Seattle, for which I gladly gave fifty cents; read to my sorrow of the sad assassination of the beautiful Empress of Austria, whom I so greatly admired at a ball in Vienna in 1887.

About one o'clock loud whistles informed us that the *Domville* was rapidly overtaking us, then came cheers from her passengers, and groans from ours, as she came alongside; a moment more and she was forging ahead. Ropes were held toward us, and there were derisive shouts of "Won't you have a tow?" Someone answered, "You may laugh now, but I'll bet you two hundred and fifty dollars we shall beat you yet." Another cried out, "We'll take your backwash today, but wait till we get to the Rapids." A cornetist on the *Domville* responded by playing *Home, Sweet Home*.

THE *DOMVILLE* PASSING US

An hour later we saw the *Domville* just ahead tied to a bank, and her passengers were all on shore with axes in hand, felling trees for fuel. Our turn at that operation would soon come, and as the engines of the *Domville* are much more powerful than ours, we knew that it was only a question of a short time before she would overtake us. Our only hope in a final triumph lay in the fact that she drew much more water than we, had already been aground two days, and that we were now to go through many shallow places where sandbars were to be seen on all sides.

We tried to photograph several Indian graves, which were built on the banks overlooking the water, the possessions which the departed ones had most prized being hung in plain view of all passersby. At last, as the moon rose in full glory, we tied to a bank, near the cabin of the Arctic Express Company, to take on fuel. There is great variety even in this work. Last night some of our passengers felled trees, while others made an enormous bonfire about them. Tonight we find the wood all cut and stacked in cords on the bank. The men form two lines which lead from the woodpile down the bank across the gangplank onto the deck; the one nearest the wood, or rather the ones at the head of each line, seize a long, heavy log, pass it on to the next, and so it goes from arm to arm until it is landed near the engine room. There is great rivalry between the two captains as to which one can pass down the greater number of logs, and the way in which it is handed over causes amusement and sometimes evokes shouts of laughter.

The moon, which was high and beautiful, caused the captain to vow that he would run all night. The passengers, all excitement, were in the bow straining their eyes for the object of the chase. Just out of sight! So the captain decided on a shortcut through shoal water. We were speedily gaining, when we felt the well-known crunching sound, and with one voice shouted "aground," while from below came the cry of "Stuck!" Backing began but was useless, so the machinery for getting off was brought into requisition with such success that in a few moments came the cry, "She's off." "Get your pole and take soundings," shouted the captain, as we advanced slowly. "Four feet, three feet six, three feet. She's stuck." "That beats me!" he cried, "how she can be stuck in three feet of water? She's done three feet and less many a time and how she can get stuck here is more 'n I can make out." "Perhaps it's only her belly that's caught," suggested another of the captains, who were all gathered together around the pilothouse, each one aching to take the wheel. "Push her on a bit." But it was no use, so after many unsuccessful trials we had to beat an ignominious retreat and go around the island to the deeper channel through which the *Domville* had successfully

168 passed. "It's all the fault of them hoodoos we took from the *Domville*; we'd never 'a' been aground but for that," were the mutterings we heard on all sides.

Inquiries were made and we found that one woman and three men, fearing that the *Domville* could not finish the trip, and having great faith in the powers of the *Flora*, had paid their passage money over again in order to come with us. We soon made the acquaintance of the woman, whose story interested us. She had been caught in the ice before, and was determined not to have a similar experience if it could be avoided, so, said she, "although I had a bunk in the *Domville*, and have only the barroom table on which to sleep here, I preferred to change. It was very lively on the *Domville*. There were six bunks in my cabin, and there were six women on board. On my side Swiftwater Bill's housekeeper had the bottom one; she's only a tiny little thing and could scarcely close her eyes because the woman in the bunk above her weighed over two hundred pounds, and every time she turned it seemed like she was going to fall through; she said she kept her hands up most all the time to ward her off; but we asked her what good her little hands could do against such a weight as that.

"My bunk was over the fat woman; on the other side were Elise and another woman. The sixth lady had an invalid husband, and preferred sleeping outside with him, even if it was among the men, and that took the bunk away from a poor fellow; when we found that he had had no place to sleep for two nights, we all felt so sorry for him we told him that after we were in bed, he might roll up in his blankets in the top bunk if he would keep his back turned, and you can imagine he was grateful! Such is life on the Yukon, in some cases and places! Elise was having a beautiful time on board. She taught W— to play cards and would keep it up sometimes till 5 AM. The first night she won fifty dollars; but the second she lost over two hundred dollars, and swore she wouldn't pay; but one of the men she owed vowed he'd sell the clothes off her back if she didn't pay him, and I don't know how it will end."

During the day the Virginian pointed out to me some horses going along a very good trail. We watched them with interest, and were finally told that they belonged to Jack Dalton and his party, and had eighty thousand dollars' worth of gold on their backs. We soon saw the famous Jack tramping over his well-known Pass, and many stories were told of his life and adventures.

WEDNESDAY, SEPTEMBER 28TH ☞ A little before nine o'clock the steward appeared with a cup of cocoa, saying, "I've been trying to get here all the morning, but have already fed over eighty, have many more to feed, and have to get a lady out who slept in the bar." At nine, one of the "boys" began a lusty song, but was interrupted on all sides by shouts of "Too early in the morning!" "Don't! You'll break my head!" "We'll throw you overboard and never give you a line."

Scarcely had I appeared upon deck when a comfortable seat was made for me out of a bag filled with blankets, and placed in front of the pilothouse. The view was fine, and the sun resplendent, taking the severe chill from the air. On the other side of the island the *Domville* was going at full speed. We were both bound for the same point in the centre of the channel. Her powerful engines were doing their work well, and we soon saw that we were again to have the "backwash," in Yukon language.

At 11:30 a cry went up, "The *Domville*'s aground again!" Such shouts, yells, and catcalls as we slowly overtook her! Her passengers were on shore, and two carpenters were mending her broken wheel. How our men tried to rival each other in such consoling remarks as the following: "What are you going to do on shore? Tend sheep?" "We'll send you a box of oranges from southern California, for you'll never see the States again."

"Do trim ship," shouted our captain. "Why do you all want to stay on the same side? Did you never see a steamer stranded before? Can't you see we're approaching the Rink Rapids? How can the sailors hear any orders if you keep jabbering so?" All this was uttered in such an excited tone, that quiet soon reigned as we found ourselves in the unusually low water of the Rink Rapids, and heard the calls six feet, five feet six, five, four feet six, four and a half, five, six, and then the suspense was over.

An hour afterwards we stopped at a lonely spot to let a passenger disembark. First one man and then another appeared, as though from underground, until a dozen or more were waiting to greet him. "Captain, will you wait five minutes, please? Sandy wants to go this trip with you, and he's running as hard as he can to get his bag." "All right," said the captain. The five minutes had almost expired when we saw Sandy in the distance, making good time, though heavily laden; the silent men stood on the bank, and as he approached, stepped up one by one to give him a last grasp—it seemed a life parting. He jumped on board, the ropes were cast off, and we were under way.

"We'll soon be at Five Fingers," said the Virginian, approaching, "where we have a drop and a narrow passage to go through between the rocks—so narrow that the steamer must graze either side. Everyone has to get off and walk around." "Even the women?" said I, in alarm. "Even the women; but you won't mind it, it's a nice, easy trail." Watching with anxiety as we approached the nice, easy trail, I saw high hills to climb and rocks, then a sharp descent. The *Flora* was tied up to a bank. "Must we get off, Captain?" said I. "Not if you will sit perfectly quiet." So with a sigh of relief, we watched the eighty or more passengers cross the gangplank and begin their scramble up the hillside. Someone called Ivan and I made no objection, thinking the exercise would be of benefit, so off he ran, following the procession. The gangplank was hauled in, and we started on our perilous trip. Soon we were in the whirl, and dashing between the gigantic rocks. As we touched the one on the port men were ready with long poles to push her off; scarcely had they done so than the captain shouted, "Pole her off on the starboard!" They had but just time to obey the order when we ran so close to a partially hidden rock that we shuddered as we saw the water rippling over it. "Well done, Captain," was shouted on all sides as we found ourselves once more in smooth water, and looked up to see our fellow passengers wending their way in Indian file along the banks. Some on high rocks were taking snapshots of the *Flora* in her perilous trip, some on the pebbly beach were waiting to come on board, but, although the entire line was distinctly visible, there was no sign of Ivan. We shouted for him and the passengers took up the call and whistled; still no sign of the noble beast. One of the crew men said, "We never wait for a dog; four were left here last time."

I rushed to the captain, who, notwithstanding his gruff voice, was indeed most kindly disposed. He said, "It's against the rules to wait, but the manager, Mr. F—, has gone back for the dog, and I can't leave without him." Sure enough, there over the hill, tramping back for Ivan were not only Mr. F—, but two or three others. But they called and shouted in vain. Ivan had gone back to the spot on which he had landed, and was waiting for the return of the *Flora*, and could not be inveigled into deserting his post. They finally had to catch him, tie their handkerchiefs around him and drag him back. As they came into view they waved their hats, and shouted, "All right," and we felt the deepest gratitude towards the men who had so kindly taken the long tramp. Everyone on board expressed pleasure, and no one objected to the detention, with one exception, and that, I am sorry to say, came from a woman who said, "What a shame to lose fifteen minutes waiting for a dog!"

"Look at the bear!" was the next cry. "No, sheep." "I'll bet you drinks." "Done." We rounded the point, and there on the banks, on the hilltops, everywhere in sight, were sheep grazing as though at home, but look where we would, there was no shepherd in sight. Another Yukon mystery! Was the scow lost? Was the owner dead? Did the sheep swim to shore? There was no way to solve the mystery. We stopped for wood, which was lying on the bank already cut. "Lucky the *Domville* didn't come along first, as there's mighty little to be had now between here and the end o' our journey," said one of the boatmen.

Edith retired at eight to get warm, so I took her place by the stovepipe under the awning, where I was soon joined by the Australian. He has been prospecting all over Alaska, but has found nothing to compare with Western Australia, where the mines, he declares, offer greater chances for investment than any others. He strongly advised a trip throughout that part of the world, leaving Sydney and Melbourne until the last, and said that the accommodations were generally good and inexpensive. We were interrupted by cries and exclamations—the beautiful northern lights were vying in splendour with the moon; three long, golden rainbow-shaped orbs filled the heavens with glory, and kept us silent with admiration.

THURSDAY, SEPTEMBER 29TH ☞ Wakened at six. Boat motionless; no sound of the axe nor of piling wood on board; no calls of six feet, five, four, three, so we are not aground and working to get off. What can it be? I unlatch the hook and peep out; the small cabin immediately fills with a fog so dense that for a while nothing can be seen, then we distinguish the railing covered with frost. An hour passes by and the tops of the trees become visible. At eight the sun's powerful rays pierce the density. Soon the banks appear, finally the battle is won, the fog beats a slow retreat, and we are in the full glory of sunshine which one never so much appreciates in any other part of the world. We steam slowly ahead, close to the banks. One could imagine oneself in Florida, as the frost has given to the trees the colouring of those covered with the grey moss so well known on the St. John's and Indian Rivers. The chilliness of the air and the falling of cinders contribute to a feeling of laziness which keeps all hands in their bunks. There is loud talking on every side, but no tramping of decks.

At 11:30 the *Golden Star* passed us on her way to Dawson. The few who were on deck responded to the cheers of those who are to be prisoners for the winter. With door slightly ajar we watched her from our bunks. Suddenly there was a crack, and the board which supported Edith's bunk partly gave way: a rip, and the canvas upon which she was lying began to tear from the nails. In an instant the door was locked and she was dressing. Hardly had she been on deck five minutes when she called back, "It's not cold out at all, and the cinders are falling on the other side, so you had better come up." Her suggestion came in good time, as the canvas holding my mattress had also given way and I was resting on the life preservers that were stacked under the bunk. Towards evening we saw in the distance many cords of wood. The cry was, "Don't let the *Domville* get it, whether we need it or not." We stopped, but were able to add only three cords to the load we already had, so many were the groans at leaving arms to aid the enemy in beating us. One lone woman stood on the bank, and holding a paper novel high in air, called out, "Will anyone exchange a book with me?" It was quickly done, and many were the expressions of sympathy as she was left alone in that dreary spot, but her face was wreathed in smiles as she waved adieu and the *Flora* passed out of sight.

Friday, September 30th ☞ The glorious rays of the moon were not only beautiful, but also of such assistance that the *Flora* was enabled to run all night. By six o'clock men were seated outside the door and the following conversation was overheard, "Well, we'll soon reach the cañon. I came through it in a scow. If a fellow once falls in he can't get out without help. I saw a fellow trying to row out for forty-six hours." "I saw a scow go to pieces there and two fellows go down like a shot. They'd 'a' been all right if they'd 'a' stuck to the wreck, but someone threw out a rope and they tried to get to it, lost it, and went down. Once you fall in, you're dead." "Not much! I swam all through it, and here I am." "Bet you're the only fellow who ever did it and lived to tell the tale." "You have to work like the devil to escape the whirlpools."

The last few days there has been no opportunity for writing. Events have crowded upon each other so fast that they leave little detailed impression upon the memory. Then came a morning on the little vessel whose side decks were so

MILES CANYON BETWEEN WHITE HORSE AND BENNETT

very narrow that men had great difficulty in using the common wash basin and maintaining their equilibrium. Suddenly there was a shout of "dog overboard" and a splash was heard in the water; as the engine was stopped and the steamer backed, I rushed to see that Ivan was safe. Just then ex-Mayor Wood appeared and he began to strike out boldly for shore through the icy water. Fortunately he was a good swimmer, as the life buoy thrown to him went wide of the mark, and he soon landed on the barren shore, which, in that particular spot was not quite so rocky and inaccessible as elsewhere. The passengers were all deeply relieved as the steamer sheered alongside and he was assisted on board. Men crowded around him all anxious to "rub him down" and dose him with remedies, but, although shivering, he laughingly assured them that no harm had been done, and that his bath was only a few degrees colder than usual, and that he felt no anxiety in regard to his sudden immersion.

There was no one on board to bring us water or to care for our cabins, so we impressed into our service one of the men who was working his passage, in order to get out of the country, and had him thoroughly clean for us an empty lard pail which was about to be thrown overboard; by attaching a rope to this, we could lower it from outside our door and have fresh water from the Yukon as often as we pleased.

The First Portage

SATURDAY, OCTOBER 1ST → We were told to prepare our bags and be ready for a tramp. We were soon tied up to the bank where we were to make the portage. Flat cars—truck cars probably they would be called, as they had no railing, only a piece at the back to hold the boxes—were drawn each by one horse, and exclamations of surprise were elicited as one heavy box after another was added to the car. The driver said, however, "Why, these horses can carry a ton each." The other passengers walked the four and a half miles over a fine road with most gorgeous scenery, while I, mounted on top of bags, shawl straps, and boxes, sat on the last of the seven cars with an umbrella over my head to protect me from the rays of the sun, which were rather powerful as we emerged from time to time from the protection of the few shade trees.

Along by the rushing, dashing, foaming torrent of White Horse Rapids, we wound our way for a time, then came a cut through a bit of woods. The driver entertained me with a short history of the road and of himself, as he stopped to put in a more secure position the gold box containing several hundred thousand dollars. The road was begun last May, cost only about three thousand dollars, and belongs to a company of ten men who have taken in twenty thousand dollars in the short time it has been running. The rails are of wood instead of steel or iron. Each driver receives four dollars and fifty cents daily, with board, and fifty cents an hour for overwork. "I've always been a jockey," said my driver, "and all my brothers are jockeys, but this pays better than the jockeying business, where you've plenty one day and nothing the next, and I've already laid by several thousand dollars; besides, I've broken every horse the company uses, and get five dollars apiece for them. Perhaps you wouldn't believe it of these meek-looking animals, but they never had a collar on before I took them in charge."

We were soon at the foot of quite a little hill. Here all the cars were waiting, the horses were unhitched, and two taken to haul the heavy load up the steep incline. I jumped down and walked on, having already been a bit nervous as we skirted the edge of the precipice, where the car tipped a little towards the dashing torrent below. It took some time for the horses to be rehitched and I was quite half a mile ahead when I saw something that looked like a bear trotting along in the distance. In a second my cowardly instincts obtained the mastery and I beat a rapid retreat, gladly taking refuge with the entertaining driver. As we approached the little steamer *Nora*, the horse, either through seeing the stable so near at hand or feeling that his master, absorbed in conversation, had forgotten him, turned off at right angles from the track with such speed and strength as almost to tip over the car with its heavy burden. With a shriek I started to jump, a dozen arms were held out to me, as there were many miners awaiting the arrival of the luggage, and I landed safely.

Being the first one on board the steamer I asked for choice of cabins for Edith, Mrs. F—, and self. "How many ladies in the party?" said the purser, rising, as he hastily finished his luncheon. "Six altogether." "Then follow me." Through the engine room we went, where the passage between boiler and boards was so narrow that my wrap had to come off before it was possible to pass, up a steep ladder to a narrow deck and into a dark room where there were three bunks on either side, made of boards, with canvas stretched, on which to lay one's blanket and pillows. "Choose your bunks," said the purser in a kindly manner. "But have you no cabin with only two bunks?" "Not such a thing on board for passengers," he replied. The lower berths, being just off the ground, were out of the question, owing to my fear of mice, so I selected the two in the middle and one on top, for which the purser wrote our three names and in which he deposited our bags. Edith had joined the walking party with Ivan as companion, while I had promised not only to secure the accommodations, but also to attend to the luggage, which had to be weighed and paid for. Great dissatisfaction was expressed by many of the owners of the boxes, as some boasted that they had stipulated in the purchase of the ticket that the luggage should be landed at Bennett, free of charge, while those who had paid the same price, but had made no such arrangement, were taxed three cents a pound portage, which made Edith's bill and mine amount to nearly twenty dollars.

At 5 PM the whistle blew and we were just starting when a shout of "A bear—a bear!" was heard. Everyone rushed to the stern and there came my bear trotting down to the water's edge for a drink as unconcernedly as though he were in the primeval forests and had never heard of his enemy, man. There was a dash for rifles. One of the mounted police was far in advance of all others, rifle in hand. Others without arms followed, shouting and yelling, so that poor bruin had no chance to quench his thirst. The small cub on board which had been kept a prisoner for weeks, whined and howled. Suddenly there was a shot, we could see the smoke and the dogs in wild chase, but were too far away to learn whether the bear had been killed or even wounded.

We stayed on deck for a short time to enjoy the beautiful view, but were soon driven away by the cinders. There was no place in which to seek protection. Below, every place was packed, so that there was scarcely gangway, and the cabins were so tiny that there was no room in them to sit. Three of the women went to bed at seven as the only way out of the difficulty. The poor "Siwash" dog who had been kept on deck from the time of leaving Dawson, not only had his long fur badly burned, but the burn went so deep that it made a large running sore, the size of the palm of a hand. To leave Ivan outside was out of the question, so I asked Edith, who manages so well with her travelling companions, to try and persuade them to allow him to sleep in the tiny corridor which was portioned off as a "washroom for ladies."

The Virginian invited me down for supper, and, although I objected on the ground of not being hungry, his arguments that he did not want to eat alone and that we would have a nice place in which to sit with no danger of being burned, quickly persuaded me. So we worked our way down the narrow ladder, squeezed past the furnace, and came to that part of the boat where eighty new passengers were huddled together, sitting on bags, boxes, and logs of wood, but singing at the top of their voices.

The manager's wife told me that small and uncomfortable as are the quarters on the *Nora*, they are now far better than in former times, when there was not even a partition for the livestock. After supper the cheering recommenced as we once more wended our way back to the narrow upper deck.

Although it was but a little after eight, there was nothing for it but to retire, so I said goodnight to my kind Virginia friend and joined the small party who were waiting for me to extinguish the light of the kerosene lamp. The next difficulty was how to wriggle into the middle bunk. "I had to get my feet in first," said Edith, "and then draw myself in gradually. You'd better try the head first, or you run the risk of breaking your back." I tried each way, but being unaccustomed to gymnastic performances, was in despair. Finally the feat was accomplished, the light was out, and we tried to settle down to sleep, but through the cracks in the floor we could see the motley crowd below and hear their songs. They kept it up until 5 AM.

The Skaguay Pass

SUNDAY MORNING WE ARRIVED at Bennett, of which we had
read so much. A heavy snowstorm greeted us and we groaned, fearing that we could never get over the Pass. We all went to the Hotel Dawson for breakfast, and as we sat on the benches waiting for food, the discussion began as to whether we should take the Chilkoot or the White Pass. Neither Edith nor I felt equal to the perpendicular descent of the former, but many of the men preferred it owing to its being so much shorter. We used all our persuasive powers to urge them in favour of the White Pass, feeling that we should be so much safer in their company, and finally, as the blinding snowstorm became more fierce, we were successful, as no one dared attempt the Chilkoot under such circumstances. The runners for Dyea did all in their power to dissuade us, telling us that one of the lakes was frozen, navigation stopped, the railway not running, etc., but in the face of all these announcements our decision was unalterable. An agent for a new transportation company started by the railroad, which wished to make a record for itself, came to get our luggage to be landed in Skaguay for ten cents a pound, and promised that we should have everything the following day at two o'clock. Mark the result. We booked all through except our blankets and toilet bags which were specially marked for the Old Log Cabin Hotel, eight miles farther on, where we were to spend the night. A man "going in," seeing the fine quality of our blankets and noticing the newness of them, was most anxious to purchase them, telling us that we would find bedding all the rest of the trip, but we said that nothing would induce us to sleep in any but our own.

At 10:30 the party started. Edith's escort was a charming Englishman, a Captain T—, who had been eight years in command of one of the Mitsu Bishi steamers in Japan, and who was well acquainted with Edith's brother. Consequently, there was much of interest for them to talk over during the eight-mile tramp. My escort was a Mr. T—. We passed the steamer that we should have taken had we gone via Dyea, skirted wonderful Lake Linderman, and I was so intensely interested in the gorgeous scenery that suddenly one leg was up to the knee in a deep marsh. Pull and tug as I would, I could not extract it; we had been walking single file and my escort was a little in advance. Happening to turn, he saw my predicament, and notwithstanding his heavy load, he was soon back, pulling with all his might as he firmly gripped my hand. For a short time the suction below was greater than the force from above, and it seemed as though the boot at least must be left as a memento on the trail, already covered with the dead bodies of more than horses; a last effort, and boot and all came slowly, slowly from the marsh, while the perspiration rolled in streams from my forehead.

I had read so much of the icy atmosphere of the summit, that I had prepared for it by wearing two thick suits of woollen flannels, a jersey, cloth jacket, and sealskin wrap and collar. [Another word of warning! Never overburden yourself with heavy clothing for an eight-mile tramp even to the summit, as each pound becomes an insupportable burden with each step.] My escort kindly offered to carry the sealskin, but his pack was sufficiently heavy as it was, so I staggered on until finally we were overtaken by the newspaper boy, lightly clad, and with nothing but a few papers to carry. I asked him if he wanted a job of packing, promising that he should be well paid for it. He willingly took the wrap, but was off before remuneration could be offered.

The trail wound uphill, over rocks, across swamps, and over log bridges which threatened to turn as we stepped on them. We picked up our short skirts and waded through shallow streams (bloomers are much safer without the skirts), reaching hilltops from which we could see the advance guard and those far in the rear, went down into ditches and swamps from which no sign of the trail was visible, and here Ivan came to our assistance, as it was only necessary to say to him, "Run ahead, good doggie," and, by following him, we soon had the leaders in full view again. Half a mile before reaching our destination we stopped at a tent on which we saw the sign "Restaurant." Never did oranges seem more delicious than those which Mr. T— presented to us! No thirsty, fever-parched patient could have enjoyed them half so intensely.

Refreshed, we continued our tramp, reaching the Old Log Cabin Hotel just as the more rapid walkers in our party had finished dinner. Their shouts of welcome were pleasant to listen to. Edith and her escort arrived an hour later; she was thoroughly exhausted, and delighted to find that we were to go no farther that night. The quarters were crowded to overflowing. We looked at the bunks, one above the other, and felt that it was no place for the night. After a short talk with the proprietor, he accompanied us to a small tent, one hundred and fifty yards beyond, a new American Hotel and Restaurant. We passed through the latter, entering a long canvas-covered room, containing thirty-two bunks, sixteen lower and sixteen upper, within places made for two in each; all were of logs over which, as usual, canvas was tightly stretched. The part to be occupied by each person was clearly defined, as a pole was lashed down the centre, although the same blanket covered both individuals.

I immediately engaged the bunk in the corner, which was curtained off by a bit of canvas, for Edith and me. At the foot of the bed was a small space in which some old bags were stored, and this I secured for Ivan. Shortly after, the other members of the party (feeling that the night was to be a noisy one at the Old Log Cabin Hotel) followed my example. The five women engaged lower bunks and had them curtained off, then came the men of the party who also desired a quiet night's rest. The place I had secured for Ivan was coaxed from me as a dressing room, all gladly consenting, however, to allow the dog to remain.

After dinner the men joined us and we sat around the stove on boxes telling stories. We had seen the bodies of horses lying all along the road, and were told that over three thousand have perished since June one year ago. From what we had read, we had fully expected the odour to be almost unbearable, but, fortunately, were disappointed.

Captain T— came in and announced that if we wanted to catch the train at the summit we must be ready to start between five and six o'clock in the morning. This so startled the slow walkers that they insisted upon being allowed to retire at once. Although our part of the tent was well screened off, we demanded that the men should clear the cabin and wait until they were called in. We undressed rapidly, realising that it was icy cold outside, and were soon rolled up in the blankets we had sworn not to use. "Come," shouted Mrs. M—. There was a pell-mell rush and a kicking off of boots. Funny stories were told, which elicited peals of laughter from women as well as men. Someone commenced filling up the stove with wood, at which we shouted loudly in protest, and, finally, requested one of the men to stand guard over it. The laughter became almost hysterical; it seemed like a lot of girls at boarding school. At last all was quiet. We were just about to doze when Ivan stretched his weary limbs, giving such a grunt of satisfaction at being in warm quarters once more that there was a general shout and the laughter recommenced.

At five the alarm clock sounded, and the men began dressing. As soon as the last one was out of the tent, we made as much of a toilet as was possible without the aid of toilet articles, washing with one handkerchief, drying with another, combing our hair with hairpins, and arranging it without a mirror. Breakfast consisted of beefsteak, potatoes, coffee, bread, butter, and applesauce, and then we were off on the trail once more. As we were among the slow walkers, one member of the party after another passed us and disappeared from view, so that when we had accomplished our tramp of two and a half miles along Shallow Lake, and had reached Middle Lake, we found the sailboat, the Peterboro canoe, and the party all waiting for us. A sail of five miles brought us to another portage of one and a half miles over a hilly, rocky, but not too difficult road. Nevertheless, it took us so long to cover the distance that we failed to reach Summit Lake in time to join the party who had sailed away nearly half an hour before our arrival.

Being much refreshed, however, by an hour's sail through the beautiful islands, we changed our minds in regard to remaining overnight at the first stopping place, and decided to push on to the Ford, two miles distant, where we were to lunch. These two miles we found to be the roughest part of the journey. After a luncheon of egg sandwiches and lemonade, we started over rocks, climbed a steep hill, finally coming to a long stretch which was being graded for a railway. We welcomed level ground once more with great joy, and were quite certain that as we had only five miles ahead of us before reaching the train the remainder of the journey would be easy walking. Alas! The grading soon came to an end, and a turn in the road brought us to the brink of a steep precipice—absolutely perpendicular. Down, down, we looked upon the immense rocks far below us, and on the other side could see the narrow trail clearly defined, but how to reach it! Evidently we had come too far. It resolved itself into a question as to whether we should retrace our steps for a mile or more or try the dizzy descent.

Poor patient Captain T—, who had been kindness itself, was ready for either, but to impose upon him all that additional tramp seemed selfish and cruel. So we screwed up our courage and began the descent, the captain taking the lead. How he found a place to rest even the toe of his foot, much less the sole, is beyond my comprehension. Each rock or stone upon which we tried to depend immediately proved treacherous, slipped, and rolled until we heard the thud far below. Slipping, sliding, sitting down at times while feeling for something solid, we gradually descended, holding our breath and making no sound from very terror. The bottom was finally reached, then began a scramble, pulling, slipping over the rocks until at length, with a feeling of the utmost satisfaction and relief, we were on the other side, and were complimented by the good captain, who said that his heart sank when he first saw the precipice, as he did not believe that we could possibly accomplish so perilous a descent.

Edith said that her great terror had made her quite forget her lameness, and she felt much better for the unusual experience. Gaily we walked along, thank-

ful for a level road once more, enjoying the dashing torrent below the tremendous rocks overhead on the other side, when, suddenly, there was a noise as of
thunder; we stopped; another blast, followed by a third, and down came some
gigantic rocks, down, down, almost by our very feet and into the chasm below.
That we were not crushed instantly was not the fault of the railroad employees,
as no lookout had been stationed on the path and no word of warning given. A
white flag was to be seen on the mountaintop, but we did not know the meaning of the signal. A sort of yodel we had heard also and answered, thinking
that it came from other members of our party, but it seemed to us that lives
were endangered both carelessly and needlessly. From that time on, the blasting was almost continuous, and as we could not tell in which direction to look
for danger we tramped steadily on, trusting to the Lord for protection.

Two men appeared in search of a packhorse which had rolled down the
precipice with his load. We looked carefully but could see no trace of horse or
pack; one more carcass added to those which already strew the White Pass! At
last the railway could be seen through the loop in the mountains as we crossed
the bridge and went along the main street of White Pass City or Heney, passing
tents and houses. A member of our party approached, greeting us with loud
shouts of welcome. "We've been so worried about you we were about to send
some of the party back; we thought that you never could do the precipice. The
ladies are all in that hotel resting, as the train does not go till five and there are
still three hours to spare." As we entered the small building honoured by the
name of hotel, the four women of the party jumped from their beds to greet us
as though we had risen from the dead.

Thank the Lord, we've accomplished the terrible White Pass, and our tramping is at an end forevermore! We wouldn't have missed it for the world; neither
would we do it over again.

The proprietor and his wife begged me to do them the honour of naming
their hotel, but as the one opposite was called "Ham-Grease Saloon," and
seemed to be very popular, I did not feel equal to competing where such names
were in favour. After resting a while, Captain T— accompanied me to the railroad station to attend to the luggage, and to purchase tickets. The station was at
the bottom of a hill seven hundred feet high, the train at the top. "Do you mean
to say we must climb that to reach the cars?" I asked of the agent. "Why, that is
steeper than anything we have done on the entire Skaguay Pass." "You might go
up in the car with the luggage," he replied. "I don't advise you to try it, lady," said
a bystander, "coz sometimes it slips back."

We went out to inspect. It looked perfectly safe, while the climb seemed a
dizzy and a dangerous one. Edith arrived, and said that the latter she could not

do, so she decided that she would take the risk of going up in the car. When the car had reached the steepest part of the road, more than halfway up, the cable suddenly slackened, allowing it to slip backwards. "Jump for your lives," shouted the man in charge. Poor Edith was imprisoned by a trunk which the employees had scarcely time to remove and extricate her from her perilous position before the car dashed down to the bottom of the steep hill. Two men helped her up to the top. This accident prevented all others from entering so dangerous a conveyance.

To those of us who had congratulated ourselves too soon upon having reached the end of all fatiguing exertion, this seemed in reality the last straw. We gazed upward and shuddered. Two men kindly offered me assistance, which I most gladly accepted. The entire trail seemed as nothing in comparison, for we dared not use the rails, with the cable now slack, then tight, then flapping so that we were in danger of being caught by it if we approached too near. There was not even a rolling stone on which to rest the foot for an instant, and, as we neared the train, it was by main force that the two stout men carried my weight until some of the employees leaned over the embankment and drew me up. I sank into the first seat at hand, and looked down the steep hill of which no photograph can give a realistic picture.

At last the whistle sounded. "All aboard!" was shouted. Then the Klondike "boys" began to exclaim joyously, "A train at last after all these years!" "How long since you been in one, Jim?" "Too long to talk about," said Jim, as the tears rolled down his weather-beaten cheeks.

Some stiff, stately persons seated in front of us drew themselves together, their noses high in the air, and gazed contemptuously upon the noisy rabble. They could not see the pathetic side of the picture—of how the poor "boys" had tramped, footsore and weary, for days, months, and even years; putting up with privations of all descriptions, suffering from lack of proper nourishment, half frozen in winter or risking their lives in going to the assistance of a less fortunate comrade, or they would not have frowned upon those shouts of joy at being once more within the bounds of civilisation. A sudden whistle! "A cow on the track, boys! Let's get off an' look at her. I've forgotten how one looks." We listened to *Suwanee River, Old Folks at Home*, everything which suggested itself to the "boys," until at last "Skaguay" was called out.

How odd it seemed to descend from a railroad train and see signs of "Beer, ten cents," instead of one dollar, and "Peaches three for a quarter." All signs were read aloud by the leaders of our procession and comparisons made. We soon reached "Brannick's," where the ladies of our party had determined to stop for the night. What luxury! A frame house, not one built of logs! Carpets! Plenty of lamps and curtains! A book was moved towards us and we were asked to register, another unusual proceeding. How pleasant to see once more a "four-poster" with spring mattress, sheets, and pillowcases! "What is the dinner hour?" we asked. "We only let rooms, but there are several restaurants and an oyster-house very near." "Oysters! We must go and get some at once, before we forget how they taste." So Edith and I started on ahead. Accustomed to Dawson and the deep respect with which we had been treated by the brave, honest miners, we were quite astonished to have the Skaguay men stop and stare at us as we passed, although it was not yet 8 PM, so we hurried into the first restaurant, ordered oysters, salads, and many other things that we had been deprived of so long, and begged for the newspapers while waiting. We were greatly interested in the wonderful letters in the papers describing life in Dawson, and were much amused at the exaggerations which we found in each article.

MRS. HITCHCOCK WITH IVAN

184   **Tuesday, October 4th** ☜ At last our tramp is at an end, all perils are over; the terrible White Pass has been traversed, and we look back upon it with a shudder, wondering how we ever dared attempt such an undertaking, yet glad at having accomplished it. Edith and I have both vowed that nothing under heaven would ever induce us to make such a trip again, and yet we are proud of ourselves for having mustered sufficient courage to surmount the dangers of which we had read, and we would not for the world have missed such an experience.

The weary Klondikers were aroused at an early hour this morning from their luxurious slumbers in comfortable beds, after months of rolling up in furs and blankets, by the loud and persistent lamentations of a passenger who had missed a steamer. Sleep being out of the question, I arose and soon became so absorbed in writing that twelve o'clock came before I was aware. Edith rushed in, saying, "There is a steamer to leave at three this afternoon—can you be ready at such short notice? If so, I'll get the tickets, as the luggage has just arrived. We can go by this and see Sitka and other interesting points, or wait until tomorrow and go directly to Seattle." "I'll be ready." So Edith went off for the tickets, then returned to go with me to the restaurant. We stopped to purchase photographs which we had not time to take ourselves, and were in the carriage on our way to the steamer *City of Topeka* just as the hotel proprietor said she was blowing her last whistle.

The purser had told Edith that the top or third berth in our stateroom would probably be unoccupied, so she did not purchase it. As we started, however, we saw extra bags in our cabin, and hung about to see our new travelling companion. She proved to be a nice, quiet, but entertaining little woman who fitted in most agreeably. Although it was quite cold we walked the decks (where there were scarcely any seats to be had, everything was in such an overcrowded condition) until late, admiring the great contrast between the snow-capped mountains and the beautiful verdure-covered islands. We asked the purser for seats at table, but his reply was, "Sit anywhere." The rush was so great when the gong sounded, that we stepped back, preferring to let "the pushers" enjoy their feast while we waited for the second table. We had the luck, however, to get an unusually good waiter, who promised to reserve the same seats for us during the entire trip.

32

A Day in Sitka

WEDNESDAY, OCTOBER 5TH ❧ As the shutter was opened, beautiful verdure on all sides gladdened the eye. Mrs. B— was up and dressed almost before we were awake. Edith and I had determined to be lazy and to get up only in time for luncheon, but when Mrs. B— rushed in, saying, "We shall be in Sitka in half an hour," we scrambled into our clothes as rapidly as possible. As we landed, Indian women hurried down to the wharves and seated themselves along the road, spreading out their wares on the ground before them—curios of all sorts and descriptions. I decided to do the town first, examine everything, then select the very best. This was a mistake, as the supply was so small and the demand so great that soon all the best things had been taken and prices were going up materially for the few remaining articles. I secured two walking sticks, the handle of one an eagle's claw, of the other a deer's hoof, a curiously carved pipe, which must have been so heavy as to have detracted from the pleasure of the smoke, a carved salad fork and spoon, a beaded bottle, finely braided basket, and one of the daintiest pairs of moccasins I have ever seen.

The next search was for photographs. We stopped at the Hotel Millmore long enough to see what a hotel in this part of the world looked like—very primitive and old-fashioned, but comfortable. We went through the Indian village, stopping to talk with the most interesting natives. Many times my camera was turned towards them but as they generally objected, I did not press the subject, nor the button. I questioned one woman as to the cause of her objection. She explained to me, in sign language, that if I would wait for her to change into her Sunday costume she would give me the great privilege. Edith was just about to snap a most picturesque group of children, when the mother came rushing upon her, shaking her fist. Edith told the children to look in her camera and see the reflection and as they were standing about her, peeping into the top of the

186   camera, their expressions of surprise brought the mother, who wanted to see also. While she was investigating with them, I snapped the group.

A little farther on, we found an Indian carving a salad fork and spoon; the design seemed so much more unique than on those I had bought that I waited for him to finish and sandpaper his handiwork. His wife soon made her appearance with her head bandaged, and apparently in such pain that she could neither sit nor stand, but moaned and walked, moaned and sat down, only to start off again. From her description in broken English and in signs, I inferred that she had had no physician, but had suffered agonies from neuralgia. "Come with me to the steamer," said I to the husband, "and I will give you a cure which will relieve her of all pain in a few hours." He caught up his cap and followed. During the walk some Alaska dolls attracted me and I stopped to purchase them; the Indian looked sternly at me and grunted, "Medichin." On we went until an article made of deer's nails, to be used either as a plaything for children or by a warrior in his dance, was more than I could resist; fearful lest some-

═══   Our roommate Mrs. B—   ═══

one else should secure it, I was handing the money for it, when a reproachful voice called out "Medichin." Quite near the steamer sat a woman with unique curios—another temptation to which I yielded, but the voice grew threatening as I heard "Medichin" for the last time. The Indian followed me up the gangplank to my cabin, where I opened the bag and handed to him four of my precious tablets, explaining to him just how they should be used. He listened attentively. "Cover," said he. I wrapped them for him, he turned on his heel without a word of thanks or salutation, and soon disappeared from view.

Having seen the natives, their homes, their handiwork, their wonderfully beautiful harbour with Mount Edgecombe, an extinct volcano, a little over twenty miles from Sitka, clearly to be seen, my attention was turned to the government buildings, consisting of United States courthouse and jail, located near the wharf on the southeast side of an old Russian log building, containing courtroom, jail, and quarters for government officials.

I went first to the mission, being most courteously received by Judge K—, who showed me through the large, bright sunny schoolrooms, where the children looked happy and interested in their studies. After a short chat with the teachers, we paid a visit to the culinary department, which looked large and clean and attractive, after the makeshifts of Dawson. A short visit to the spotless dormitories—a few words of thanks and encouragement to Judge K—, who has spent so many years of his life so far away from home, and then on with a fellow passenger for one of the most romantic walks imaginable to the Indian River and along its banks. It reminded me greatly of "Flirtation Walk" at West Point, so dear to the heart of the cadet.

We went next to the Russian church, with its beautiful Russian paintings, many of which were covered with gold and silver. Everywhere we met Indians wearing the large "Dewey button."

Killisnoo

THURSDAY, **O**CTOBER **6**TH ❧ We left Sitka at 6 AM, reaching Killisnoo at one. "Five minutes will be more than enough for this place, so don't hurry," called out one of the passengers, but we were not deterred from starting on a voyage of discovery, and were fully justified in not heeding the warning. On our way to the Russian church, we were told that many years ago some Americans visited this town, but were attacked and killed by the Indians. Immediately afterwards a man-of-war was sent in, which bombarded the place. We searched for a book, pamphlet, or paper from which to gain some reliable information, but in vain.

I climbed thirty or forty steps to photograph the little church, but as the day was dark, could not hope for good results. There was nothing more to be seen or done except to buy a curio in the shape of a tiny canoe with two men in fur—one paddling, the other with spear in hand.

Just as I was going on board followed by the faithful Ivan, who had attracted the usual amount of attention, someone called, "Bring your camera quick—here's the chance of a lifetime," and I hastened to the edge of the wharf to see a scow so laden with silvery herrings that men were standing knee-deep among them, scooping them into receptacles which were hauled up over a bridge, from which they were emptied in a shower into a waiting car. The car was then hauled by cable to the warehouses, through which the headman soon escorted me saying that it was the only establishment of the kind on the Pacific coast. They caught one hundred and thirty-five tons of fish in a net one hundred and forty fathoms long and seventy feet deep, yielding one thousand three hundred and fifty barrels. The oil is used by miners, as it is non-explosive, and is also boiled for paints. The processes, as we followed them, interested us greatly, and we left, deeply impressed by the industry of the Alaska Oil & Guano Company.

At four o'clock we were off again and watched the wonderful scenery until dinnertime. The captain says we shall reach Juneau after midnight, leaving by 6 AM, so that we shall not have the desired opportunity of visiting the famous Alaska-Treadwell mines.

FRIDAY, OCTOBER 7TH ☞ Through the window this morning we saw small icebergs, some in the shape of beautiful swans, others resembling animals of different descriptions. At nine came a knock on the door and an inquiry whether the ladies were in, as a big paper bag was handed to Edith. We peeped to see the contents as eagerly as children, shouting with exclamations of delight and surprise over bananas, peaches, even grapes, bonbons, peanuts! "A souvenir of Juneau," as Mr. M— (the kindly fellow passenger who had provided Edith with an awning during the previous trip) modestly put it.

KILLISNOO

190   The rain was falling, the steamer overcrowded, and there was not a place to sit and be comfortable, for even the dining room chairs were all in use, and when the hour approached for laying the tables, their occupants were obliged to stand, or go to their cabins. Edith and Mrs. B— went to breakfast, after which the latter returned and entertained me with stories of her camp life. To have spent two years in that country, without paying a visit to Dawson, was the part that astonished me.

Farewell to Alaska

ALTHOUGH THE RAIN WAS STILL FALLING, we prepared to go on shore at Wrangel, and passed the time before arrival chatting pleasantly with Captain T—, who is still obliged to sleep on the dining room table, although it is loudly whispered that there are a number of vacant bunks on board. The first time he asked the purser for one of them, he was told that it had been partially promised to another man; the second time, that he might have it "if the other man did not apply before night"; the third, that if he could discover which bunk was vacant he might put in an application; so, rather than be subjected to further indignities, he decided to endure being ordered from his short repose on the table at four each morning. As we tied up to the dock at Wrangel, the night was black, and the rain still falling in torrents; although we landed, we were not able to see our way into the town without the aid of a lantern, which it was not possible to obtain. Fortunately, a man came on board with samples of rocks from the Stickeen River, in which were embedded large garnets, and I managed to secure some fine specimens as souvenirs.

SATURDAY, OCTOBER 8TH ⋈ A rainy, nasty day! We reached Ketchikan at six o'clock, too early to dress and go on shore, and after that, were only to stop at Mary Island for a few hours to leave there the winter's supply of coal. "Absolutely nothing to see," Mrs. B— assured us. "We do not even go to a dock, as there is none to go to, and the coal is put off in bags, on a boat." We had heard most alarming stories of the roughness of the waters at Dixon Entrance, so we three concluded to be on the safe side, and remain in bed. Our suspicions of "a bad day before us" were confirmed by the unusually early arrival of the man in charge of filling the lamps, who said, "I must do them now, as it may be too rough later." One of the stewards looked in, to see that everything was well secured, telling us that, on a previous trip, a tremendous wave had knocked in the door of this very cabin, split open the bunk in which I was lying, and washed out a mother and babe, who were in Edith's bunk.

After such preparations, the reality was indeed tame, for we had but a gentle rocking motion which lasted only a few hours, and soon rounded the point and were in smooth water again.

Monday, October 10th ⁎ A rough night! Reached Departure Bay at 9 AM. The captain decided not to stop at Victoria, owing to the fact that only three passengers were booked for that port, and the cost of wharfage was very great. Late in the evening we made Port Townsend, reaching Seattle after midnight.

Tuesday, October 11th ⁎ We three women suffered veritable torture last night! We were shut in a cabin six by eight, with bunks so near each other that to sit up was an impossibility. One or two of the passengers who had not been able to procure extra blankets had asked to have the steam turned on, and turned on it was! At midnight, we compared notes and found that no Turkish bath could have surpassed in temperature that which we were enduring. There were no bells to ring, and no one to call. How we longed for morning! At four o'clock I could bear it no longer, got up, dressed, and sat on deck, and the others were not long in following my example. At the same time, I must in justice add that the steamer was clean and the service wonderfully good, taking into consideration the fact that there were three sets of passengers for each meal, so overcrowded was the ship; the cuisine was really excellent. The only other cause of complaint is the way in which the three bunks are crowded together one above the other, but that seems to be a custom of the Pacific coast.

We reached Hotel Butler in the early morning and were soon surrounded by reporters, many of whom it would perhaps have been advisable to see, in which case they would not have written, "The ladies were obliged to travel through the Klondike in men's clothing," or, "The ladies astonished the miners with their silks and satins, laces and diamonds."

We soon received many invitations, and were shown that cordial hospitality for which Seattle is famous, but we could not tarry long, as we were anxious to reach our own firesides. Our trip had come to an end, and although the privations had been many, they had been more than compensated for by the kind friends we had made, by the insight we had gained into a phase of life hitherto unknown to us, by the magnificence of the scenery, and by the novelty of the experience.

INDEX

Note: Page numbers in *italics* refer to illustrations. References to Mary E. Hitchcock are abbreviated MEH; references to Edith Van Buren are abbreviated EVB.

A

accommodations: in cabins, 79–80, 81
 in Dawson, 45, 154
 on the trail, 78, 80, 84, 178–179
 aboard watercraft, 21, 22, 95, 157, 168, 176
Adams, Fort, 34
Alaska Commercial Company, 117, 142, 150–151
 reputation of, 2, 62, 154
 service of, 11, 48, 157–158
 steamers of, 14–15, 33, 92
 warehouse of, 70, 159
Alaska Oil & Guano Company, 188
Alaska-Treadwell Company mines, 112, 189
Alice (steamer), 29
Alliance (watercraft), 48
American Hotel, 179
Andreafsky, 27
animatoscope, xviii, xix, 104, 107, 108, 109, 118
 Arizona Charlie's, 114, 115–116, 139
 problems with, 123–124, 131, 138–139
 success of, 141, 142
Aphoon River, 27
Arctic Express Company, 161, 167
Arizona Charlie, 116, 139, 142, 150
Armstrong, Nevill, xv
aurora borealis (northern lights), 164, 171

B

Barr. See John C. Barr (watercraft)
Bear (watercraft), 9
Bear Creek, 94, 105, 111, 143, 147, 148
Bella (watercraft), 20, 56
bench claims. *See* claims
Bennett, 175, 177
Berton, Pierre, xvii
Big Alex. *See* McDonald, Alexander
Big Tent, xiv, 50, 51, *58*, *64*
 condition of, 37, 67, 70
 curiosity about, xiv–xv, 51, 53, 58, 63
birds, 147, 161, 164
 in the Big Tent, 51, 58
 at St. Michaels, 13
 travel with, 21, 39
 See also parrot; pigeons
blasting on the Skaguay trail, 181
bloomers, 103, 178. *See also* clothing
boats: prices of, 50
Bonanza, 72, 79, 81, 128, 142, 148
bowling alley, 104, 107, 109, 110, 117, 134
Brannick's (Skaguay hotel), 182–183
business: in Dawson, 48, 92
business schemes, 104, 106–107, 108, 131, 141
burial practices: of miners, 124–126
 along the Yukon, 27, 167

194   **C**

cabins: construction of by MEH, 113–114,
    135, 139
  in Dawson, *46*, 147
  provision, 161
  See also accommodations
Canada: crossing the border of, 41
  See also taxes: Canadian
cannibals, 69
canoes: birchbark, 29
  Peterboro, 55, 180
Castelmenardo, Gennaro Vessicchio de
    (husband of EVB), xxi–xxii
cemeteries, 8, 27, 125, 167
Chandler, William E., xi
Chilkoot Pass, 60, 140, 177
churches: Russian Orthodox, 27, 28, 187, 188
church services, 73, 74–75, 87, 110
Circle City, 37, 38, 39, 104, 108
City of Topeka (steamer), 184
claims, 42, 78–80, 111, 142, 143, 147, 159
  of Alexander McDonald, 72, 79, 80
  of Hank Summers, 35
  of MEH, 19, 65, 87, 94, 111, 148
  recording, 78, 94, 105–106, 128–129
  staking, 77, 87, 147
  See also Bear Creek; gold panning
Clara (watercraft), 154, 155, 156, 157, 160
clean-ups, 72, 80–81, *82*
  defined, 72n
clothing, 128, *186*, 192
  in Dawson, 54
  of miners, 20
  worn by women, 61, 63, 103, 178
coal, 34, 191
Columbia Navigation Company, 15, 32
Columbian (watercraft), 141, 144, 148–150,
    151, 165
Combination Company Theatre (Dawson),
    65–66, 68, 142
Constantine, Fort, 42
Copper River, 38
Criterion (music box), xv, 1, 54
Cudahy, Fort, 42

D

Dalton, Jack, 168
dancing: in Dawson, 47, 67
Dawson: departure from, 160

description of, 44
illness in, 24, 29, 35
prices in, 16–17, 39, 57, 110, 127, 152
reports about, 19
sanitary conditions of, 39
Dawson Annex (West Dawson), 51, *64*, 107,
    136, 139, 140, 143
  description of, 46
Departure Bay, 192
Dixon Entrance, 191
dogs: native, 22, 31, 34, 176
  aboard the *St. Paul*, 4, 5
  travel with, 21
  See also Ivan (Great Dane); Queen (Great
    Dane)
dog teams, 161
Dominion, 88, 136
Domville (steamer), 153, 163, 165–170, *166*
Dutch Harbour, 9
Dyea, 59, 177, 178
dysentery, 143

E

Eagle City, 108
Edgecombe, Mount, 187
El Dorado, 35n, 72, 80, 94, 97
electric lights, 95
Entertainment Club, xxi
Episcopal Mission at Fort Adams, 34
Eskimos: conflicts with Indians, 29
  description of, 13
  use of watercraft, 18

F

Fairview Hotel (Dawson), 45, 94, 156
Flora (watercraft), 149–150, 151, 153, 155,
    156, *157*, 161
  races with the *Domville*, 165, 168, 170, *172*
Five Fingers (Five Finger Rapids), 169
food: attitudes toward, 99–100
  at dinner parties, xv, 75, 88, 94
  preservation of, 60
  price of in Dawson, 45, 49, 71, 134
  price of along the Yukon, 39, 43
  eaten or served by MEH, 54, 55, 60, 62,
    71, 102, 106, 108, 109, 110, 111
  served in Dawson, 65
  in Skaguay, 183
  sold by MEH in Dawson, 131–132, 134

aboard steamers, 3, 160, 192
  on the trail, 77, 80, 179
Forks, 73, 77
Fort Adams, 34
Fort Constantine, 42
Fort Cudahy, 42
Fort Hamlin, 35, 37
Fort Selkirk, 148, 149, 162, 163
Forty Mile, 42
Front Street (Dawson), *66*

G

gardening, 29, 38, 49
Gates, William C. ("Swiftwater Bill"), 95
goats, *60*
Golden Star (watercraft), 171
gold panning, 41, 42, *42*, 79, 81
  See also claims
Gordon's Camp, 78
Grand Forks Hotel, 72, 79
graphophone, 1, 51
grub-staking, 35
  by MEH, 19, 31, 45, 65
  See also claims

H

Halfway House, 77, 82
Hamlin, Fort, 35, 37
Harriman, Frederick C. (son-in-law of
  MEH), xi
Hitchcock, Harriet (daughter of MEH), xi
Hitchcock, Mary E., ix, *xxx*, *93*, *183*
  business plans of, xviii–xix
  birth and death of, x, xxi
  clothing of, xv, xix, 192
  cooking of, xiii, 146–147
  crosses White Pass, 177–181
  decision to go to the Klondike, xii
  departure from Dawson, 160
  desire for gold of, xviii, 22–23
  as an explorer, xx–xxi,
  friendship with EVB, xi
  marriage of, x
  meets Alexander McDonald, 72
  perspectives on the Klondike, xiii, xiv, xix
  early travel experiences of, x–xi
  use of initials, xiii–xiv
  visits claims with Alexander McDonald,
    77–79, 81

writing projects of, xi, xix–xx
Hitchcock, Roswell D., Jr. (husband of
  MEH), x
Hitchcock, Roswell D., Sr. (father-in-law of
  MEH), x
Holy Cross (Koserefsky), 29
Hotel Butler (Seattle), 192
Hotel Dawson, 177
Hunker, 88

I

ice cream, 32, 97
Ikogimiut (Russian Mission), 28–29
Iliuliuk, 11. *See also* Unalaska.
illness, 20. *See also* dysentery; typhoid fever
Indians: encounters with, 112, 186–187
  selling curios, 185–186
Ingaliks, 29
Isaacs (servant): 89, 155
  hired by MEH, 56
  problems with, xvi, 68, 86, 92, 93–94
  seeks work, 96
Ivan (Great Dane), *xxx*, 1, 22, 27, 34, 55, 98,
    116, 170, *183*
  admired in Dawson, 129, 134
  prepares to depart, 155–156
  steals bread, 122

J

Jesse Lee Home (Unalaska), 8
Jesuits, 29. *See also* missionaries; priests
John C. Barr (watercraft), 38, 40–41, 163
Johnson-Locke Company, 93, 104, 139, 141
Jones, John ("the sick boy"), 57, 58–59, 69
  kindness of, 96, 99
  offers for EVB, 122–123
Joseph Ladue Company, 93
Juneau, 189

K

kayaks, 18, 29
Ketchikan, 191
Killisnoo, 188, *189*
King Island, 9
Klondike: richness of gold in, 22–23, 80–81
Klondike Edition, 105
Klondike Fever (Berton), xvii
Klondike Kings, 49, 72n. *See also* Ladue,
  Joseph; McDonald, Alexander

196 *Klondike Nugget*, xvii, 51, 75, 88, 122n, 161
Klondike River, 44, 46
Kollik, 27
Koserefsky (Holy Cross), 29
Koyukuk River, 19, 31

L

Ladue, Joseph, xii, 22–24
Lake Bennett, 124
Lake Linderman, 137, 178
Leah (steamer), 41, 42
Lousetown, 85
Lynch, Jeremiah (diarist), xiii

M

magic lantern, 107, 108, 142, 151
mail service, 39, 70, 91, 116, 136
  to Dawson, 18, 48, 161
Main Street (Dawson), 65, 85, 106, 107, 136, 141, 149
malaria, 22, 35
Mammoth Island, 37
Margaret (watercraft), 33
Mary Island, 191
mattresses, 52, *52*, 89, 98
May West (watercraft), 122
McCook, James C. (consul-general), 75, 95
McDonald, Alexander ("Big Alex"), 72n, 88, 111–112, 120–121, 153
  accompanies MEH and EVB to claims, 76–81
  claims of, 72, 77, 79, 80
  hosts dinner, 94–95
  meets MEH, 72
  plans to tour mines with MEH, 72–73
McQuesten, Leroy Napoleon "Jack," 39, 39n
Middle Lake, 180
Miles Canyon, *172*
miners: burial of, 124–126
  justice of, 103
  manners of, 47, 53, 78
mining. *See* claims; gold panning
missionaries, 26, 29, 40, 163
missions, 8, 9, 28, 29, 34, 42, 187
Monarch (watercraft), 38
Monte Carlo Theatre (Dawson), *47*
mosquitoes, 18, 27, 28, 37
Mount Edgecombe, 187

music: in the Big Tent, 54, 55, 90, 98
  in Dawson, 65, 67
  aboard the *St. Paul*, 6
  on Sundays, 28, 73

N

Nora (steamer), 161, 175, 176
North American Transportation Company, 38, 95, 135, 148, 154
Novikakat, 32
Nulato, 31

O

Oatley Sisters' Theatre, 108, 116, 123, 141
Old Log Cabin Hotel, 177, 178–179
Ora (steamer), 95, 116, 120, 124, 141, 161, 163, 166

P

Paimut, 29
parrot, 91, 112, 116, 118, 137, 162–163
Pass, the. *See* Chilkoot Pass; White Pass
photographs and photography, 27, 74, 110
  of Eskimos and Indians, 12, 18, 31, 185–186
  as souvenirs, 184
pigeons, 56, 63, 85–86
Pioneer Hall, 106
Portland (watercraft), 15
Port Townsend, 192
prices, 89–90
  of fur, 71
  on the Yukon, 24, 25
  See also food, price of; Dawson, prices in; wages; wood, price of
priests, 6, 9, 13, 29
  See also missionaries; missions

Q

quartz, 89
Quartz Creek, 105
Queen (Great Dane), *xxx*, 1, 22, 24

R

Rampart City, 34
Rideout (steamer), 104, 110, 115, 154
  arrival of, 109
Rink Rapids, 169

Roanoke (watercraft), 15, 17
royalties, 19, 35
Russian Mission (Ikogimiut), 28–29
Russian Orthodox churches, 27, 28, 187, 188

S

Saint Anne, Sisters of, 29, 49, 70
Salvation Army, 114
San Francisco: outfitting in, 1, 52
Sarah (watercraft), 158, 159
Schley, Winfield Scott, 92, 92n
scurvy, 20
Seattle, 192
Selkirk, Fort, 148, 149, 162, 163
servants, xv–xvi, 94
Shallow Lake, 180
Sheep Camp, 70
Sisters of St. Anne, 29, 49, 70
Sitka, 184, 185–187
Skaguay (Skagway), 177, 182
Skaguay Pass, 181
Skookum Creek and Gulch, 79, 81
souvenirs, 184, 191
    from Sitka, 185–186
Sovereign (watercraft), 37, 38
Spanish-American War: news of, 3, 42–43,
    102
Stickeen River, 191
St. Michaels, 11, 13, 17, 158
St. Paul (steamer), 2
Sulphur Creek, 73, 101
Summers, Hank, 35
Summit Lake, 180

T

Tales Out of School (Hitchcock), xi
Tanana Valley, 69–70
taxes: Canadian, 19, 35
telephone: in Dawson, 153
tents. *See* accommodations; Big Tent
Tillamook (steamer), 104, 141
travel, ix–x, 2, 25, 182
    See also accommodations
Two Women in the Klondike: critical
    reception of, xx
    as memoir, ix–x
    publicity surrounding, xix, xx
typhoid fever, 35, 99, 143, 150, 152

U

Unalaska, 7–8

V

Van Buren, Edith, ix, xi–xii, xxii, *xxx*, *77*,
    93, *130*
    falls into the Yukon, 144, 146
    friendship with MEH, xi
    marriage of, xxi–xxii
    pans for gold, 42
    travel experiences of, xii
Van Buren, Thomas (father of EVB), xi
Victoria (British Columbia), 192
Victoria (watercraft), 35, 36, 37

W

wages, 78, 86, 90, 113, 114, 141, 174
war: news of, 33, 42–43, 102
West Dawson (Dawson Annex), 51, *64*, 107,
    136, 139, 140, 143
    description of, 46
Wheeling (man-of-war), 19, 23
White Horse (Whitehorse), 156
White Horse Rapids, 174
White Pass, 95, 121, 140, 141, 151, 177, 184
    dangers of, 41
White Pass City (Heney), 181
Willie Irving (steamer), 149, 153, 162
women, ix–x, xvi, 13
    See also clothing: worn by women
wood: driftwood, 27, 37
    price of, 33–34, 36
    taking aboard, 27, 37, 38, 162, 167, 171
Wrangel (town), 191

Y

Yukon Flats, 37, 38
Yukon River, 37, 40